Low-Key Politics

LOW-KEY POLITICS

Local-Level Leadership & Change in the Middle East

RICHARD T. ANTOUN

State University of New York Press Albany, 1979

Low-Key Politics
First Edition

Published by State University of New York Press
Albany, New York 12246

Printed in the United States of America

Library of Congress Cataloging in Publication Data
Antoun, Richard T.
Low-key politics.
Bibliography
Includes index.
1. Kufr al Māʾ, Jordan—Politics and government.
2. Local government—Jordan—Case studies.
I. Title.
JS7499.J653K342   1978   320.9'5695'4   77-19018
ISBN 0-87395-373-8

Contents

Tables, Charts, Maps

Tables

Charts

Maps

Transliteration of Arabic Letters and Symbols

ا	a
ب	b
ت	t
ث	th
ج	j
ح	H
خ	kh
د	d
ذ	Th
ر	r
ز	z
س	s
ش	sh

VOWELS

	(short)	(long)
◌َ	a	ā
◌ِ	i	ī
◌ُ	u	ū

Other Symbols

ّ	indicated by the doubling of the letter
ّ	indicated by the doubling of the letter followed by a vowel
ء	indicated by '

The voiced velar stop characteristic of Transjordanian (but not classical) Arabic and pronounced as the "g" in the English word "goat" will be transliterated by the letter "g".

Key Arabic words frequently repeated in the course of the text will not be italicized and their long vowel marks will not be transliterated after first mention. Place names will be spelled according to the

ص	S
ض	D
ط	T
ظ	TH
ع	ʿ
غ	gh
ف	f
ق	q
ك	k
ل	l
م	m
ن	n
ة	h
و	w
ى	y

most common usage found on maps. Proper names will be transliterated with vowel marks in Table 3 but not in the text.

Preface

In evaluating any book it is useful for the reader to know how it came to be. I originally carried out field-work research in a Transjordanian village over a full year in 1959–60. I intended to conduct an ethnographic study of a Sunni Muslim peasant community. My training and interests leaned heavily toward the study of social relations rather than other aspects of culture, a fact that was reflected in the subtitle of the Ph.D. thesis I finally submitted to Harvard University in June 1963: "A Study of Social Structure and Social Control." When I returned to the same field-work milieu in 1965 and subsequently in 1966 and 1967, it was to fill in the ethnographic and social relational gaps of the earlier study. Specifically I aimed to examine more closely such topics as rural-urban migration, tribal law, and Islamic law and ethics in its local environment—the village. Although I had a peripheral interest in local-level politics, it was not my main focus from either a theoretical, methodological, or substantive point of view. Moreover as a western observer of a Middle Eastern culture there was little culturally familiar behavior to lead me to believe that politics was a cultural focus of the people themselves: political party activity was absent, competition for the mayorship seemed minimal, and elections at the local level did not take place during my stay.[1] When the men gathered in their guest houses in the evening, they discussed agricultural conditions, folklore, tribal law, the contraction of marriages, and local gossip, but rarely political affairs. When they did so, surprisingly, it tended to be commentary on the latest international news rather than on national or local-level political affairs. When the preacher delivered his Friday congregational sermon from the village mosque, it seldom concerned politics at either the national or local level. This contrasted sharply with the political content in sermons delivered in many urban mosques.[2]

There was no doubt in my mind, however, that some kind of competition, albeit muffled, did exist between the two mayors, each of whom represented the village but each of whom seemed to have a separate clientele or following, mainly based on his own clan. My interest in this competition was piqued when I discovered on my return to the village after a five-year absence that both mayors still occupied their positions and that some degree of estrangement existed between them. I was also struck and puzzled by the fact that one of the mayors, whom I had always regarded as ineffective, continued to be supported by his own backers, perhaps more strongly than ever before. These were interesting facts, but pursuit of their implications did not occupy much of my time during my second field trip. It was not until my third and fourth field trips, both short-lived, that I paid much attention to the subject of local-level politics.

I had not, in fact, undertaken field research initially or at any later stage with any particular conceptual framework for the study of politics or any explicit hypotheses in mind. The specific concepts discussed in this book are mainly those developed by F. G. Bailey, a social anthropologist who has conducted the great bulk of his field research in India. I first became acquainted with these concepts during my third field trip and only fully digested them after my last field trip in 1967, so I did not collect data during my various field trips with them in mind. More generally and perhaps more important I did not select a location for research because of any problem or problem orientation relating to politics. From a strict social science point of view this set of circumstances may be regarded as unfortunate, since many social scientists find it difficult to conceive of conducting research without the elaboration of hypotheses in advance of field work, the selection of a field location on the basis of problem relevance, careful sampling, the precise stipulation of operational procedures during the collection of data, and the statistical validation of relationships claimed to exist among the phenomena investigated. However there is one supreme advantage of testing a hypothesis, or in this case applying and refining a conceptual framework, in a situation where such a framework or hypothesis seems inappropriate: it provides a more substantial test of the usefulness of that framework or hypothesis. As Levine has astutely observed:

> If every anthropologist were to become interested in a particular institutional pattern and did field work only where that pattern were most elaborated or developed, cross-cultural studies of those patterns would become impossible, for it is from variations in the magnitude of institutional factors that

we test hypotheses concerning the functional relations of those factors with other variables. . . . Studies of politics in stateless societies, of descent groups where there are no lineages, of leadership where there are no chiefs, prices where there is no money, of aggression among peaceful peoples, of history and science among the nonliterate and technologically primitive— represent some of the most significant and subtle advances in anthropological understanding.[3]

In the present instance the value of studying politics in this particular village is precisely that politics is not a cultural focus for the people themselves and was, indeed, difficult for the investigator to identify and observe. Politics is muffled and "low-key"; it falls so far toward one end of the continuum that any successful attempt to analyze it with a particular set of concepts is doubly meaningful. The significance is enhanced by the fact that the concepts were originally developed in Indian peasant communities. Applying them in a totally different setting—a Middle Eastern setting where the ideology of egalitarianism is as well rooted as the ideology of caste is in India—provides a staunch test of their utility. This book, then, is not intended simply as another detailed case study of another peasant community somewhere in the developing world—though such studies are by no means trivial or insignificant for social science. It illustrates the value of serendipity—when systematically pursued—and provides a good test of a particular conceptual framework.

I would be very remiss at this point if I did not thank all those individuals, institutions, and foundations who have helped and encouraged me in my research, though they are in no way responsible for its conclusions. An extended leave of absence from Indiana University from 1965 to 1967 allowed me to return to the original locus of field research. During part of this period I served as a Visiting Lecturer in the Department of Sociology and Anthropology and the Department of Cultural Studies at the American University of Beirut. The chairmen of these departments, Samir Khalaf and James Peet, extended me their full cooperation in arranging my academic schedule so as to make my research trips possible. A grant from the International Affairs Center at Indiana University covered transportation costs to and from Jordan and a grant from the Joint Committee on the Near and Middle East of the Social Science Research Council covered the expenses of field research. I wish to thank the many Jordanians who aided me in my research including the judges of the local, civil, and religious courts, the subdistrict and land regis-

try officers, the agricultural inspectors, and, above all, the people of
Kufr al-Ma, who responded to the intruder in their midst with patience, warmth, and generosity.

I also wish to thank my students at the State University of New
York at Binghamton who provided continuing stimulation by discussing many of the concepts dealt with in this book in various
seminars in political anthropology. In addition I wish to thank the
State University of New York Press, particularly its director, Nor-
man Mangouni, and his editorial assistant, Margaret Mirabelli, for
guiding the manuscript to its final form. Finally I wish to thank all
of my friends and colleagues, those at other universities as well as
those at the State University of New York at Binghamton for taking
the time out of busy schedules to read the manuscript in whole or in
part and to offer many helpful comments and criticisms. In particular, I wish to record my thanks to Leonard Binder, Jeremy Boissevain, Brian Foster, Paul Friedrich, George Grassmuck, Iliya Harik,
Michael Horowitz, Alan Horton, Albert Hourani, Fred Huxley, Fred
Plog, William Quandt, June Starr and Terence Turner. Special
thanks are due to Fred Bailey who offered good advice and encouraged the enterprise at every stage.

Binghamton, New York
March 1976

Introduction to
the Study and its
Conceptual Framework

This is a book about local-level politics. Its aim is fourfold: first, to provide a detailed case study of the actual process by which such politics occurs in a Middle Eastern setting; second, to identify and document one particular type of political process, a type generally neglected by students of politics—"low-key politics"[1]; third, to test the usefulness of one particular conceptual framework for the study of politics by applying it in an area outside of that where it was originally conceived; and fourth, to refine that framework by focusing on certain key concepts, reworking them, and evaluating their worth. Although certain chapters of this book stress some aims more than others, a reading of any particular chapter will reveal that they are all intertwined. That is, the detailed case study provides the foundation for the realization of the other aims and it is the realization of these other aims that gives the case study added significance.

Politics is a process that is conceived to be only one aspect of political systems. It is the process of competition for scarce ends. To study this process the investigator must focus on the strategies competing coalitions pursue, taking into account the constraints imposed on them by geography, numbers, ideology, economic differences, the overarching political structure, and the nature of the competitive situation itself. Other aspects of political systems include administration, law or more broadly social control, and political theory. Their neglect in this monograph does not indicate their unimportance. Indeed they are discussed at length insofar as they impinge critically on the local-level political process (e.g., administrative rules and roles in chapters four and five), but they are not the focus here. Likewise, although politics involves competition for power or its concomitants and hence involves disputes, this book does not focus on the sociology of dispute or social control. It does not trace the process by which individuals or families achieve accommodation and reconciliation after disputes or demonstrate how community norms are upheld. As I have indicated elsewhere,[2] the process of social control is an important part of the environment of politics and constitutes an important independent variable determining its forms and boundaries. However this study assesses disputes for their effect on the competition and the substantive balance of power within the village. Finally, although considerable data on the social structure of the village is introduced in chapter two, it is introduced as background material for the following analysis and in no way represents a systematic attempt to describe the social structure of the community. That task has been undertaken elsewhere.[3]

If politics is the process of competition for scarce ends—power, dignity, prestige, honor, purity—by particular means and by the utilization of resources that are also scarce—land, money, men— one key element in understanding the political process is to appreciate how certain kinds of resources—land, money—are converted into others—honor and prestige (which are simultaneously the ends sought).[4] Although they may be separated analytically in the behavioral sequence, ends, means, and resources are caught up in an interdependent feedback process. In these terms politics can be studied at any social structural level, e.g., within the family as well as within the nation-state. The politics examined in this book is at an intermediate level—the village. Moreover the book examines public politics: it focuses on the competition by coalitions for control over certain public institutions identified with the community as a whole—the village school, the village council, and certain public offices, such as subdistrict officer, directly concerned with village affairs.

The assumption I have made is that all village men or, more specifically, all heads of households must play the political game. This is not to say that all such men are active or even latent political entrepreneurs seeking power, position, or the advantages they offer. As one political scientist has pointed out, for most people, "Politics is a sideshow in the great circus of life."[5] But all heads of households must establish a connection with a mayor (there are two in the village) in order to deal with government officials about ordinary matters—marriage, divorce, inheritance and job applications—and extraordinary matters—government handouts, water shortage, and cases of honor. By doing so, willy-nilly, they take sides or are regarded as having done so. The focus, then, is on the competition between village coalitions for the control of its public institutions.

It should be noted that I have not said competition between "corporate descent groups." It would have been easy enough to describe the competition as one between particular descent groups or clans. Indeed a substantial core of clansmen does compose each coalition and most of the competitors themselves view the competition in this way. But as I indicated briefly in *Arab Village* and as others have argued at length and eloquently (e.g., Smith, 1956, Barth, 1959, Peters, 1967, Boissevain, 1968), to view political competition as occurring between discrete corporate groups organized into segmentary systems is to oversimplify and to distort. By focusing on the formal attributes of such groups—clans, lineages, age grades, tribal sections, village quarters—and the functions attributed to them, a generation of social anthropologists has been led away from studying the composition and dynamics of the units of competition. This study does not assume that the basic kinship units constitute the fundamental building blocks of the system of political competition. On the contrary, it makes the recruitment, composition, and operation of such units problematic and a principal subject of the investigation. If this book holds any message for political anthropologists and students of politics in general, it is that we cannot advance in the study of politics until we have carefully described and analyzed the composition of the minimal units of competition and the process by which that composition is altered or transformed.

What this assumption implies about the kind of social structural level of analysis is clear. Although local-level politics itself is the competition between coalitions over the control of public institutions, the strength of such coalitions reflects the size, spatial dispersion, ideology, economic resources, marriage alliances, and grudge relationships of its component elements, whether they are groups, social networks, or dyadic relationships. In many small face-to-face communities of the kind analyzed in this book—and they still form the majority of the world's community types—the strength of any particular tie between a leader and a follower reflects the multiplex and, thereby, ethical ties of the community at large; more specifically, the social links within and among particular families forged by the vicissitudes of their history. It is, therefore, impossible to judge the strength of the competing coalitions or to analyze local-level politics without undertaking a detailed microhistorical (with respect to time span) and microsociological (with respect to level of social structure) study. Chapter six carries out such an analysis and demonstrates its importance.

What conceptual framework available for the study of politics most suits the needs of the social anthropologist, whose two or three years of field research requires a framework neither too general, too abstract, nor too difficult operationally to permit collection of the required data? Although I would not reject Laswell's view that politics is the study of influence and the influential—the analysis in chapter seven reflects this view—most of Laswell's categories are too general to fit the detailed data collected.[6] On the other hand I had insufficient data to utilize Gamson's admirable attempt to make the concept of influence operational by developing indices of influence through the application of different approaches (relative frequency, subjective probability, influence attempts).[7] Easton's conceptual framework focuses on too broad a problem—the persistence of political systems—and it embraces societal systems rather than local-level ones.[8] Because of its manifestly manipulative approach a classic work such as Machiavelli's *The Prince* precludes the development of a systematic conceptual framework for the study of such competition.

In the recent literature of political anthropology M. G. Smith has advocated studying comparative politics through the analysis of "publics," enduring groups with determinate boundaries, membership, internal organization, and procedures.[9] Boissevain, on the other hand, argues that students of politics should focus on "non-groups," egocentric networks recruited on diverse principles.[10] Since such networks are inherently unstable, this necessarily leads to a more perceptive analysis of political process. My analysis of core and support elements in chapter three and the episodes of competition examined in chapter six substantiate Boissevain's insight that competing political units are usually in a state of transition and that to view them as solidary corporate groups not only distorts reality but interferes with analysis. But it would also misrepresent reality if the author were to claim that the notion of corporate groups or "publics" was wholly irrelevant to political competition in Kufr al-Ma.[11] Although not corporate groups in the full sense, clans are discrete units with regard to membership, and they exercise on-going corporate functions such as social control. Since the competing coalitions have clan cores, it is by no means clear that analysis of competition in terms of "non-groups" or "social networks" at the expense of "publics" or corporate groups is the best course to follow. Indeed the significance of the political situation in

Kufr al-Ma lies precisely in the fact that although the concept of the corporate group is becoming less relevant and the concept of the quasi- or non-group is becoming more relevant, neither can wholly explain the composition and operation of coalitions. However by describing coalitions in terms of core and support elements and episodes of competition, we can avoid the confusion arising out of the exclusive use of either Smith's or Boissevain's conceptual frameworks.

In a very different approach Barth has advocated the construction of "generative models." He argues that by the systematic manipulation of a few key variables the analyst can generate the empirical types of social and political organization and, more important, explain the process by which they came into being.[12] Asad, on the other hand, has argued for an analysis more sensitive to the concept of class—more oriented to the examination of horizontal than vertical cleavages. A class analysis, he argues, not only adds a historical perspective but also relates the macropolitical order to microlevel decision-making in a way precluded by other conceptual frameworks, including that of Barth.[13] Both Asad's class analysis and Barth's generative model provide interesting frameworks, but I lack the historical data to apply Asad's formulation and I am not convinced that class differences are necessarily the most significant factors in the situation under study. To some degree I have applied Barth's generative model in chapter three, which records frequency distributions for different kinds of political contracts and in chapter four, which examines the implications of these contracts for different kinds of political strategy and tactics. In a sense this stands Barth's model on its head, for I have first noted the frequency distributions and then analyzed the strategies appropriate to them. Still another anthropologist, Abner Cohen, has studied local-level politics in relation to ethnicity among the Hausa of Ibadan. In his pioneering book *Custom and Politics in Urban Africa*, he argues that ethnicity has the latent (and perhaps manifest) function of allowing an occupational group to defend its interests against another in a situation where resort to formal political organizations is ineffective. However the book fails to investigate the cultural content behind the "ethnicity," the manipulation of which the author describes so well. The present study does not utilize Cohen's conceptual framework, for the community studied is ethnically homogeneous and operates within a larger political framework that is also ethnically homogeneous.

Most recently in his study of the Sicilian Mafia, Anton Blok has argued that politics at the local level should be studied in terms of a long-term historical perspective in which the different stages of state-formation are the critical explanatory concepts for analyzing particular competitions.[14] Blok's approach does not provide a substitute for the kind of study pursued here—a study mainly concerned with the detailed analysis of the oppositional context of competition at the local level. On the contrary, the two approaches complement one another: microhistorical and microsociological studies illuminate, enhance, and perhaps correct social historical studies with long-term evolutionary implications and vice versa.

Taking into consideration generality, level of abstraction, and difficulty of operationalization, then, F. G. Bailey's conceptual framework proved to be most satisfactory for my material. Central to his analysis of politics is the concept of "competition," that is, rivalry as governed by rules, explicit or implicit, that define who may enter the competition, what resources may be called upon, what the pertinent prizes are, and what tactics may be used to win them. Politics is a competition and not a "fight" (which, Rappaport observes, is truly characteristic of hostility between dogs).[15] However when the competitors increasingly disagree about the rules that govern personnel, tactics, and prizes, then competitions take on some of the attributes of fights. The competition takes place in an "arena," the locus of conflict-interaction for the gaining of a given prize.[16] The arena is defined by the prize offered—e.g., chairmanship of the village council, control over community land, or in Bailey's Indian case, access of untouchables to the village temple. A "team" is one competing coalition. It contains a relatively permanent "core" or nucleus, and a more unstable "support" element, sometimes recruited for each separate contest.[17] Teams can become arenas and vice versa depending on whether the main prizes shift to different levels of the social structure. A genuine competition for the village mayorship at one stage may become a bogus competition, if, in fact, one competing group in the village regularly monopolizes the position. The genuine arena in this case becomes that group rather than the village as a whole.

Bailey generally characterizes competing coalitions as having the attributes of either "movements" or "machines," although he recognizes that these concepts are ideal types and that any particular coalition has attributes of both with the weighting to one side or the other. Movements recruit on the basis of loyalty, habit, and a sense of the rightness of the cause, machines on the basis of calculated mutual advantage; the former tend to be open, mass-produced, stable in membership, and characterized by substitutable leadership, while the latter tend to be secret, craftsmen-made to suit local conditions, unstable in membership, of limited size, and focused on a single, indispensable leader.[18] Competition takes place in three modes that are usually sequential: "subversion," "confrontation," and "encounter." Subversion is the process of altering the balance of support in one's own favor by recruiting neutrals or rivals to one's own side; confrontation is the process of signaling one's command over resources—it often simultaneously challenges the opponent to respond; the absence of such a response, a "bye," constitutes a tacit victory for the challenger; but a response brings about an encounter, which always terminates an "episode" and, more important, results in a substantive shift of resources from one coalition to the other.

Since the rest of this book will be devoted to exploring, spelling out, and evaluating Bailey's conceptual framework, particularly these concepts, it is appropriate here to mention the disadvantages of this framework. As Gamson, among others, has pointed out, politics in the wider sense can be studied from either the point of view of "the authorities" or that of potential "partisans."[19] The former, the study of social control, investigates how authorities—those who make binding decisions—utilize various mechanisms, e.g., sanctions, persuasion, insulation, to alter the views of potential partisans. The latter, the study of influence, examines how partisans—those affected by a given decision in a significant way—mobilize support to challenge the authorities and alter their decision-making. Gamson points out that those who are commonly regarded as authorities can, when they change their point of view, become partisans and vice versa. Although Gamson identified the two points of view, he attempted to treat them within the same conceptual framework. Yet their very different implications readily lend themselves to quite different conceptual frameworks—one addresses the problem of order and the other addresses the process of competition. Social scientists have given a great deal of thought to the former, beginning with the classic works of Durkheim and Weber up to the more recent work of Coser, Gluckman, and V. Turner. Turner's *Schism and Continuity in an African Society* outlines in great detail the competition for the headmanship of a Central African village, but the conceptual categories focus on concepts such as "social drama," "redress," and "ritual resolution," not "contest," "prize," and "encounter." Turner takes the community's point of view and emphasizes those events which resolve disputes and restore social solidarity. Social scientists in general have given much less thought to the nature of competition than to the mechanisms for conflict resolution. Bailey's work deliberately attempts to right this imbalance and to investigate the process of competition itself, or what one of his critics has called "practical politics."[20] Bailey neglects social control, with all its implications. To be sure, one of his latest works briefly discusses "umpires" and "collusion," i.e., factors dampening or controlling competition, but he always concentrates on the contest.[21] His framework assumes one side must win and the other lose—more, that at any given moment one side is winning and the other is losing. He refines his framework to make possible a better assessment of just what the score is at any point in time. Of course as James Reston observed, the game format has always had a powerful attraction: it follows clear-cut, uniform rules (cheating can always be identified), has a beginning and an end, and produces identifiable winners and losers, who by extension and with interpretation, become heroes and villains (heroines and witches).[22] The drawback of using a game format is twofold.[23] It oversimplifies reality and presses it into inappropriate categories—it is not always clear at the behavioral level who the competitors are, what constitutes the core element of the team, and what role the leader of the coalition is playing at any given moment. The game format also by definition precludes looking at politics from an overriding societal point of view. This might not be a serious drawback—the choice of any conceptual framework always precludes the use of others—but in this particular instance there is considerable evidence that the process of social control does affect political competition. Indeed, as I have argued in "Pertinent Variables," the kind of political competition is determined by the existence of a "community of social control," the intensity of its activity, and the precise location of its boundaries. As the pattern of grudges in Kufr al-Ma reveals, the success or failure of particular mediation attempts has consequences for the mobilization of core and support elements at later stages in the competition. Moreover local-level political competition is sometimes converted into "encounter-by-mediation." Thus the outcomes of social control and the outcomes of political competition have empirical as well as conceptual implications for one another.

On the other hand, there is empirical evidence both in this and other studies that many conflicts associated with the process of social control are treated quite separately from those associated with political competition. Middle Eastern communities, for instance, tend to deal with cases of honor quite separately from political competition. In Kufr al-Ma individuals belonging to competing coalitions willingly join together to pay an offended group compensation. Factional rivalries are simply irrelevant to the matter of compensation or the process of tribal law generally. The separation of political competition from social control does, then, have some empirical basis, at least in the Middle East. But even if it did not, there would still be justification enough for focusing on competition to the exclusion of other problems. An important obstacle to progress in the social sciences is that analysts fail to seize upon a particular conceptual framework and to refine it both deductively, by following its logical implications, and inductively, by working it out through a larger body of data. In this sense Bailey's act of exclusion is not only justified but also much to be desired.

A second and quite different drawback—at least in his recent published works—is that Bailey fails to consider the environment of politics. One critic has pointed out that although his conceptual framework specifically stresses the importance of the political environment, including social institutions (such as economics, the family, and religion), political institutions (such as the state), and constraints of the physical environment and demography, in fact his recent works do not examine their impact on political competition.[24] This is all the more remarkable, for Bailey's first three major works took such factors into account in a detailed and sophisticated manner.[25] This deficiency, then, is not part of the conceptual framework itself or attributable to Bailey's ignorance or neglect. It probably stems from his absorption in working out the implications of the competitive situation for the rival actors and coalitions. Whatever the reason, it is an unfortunate tendency and this book certainly attempts to include such important, environmental factors as the state and its administrative officers, the occupational structure, the social relations of households within the village, religious and secular political ideologies, demography, the physical environment, and differences of personality.

Every social scientist, whether he defines "science" broadly, as Kroeber does, in terms of its nomothetic goals and its characteristic method of breaking down and reformulating phenomena into abstract concepts, or more narrowly, as Northrup does, in terms of the postulational set, must address himself to the problem of validity.[26] Of necessity this problem involves philosophical questions about the nature of reality and knowledge. I believe that reality is not of a single piece; any set of concepts—any classification—reveals part of reality but not the whole. One may imagine a prisoner in a dark cell for whom every additional aperture sheds a ray of light, with the several rays combining to illuminate the room. To select a single point of view, here the point of view of the contest, gives weight to certain facts in an arbitrary manner. I do not claim that this is the only point of view or even the best to take for the study of politics, but by taking it, we gain certain insights into human behavior that would otherwise remain hidden.

While conscious of the problem of validity, this study does not pretend to establish the correctness of its conclusions by strict application of the postulational set, by the elaboration of hypotheses before field research and their systematic falsification through formal tests of validity or even controlled comparison. It is, quite frankly, *ex post facto* analysis.[27] The validity of its conclusions rests upon the internal coherence of the argument, the detailed synchronic and diachronic data which provides the evidence, and the close fit between the evidence and the concepts used—in short upon a well-documented case study. Its main value for students of politics is heuristic: it investigates the possibility of analyzing the political process, in particular the choice situation itself and the range of alternatives and strategies given the resources available to the competitors and the constraints and the opportunities provided by the environment; it investigates the possibilities of analyzing this process in terms of such concepts as core, support, encounter, confrontation, arena, and external resources. I hope this case study will stimulate other detailed case studies using and refining the same concepts and will eventually lead to more systematic comparative studies. However since anthropological research has humanistic as well as social scientific significance, this study also stands on its own merit as another example of human variety.

Since this book analyzes social process rather than social structure, a brief comment on the notion of process and the limitations of this study with regard to it is in order. Process can be understood in terms of stability as well as change. That is, certain mechanisms bring about the persistence of forms and generational continuity. When processes are involved in change, that change can be conceived in terms of stages—stable periods of time followed by macrochange; in terms of feedback—where the same factors are mutual cause and effect; or in terms of contradictions—where conflict is always recurring as a result of inherent social structural incongruity. Whatever the conception of process entertained, its study assumes a change of condition between some beginning point and some end point. In order to substantiate that this change has taken place a set of readings should be taken at a number of points between the beginning and the end of the relevant sequence. I have done this in a very limited fashion at only four points in time, with each subsequent investigation being for a shorter period than the previous one: one year in 1959–60; two and one half months in the winter of 1965–66; one month in the summer of 1966; and one week in the spring of 1967. A larger number of readings over a longer period of time are to be desired for any accurate delineation of process. This is particularly so in the present case, for the last two readings, in the summer of 1966 and the spring of 1967, led me to modify my earlier assumptions of linear and cumulative change towards a more cyclical notion of change. Later readings might have led to further modifications or even substantial change, which is only another way of saying that the study of process is hardly ever based on a sufficient number of observations and is almost always incomplete.

The Social Structural Background
of the Political Process:
The Village and Clan as
Movement and Machine

Kufr al-Ma is an Arab village located in the denuded eastern foothills
of the Jordan valley. It is one of the 200 cereal-growing villages of the
Ajlun district of northwestern Transjordan. Its two thousand people
are all Sunni Muslims. Approaching the village along a dirt road
from its eastern side, one sees that only a few ancient olive trees
soften the unrelieved bleakness of the stone-strewn soil. Nothing in
the outer aspect of the village itself suggests that it differs from the
hill settlements which surround it—neither its close-jammed,
brown, clay-covered houses, its dusty paths, nor its gardens and orchards.

Unless the traveler passes through the rolling hills in the late
spring or early summer, when the verdure of the winter crops covers
the landscape, he would never suspect that peasants could eke out a
subsistence in these surroundings. No streams exist to resuscitate
crops from the summer heat and the blasts of desert wind. Although
a number of ravines and gullies dissect the landscape, no springs
provide water for wells from which men or animals might drink.
Each family in the village has dug a cistern to catch the precious
winter rains. In July, when these cisterns run dry, the peasants of
Kufr al-Ma must trudge to the nearest spring in the adjoining village
of Deir Abu Said. There they purchase water from the residents, load
it on their donkeys, and return along the dusty track to their village.

However barren its outer aspect, Kufr al-Ma lies in the center of a
populated cereal-growing region. Its manner of sedentary subsist-

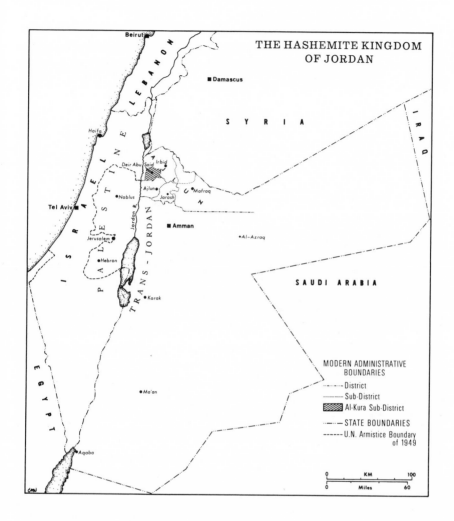

THE HASHEMITE KINGDOM
OF JORDAN

■ Damascus

S Y R I A

Haifa

Deir Abu Said Irbid

Ajlun ● ●Mafraq

Nablus Jarash

Tel Aviv ■

■ Amman

Jerusalem ●

●Al-Azraq

●Hebron

SAUDI ARABIA

Karak

MODERN ADMINISTRATIVE
BOUNDARIES
District
Sub-District
Al-Kura Sub-District

STATE BOUNDARIES
U.N. Armistice Boundary
of 1949

●Ma'an

Aqaba

KM   100
Miles   60

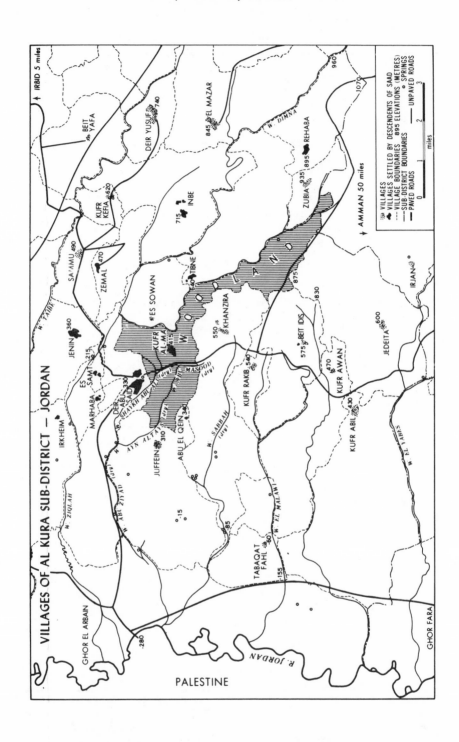

VILLAGES OF AL KURA SUB-DISTRICT – JORDAN

ence agriculture is, apparently, of some antiquity, as the ancient ruins of towns such as Jerash and Pella attest. An estimate of the population per square mile of cultivated area is about 780, making this corner of Transjordan one of the most densely settled areas in the Middle East.[1]

The village itself, like its sister villages, is located on the side of a hill. The visitor approaches from the main road at the bottom and, transversing this rough dirt track bordered by prickly pear and fig orchards, gradually makes his way up to a wide open area at the center of the village, on which front four village shops. As he ascends, the proximity of the houses to each other increases, until at the top, below the cemetery and three-eighths of a mile from the entrance to the village, he is surrounded on either side of the narrow lane by houses abutting one another.

Each of the surrounding hill villages—namely, Khanzira, Abu el-Qein, and Tibne—present the same aspect. They stand between one and two miles from Kufr al-Ma, separated from it by an expanse of cultivated land and one or more dry ravines. But significant differences in altitude exist between villages as the traveler moves from the northwest to the southeast. Tibne, for instance, at 2,080 feet above sea level and surrounded by treacherous ravines, provided refuge against the depredations of the Bedouins and extortion by Ottoman Turks while the other villages were victimized. Deir Abu Said looks like the adjoining villages, however it contains a larger population (3,000) and serves as the administrative center of the subdistrict, Al-Kura. As such, it houses the subdistrict officer, the forest ranger, the land registrar, the religious judge, the civil judge, the tax official, and the doctor. Although its main street is paved and its coffeehouse caters to the government officials who are forced to reside there, Deir Abu Said still resembles an overgrown village. Despite the vegetable stands which adorn its main street and its weekly livestock market, Deir Abu Said can hardly be considered a market town.

Kufr al-Ma lies in the center of Jordan's grain-producing area, the Transjordanian plateau. Here the bulk of Jordan's population lives, cultivating most of the million acres devoted to rainfed cereals. In Kufr al-Ma and its adjoining villages wheat, barley, and legumes (for fodder) are the chief winter crops, while maize and sesame seed are the chief summer crops. These cereals are grown for subsistence. Only the straw from the winter crops and the sesame seed are sold. Trucks pick up these commodities in the village and transport them to Palestine for sale. In a bumper year some peasants will harvest surplus grain, which they use to pay off their previous debts at the village shops; it is also stored against future purchases and expended for marriage payments. The leguminous crops include vetches, kersenneh, chickpeas, and lentils, but in Kufr al-Ma, only kersenneh takes up substantial acreage. In the hills of southern Ajlun, where rainfall is greatest, vineyards produce grapes and raisins. Tobacco is also grown there for home consumption.

The peasants of Kufr al-Ma practice what geographers have termed "dry land farming." This can be defined as crop production under conditions of deficient rainfall.[2] In Jordan dry farming is associated not only with low rainfall, but also with uneven falls of rain, long intervals between rains, scorching winds, and large daily oscillations in temperature. Since water is the overall limiting factor in crop production, efforts center around the conservation of moisture. Ploughing, fallowing, and weeding are three aspects of this conservation effort.

In addition to rainfall and altitude differences between villages, microecological factors such as soil and topographical differences within a given village can bring bounty to one peasant when all of his neighbors are suffering dearth. Thus in 1960, a dearth year, one of the village mayors reaped only half the seed he planted; a second peasant planted one sack of grain and harvested two; a third planted one sack and harvested six; and a fourth planted a sack and harvested twelve (a twelvefold return on seed is considered bounty).

Al-Kura, the subdistrict in which Kufr al-Ma lies, was one of the few areas in Ajlun that Bedouin tribes did not subjugate. This was due, in large part, to the development of a district organization centered in Tibne and led by the Wazir family. Wazir Rabba'a's grandfather originally settled in Tibne after coming from the Hauran in Syria. He married the daughter of Amir al-Mahaydi and succeeded his father-in-law as the leader (*shaykh*) in Al-Kura subdistrict. As Shaykh[3] he not only exercised political authority, but also judged between villagers in the settlement of their disputes. Disputants would go to the Shaykh's guest house "to demand justice" (*li Talab al haqq*) in the presence of the assembled elders. Although the Shaykh's important day-to-day function was arbitral, his role was essentially political; his authority extended beyond the acceptance of his decision in arbitration. The Shaykh made war and peace and collected taxes. The villagers in his district constituted a potential military following that could be called on in any crisis. His principal political function was protection, in return for which the Shaykh demanded annual economic contributions at harvest time from the villagers as a mark of their allegiance. He appointed members of his family as headman in area villages and frequently the villagers welcomed a member of the Wazir family to the village and even granted him a piece of land if he agreed to settle there and become their shaykh. The Shaykh also constituted a redistribution point for economic surplus by offering hospitality. He earned his reputation as a wise man by his skill in settling disputes and his reputation as a good man by slaughtering sheep for guests who came to pay him homage or ask for advice and aid. Since tribal custom demanded the sharing of every slaughtered animal with as many men as possible, the arc of generosity was very wide indeed.

The achievement of social status through the display of generosity is related to the fact that for men such as Wazir and his descendants consumption goods were not available, nor were they needed. Men built their own houses, made their own clothing, and grew their own food. A shaykh with an economic surplus invested it in sheep which were slaughtered and served in his guest house on every suitable occasion. Such slaughterings provided opportunities to gather the whole community, and the Shaykh's guest house was the region's political center. The leader of this district network utilized the economic tribute he received (frequently sheep) to win political adherents and to achieve social status rather than to increase his own or his family's standard of living.

The importance of the Shaykh was accentuated by the absence of any functionaries from the central government in the area. No local police post existed. The Ottoman governor or *wali* of the Ajlun district lived in Deraa in Syria. Considering late nineteenth-century communication and transportation, appeal to him against the Shaykh's rule was out of the question. Moreover Ottoman authorities found it easiest to deal with a single authority who could collect taxes and maintain some sort of order. The Shaykh became recognized as the area's political overlord by his own followers, by the Bedouins, who opposed him, and by the Ottoman government, which sought his aid. The elders of Kufr al-Ma, in speaking about Kleb Wazir, the last of the Tibne Shaykhs, were unambiguous about the nature of his overlordship: "He used to loose and bind" (*kan yafiq wa yirbuT*). And the *mukhtar* (present-day village mayor) was always compared invidiously with the Shaykh of Tibne. He was only another man "from among the peasants" (*min al fellaHin*).

As late as 1922 Kleb Wazir, the Shaykh of Tibne, refused to attach the subdistrict of Al-Kura to Irbid under the new state of Transjordan being organized by Amir Abdullah. Kleb set up an independent administration at Deir Yusuf, which printed its official papers in Damascus, continued to collect taxes, and organized fifty police posts in the area. Kleb refused to travel to Irbid, which had been the headquarters of the detested Turkish authorities, to meet with officials of Amir Abdullah's administration. And when the officials of the central government came to levy a tax on sheep in Tibne, they were wounded in an exchange of fire. Another force sent to Al-Kura to arrest the culprits and subdue the region was murdered in the ravines below Tibne. It was only when British aircraft in the service of Amir Abdullah bombed Tibne in 1922 that the proud overlords of Al-Kura submitted to government control. The district organization which had risen to meet the threat of Bedouin incursion and arbitrary rule had, with the establishment of centralized government, lost its *raison d'etre*. But the supravillage network of which Kufr al-Ma was a part continued to have some significance for the daughter villages of Tibne.

The Mushā' System

Until 1939, when the lands of the village were individually registered, Kufr al-Ma held the greater part of its cultivated lands under an unofficial category of land tenure known as *mushā'*. This system has been described as follows:

> Mesha'a is a relic of joint ownership of land. Under it the properties are regarded as being owned by the community—which is always a village community—but are in the actual possession of several owners each of whom has a certain share of the joint property, though his ownership of any special area is not fixed. Usually the fields are redistributed periodically among the members of the community according to some generally accepted plan.[5]

Even during Ottoman times, however, at least one-fourth of the village's cultivated lands were exempted from musha', being individually owned.

In addition to fixed dates of planting and harvesting set by the council of elders and biennial or triennial rotation, musha' did not allow the individual peasant to sell his share of village land to strangers; he could not keep pasture idle or enclose his land; and no public or private paths or dwellings of any sort could be kept on cultivated land, for in the redistribution they would be ploughed over.

In Kufr al-Ma the musha⁾ system necessitated preharvest coordination and cooperative and consecutive harvesting. A crop watchman (nātūr), hired by the village or the respective descent groups, protected the unharvested crops from thieves and animals. Depredation was quite probable, due to the fragmentation of each landholding into a number of widespread parcels. Villagers or kinsmen banded together to harvest the crops of each individual's plot; they would finish it and then move on to the adjoining plot. A cultivator was not allowed to harvest his plot before his turn came, a prohibition enforced in order to prevent depredation by plough animals and sheep if harvesting were individually carried out on a helter-skelter pattern.[6] After harvest of the whole area, all cultivators could turn their flocks into the village fields.

The village lands were divided into three equal parts, corresponding to the three clans of the village. (The three clans were of unequal size, however, and often families from the larger clans or independent families would join the smaller clans to even up the division.) Each clan was assigned an area by lot. Then each clan would redivide its allotted stretch among its component families. Thus "every humula [clan] or family received an area corresponding to the share which was originally assigned to it in the landed property in the village."[7]

In 1928 registration of cultivated land in the name of individual owners was begun in Palestine and Transjordan. By 1943, 968,500 acres had been so allocated—84 percent of all cultivated land and nearly all land held under musha⁾.[8] Land settlement officers reached Kufr al-Ma in 1939.

Under musha⁾, village-wide cooperation in the coordination of planting, protection of crops, and consecutive harvesting of crops and pasturing of animals was necessary. With the registration of land each peasant determined for himself the crops to be grown and the time of planting and harvesting. This is not to say that under the present system—out of his own self-interest—he can completely ignore the agricultural regime followed by his neighbors. Under musha⁾, however, punishment for violations of the agricultural calendar or for crop destruction by livestock was handled by informal village or kin group consultations. Although minor cases of crop depredation still come before the mukhtar and clan elders in the guest house, many now go to the subdistrict officer or the civil court in the next town.

Today Kufr al-Ma cannot be regarded in any sense as a corporate village with control over economic resources. Land sales occur, even to nonvillagers. However the village has not yet shed its corporate history despite the formal revolution in land tĕnure. Over the last twenty years very little land has been alienated to nonvillagers. Owners of adjacent plots are usually granted the privilege of first refusal on land for sale. (Villagers have sometimes failed to buy, however.) Most sales are to neighbors on the land or to lineage mates and clansmen (often the two are synonymous). A comparison of the distribution of land plots in terms of lineage and clan affiliation in 1939 and in 1960 shows very little change. Owners of abutting land plots tend to be affiliated with the same clans and lineages (though they may not be the same individuals) as in the earlier period.

To summarize, two of the most important events in the village's recent history were the breakdown of the district political structure with the bombing of Tibne in 1922 and the termination of communal land tenure and cultivation in 1939. Land registration destroyed the corporate nature of the village, at least in its economic aspect, and in a sense freed individual households for enterprise within and mobility outside it. The remarkable fact is that despite the revolution in land tenure and despite the increase of occupational mobility, so little change has occurred whether in the actual alienation of land to nonvillagers or the agglomeration of land within the village. Its religious life remains strongly Islamic and its process of social control egalitarian and traditional. Despite considerable economic differentiation, social status differences are minimal. The existence of social stability against a background of economic change poses a fascinating problem which I have examined elsewhere.[9] What is important in the present context is that the heritage of common political action and common economic control has had positive consequences for village and clan solidarity. Despite basic economic, political, and social changes, the village and clan continue to function as frameworks for political rivalry, social status, and social control, and as the loci of kinship ties and land ownership. The following chapters will examine the basis of this solidarity and the factors working toward its dissolution.

The Occupational Structure

For the villagers who till the soil economic status remains largely determined by land tenure relationships. The term *fellāH* denotes a man who lives in the village and who owns land and derives his main income from it, whether he tills it or not; it also refers to a sharecropper who works land as an equal partner, contributing capital along with the owner, i.e., his plough animals and one-half the seeds, for a one-half share in the harvest. The sharecropper for a one-fourth share, however, is termed *Harrāth* (ploughman). He has no plough animals to contribute and offers only his labor; moreover, he often lives in his employer's house, if he comes from another village, and eats with his employer's family; he has such additional duties as feeding and watering the animals and running errands for his employer's household. The daily agricultural laborer or *ʿāmil* works for a daily wage and his employment may be summarily ended by his employer. Finally, there is the agricultural pieceworker or *qatrūz*. He is usually a young man who is hired as a sort of apprentice ploughman. His employer contracts to give him a certain number of sacks of grain at the end of the season in return for his labor on the land. A man without land who has no other permanent nonagricultural employment (army, shopkeeping, government position) is rather invidiously termed a "landless one" (*fellawti*). Each term refers to a distinct agricultural status, with the exception of fellah, which includes both owners and sharecroppers working for one-half the crop. This discrepancy may be explained by the fact that the peasant does not consider land ownership the most important factor. Kufr al-Ma is, after all, a village of very small holdings, where 61 percent of all landowners have twelve acres or less. The largest landowner owns only one hundred acres. The important factor is the investment of capital and the sharing of risks. The sharecropper for half the crops contributes animals and seeds and shares with the owner the wage costs of the blacksmith and other agricultural laborers hired in the course of the season.

The single most important fact about the occupational structure of the village is not its dominance by those employed in agriculture. On the contrary, as table 1 demonstrates, less than 40 percent of the employed men are engaged in subsistence agriculture.[10] Of the 200 households counted, 92 possessed no land whatsoever. The consequences of such an occupational structure for mobility are plain. A certain number of men (34) find employment in the village as shopkeepers, artisans, and stonecutters; many others (39) work outside the village, but in the locality, as builders, peddlers, and local laborers; the remainder (141) find employment as government clerks and ushers in government offices, as soldiers, and as laborers in distant towns, army camps, and the capital, Amman. In addition many

Table 1
Occupational Structure of Kufr al-Ma—1960

OCCUPATION	NUMBER
AGRICULTURAL	
Peasant (Owner of Land)[1]	57
Peasant (Owner and Sharecropper for one-half of crop)	36
Peasant (Sharecropper for one-half of crop)[2]	27
Plowman (Sharecropper for one-fourth of crop)	4
Daily Agricultural Laborer	1
Yearly Agricultural Pieceworker	5
Shepherd[3]	17
Total: Agricultural Occupations	147
Percentage: Agricultural Occupations	39
MILITARY	
Soldier	108
Percentage: Military Occupations[4]	29
NONAGRICULTURAL	
Laborer (Local)	23
Laborer (Distant)[5]	17
Stonecutter	16
Peddler	6
Mason[6]	10
Carpenter	1
Blacksmith[7]	2
Tailor[8]	1
Shopkeeper	14
Magician	1
Preacher (*imām*)[9]	2
Mukhtar[10]	2
Watchman[11]	2
Government Employee[12]	16
Muezzin[13]	1
Total: Nonagricultural Occupations	114
Percentage: Nonagricultural Occupations	30
RETIRED	9
Percentage: Retired	2
TOTAL NUMBER OF MEN EMPLOYED OR RETIRED[14]	378

1. Following native usage I am using the word "peasant" (*fellāh*) here to designate a man who is primarily engaged in subsistence farming, who owns and tills his land, or who sharecrops land for one-half of the crop. The critical distinction between a peasant and other men who till the soil is the amount of capital (land, seeds, animals) contributed to the enterprise rather than land ownership. These economic distinctions are reflected in the occupational terminology used by the inhabitants themselves (see discussion above). Many of the men listed as peasants, plowmen, or agricultural laborers spend a considerable part of their time working as nonagricultural laborers, particularly in years of drought. The definition of peasant used above is not meant to rule out a broader definition of peasant based upon cultural criteria. For certain purposes of analysis such a definition is more useful than the economic definition given above. (See, for instance, Richard T. Antoun, "The Social Significance of Ramadan in an Arab Village," *The Muslim World* 58 [January, 1968]; see also chapters two and three.)

2. The first three categories of peasant are lumped under a single term by the villagers—fellah—but the other categories of cultivators are designated by distinctive terms.

3. Shepherds and agricultural pieceworkers tend to be younger men not heads of households. In fact, shepherding and piecework are generally regarded as a sort of apprenticeship before becoming a full-fledged peasant landowner or sharecropper.

4. The category of soldier includes men in the army, national guard, and police.

5. Local laborers seem to be recruited from older men who are heads of households, while distant laborers are usually recruited from younger men not heads of households.

6. Kufr al-Ma "exports" masons to the surrounding villages. Most of these builders are, in fact, building outside Kufr al-Ma for most of the year.

7. Although a blacksmith is resident in the village, many peasants take their smithing trade to a neighboring village where a Christian blacksmith resides. He is regarded as being more skillful at the trade than his counterpart in Kufr al-Ma.

8. The tailor is a young man who, with his mother, works on a recently purchased sewing machine.

9. The imam is the religious specialist of the village. He is mainly supported by the villagers, who pay him in grain on the threshing ground after harvest. But he is also recognized by the government, which supplements his income with a meager monthly stipend. His primary duties are to lead the five daily prayers in the village mosque, to deliver the Friday congregational sermon, and to wash the dead and pray for them at their burial. One of the two imams listed is retired, but continues to wear the headdress of his occupation.

10. The mukhtar is the village mayor. There are two in Kufr al-Ma. They represent the village, although they are selected and paid by the members of their own clans on the threshing ground after harvest.

11. Like the mukhtar and the imam, the watchmen are paid in grain at the threshing ground after harvest.

12. Included among government employees are six law court clerks, two law court ushers, two teachers, a customs official, and an army officer.

13. The muezzin is the village crier. He calls believers to prayer on Friday from the roof of the mosque. He does not get a salary but often receives hospitality from the residents of the village.

14. The figures cited here represent approximately 85 percent of the employed men of the village. It had been my original intention to census all employed men, but this proved impossible due to the high degree of occupational mobility. It is probable that the number of soldiers and laborers make up a larger percentage of the total employed force than indicated above.

peasants, particularly sharecroppers, are forced to hire out their labor in surrounding villages or in the Jordan valley.

Kufr al-Ma has been characterized by long-distance mobility since the establishment of the British Mandate in Palestine (1920). A large majority of the villagers worked in Palestine on three or more separate occasions. Many used to leave after the harvest or during drought seasons to spend three or more months in Haifa or Tel Aviv, where they worked as fishermen, construction laborers, factory hands, gardeners, and harvesters.

With the end of the Palestinian War in 1949 and the closing of the western border of Jordan, the towns that had provided an outlet for such migration—Haifa, Akka, Jaffa, and Tel Aviv—were suddenly cut off. Long-distance migration now, to some degree at least, turned toward the north (Damascus and Beirut) and the east (Amman). But this remained a trickle as compared with the former migrant flow to Palestine.

The expansion of the Jordanian army during and following the first Arab-Israeli war counterbalanced the economic opportunities lost by the partition of Palestine. Indeed the new opportunities were so much better than the old that bribery was often the only sure means of securing enlistment into the Jordanian army. Yet only forty years earlier men had given away their lands in order to avoid service in the Turkish army!

The labor migration to Palestine had been largely sporadic. Men would leave the village after the harvest, only to return two or three months later. They might not go again for several years if agricultural production proved sufficient. The monetary returns varied, but they were, in general, small. After three months a man might return to the village with the equivalent of twelve dollars saved, at most twenty-five. Since most migrants turned to fishing, where a day's wage depended on the catch, returns were unpredictable—from nothing to about $3. As political disturbances increased, the better paid jobs within the Jewish section of the economy disappeared, particularly after the Jewish Agency in Zurich decided in 1929 to exclude Arab labor from all Jewish enterprises.

Employment in the Jordanian army, on the other hand, guaranteed a young recruit a monthly salary. For every child the soldier received an additional stipend. Of fourteen lineages examined in Kufr al-Ma, seven had a soldier as the highest salaried man, while in four, the highest salaried man worked as a government employee outside the village. The seven army men who led their respective groups in salary had annual incomes in pounds sterling as follows: 170, 192, 310, 312, 428, 444, and 580. The four government employees had incomes of 420, 480, 600, and 695. Three of these four men lived outside the village, in the town where they worked, but all had land or houses in the village or wives and children living there. In only three of the fourteen lineages did cultivators receive the highest income. Their incomes in 1960 were £186, £190, and £225 respectively. The richest farmers in Kufr al-Ma were not, therefore, able to match the income of the salaried employees; in general a gap of £100 or more separates them. The same gap exists between prosperous village grocers (who earn about as much as wealthy cultivators) and salaried employees.

After World War Two another change occurred that drew Kufr al-Ma politically, economically, and ideologically into a larger world. The region of Al-Kura was elevated to the status of a subdistrict or *qadā'*. Deir Abu Said, a neighboring village, became the administrative center, and access to government offices became easier for the peasants of Kufr al-Ma. A subdistrict officer in charge of government wheat distributions, water allocations, and school improvements resided in Deir Abu Said. The chief forest ranger, who guarded the woodlands from depredation by peasants searching for firewood and from foraging animals, established his office there, as did the inspectors of agriculture and health. A civil court, which heard all cases regarding crop damage, a land registry office, which handled all cases involving land title and sale, a dispensary, and a tax office were established there. Finally in 1953 a religious court was set up in Deir Abu Said to hear cases involving marriage, inheritance, divorce, and endowments.

There are, then, two economic sectors within the village. The first, the agricultural, is strongly affected by contingent environmental conditions which have placed a ceiling on economic differentiation and supported an egalitarian ethic rooted in religious belief. Within this sector land is the key to economic and social status. The second and larger sector, the nonagricultural, seeks its income for the most part outside the village. Within this sector economic differentiation is considerable. A poor peasant may find his closest kinsman, a brother or a cousin, earning a salary four times his own.

Two important conclusions emerge from the preceding. First, the diversified occupational structure and the resultant economic differentiation prevent classification of all village residents as "peasants" (*fellāHin*). But this is so only if the peasantry is defined in terms of economic criteria (occupation and income). If style of life is the main referent (including clothing, language, diet, recreation, education, and outstanding personality traits), then all the residents of Kufr al-Ma are "peasants." They wear the shawl and headband (and do not walk in public bare-headed), assemble in their own guest houses (not the coffee shops in town), and negotiate marriages and discuss crop conditions (and not national politics). In town circles they achieve a kind of notoriety for their rudeness, naiveté, and duplicity (rather than their knowledge or sophistication).

The Social Structure: Formal and Functional Aspects

The significant social units in Kufr al-Ma are stipulated in table 2. In order of size from smallest to largest we find the household, the close consultation group, the lineage, the clan, the village, and that part of the subdistrict identified by the phrase "the peoples of Tibne."[11] Two critical formal attributes attach to each one of these units, propinquity and patrilineal descent (the one exception being the village, in which descent is not a dominant ideology though it is, indirectly, a mode of recruitment). Patrilineal descent reflects the main principle of recruitment and propinquity allows important economic and/or political functions to be performed by the unit. There are other important social categories, e.g., sibs and subsibs, age and generational cohorts, social networks, and divisions of economic status, but all lack the attribute of propinquity which allows the members of the above-mentioned groups (village, clan, lineage, etc.) to interact on a day-to-day basis in important social, economic, and political affairs. Thus sibs and subsibs are social categories defined by patrilineal descent embracing all patrilineally related members wherever they may live. They may serve important functions, e.g., bearing legal responsibility in cases of honor and social obligation on the occasion of life crises such as funerals. But members of sibs and subsibs are usually scattered in several villages and often would not see one another more than a few times a year. Since this monograph concerns local-level politics, it will focus on *local* descent groups (listed in table 3)—those which *do* interact frequently and *do* combine in opposing coalitions, i.e., on those groups engaged in politicking—the clans, lineages, and close consultation groups of the village.

The basic social group of the village is the household. The smallest permanent economic unit in the village, it is defined by the

Table 2
Significant Social Units in Kufr al-Ma

Local Groups	Size or Number of Units	General Term of Reference for the Group	Ideology	Principle of Recruitment
Part of Subdistrict	9 Villages	The Clans of Tibne ('*Ashā'ir Tibne*)	"The People of Tibne" (*Ahāli Tibne*)	Common Historical Origin and/or Patrilineal Descent
Village	2,000	The Village (*Al-Balad*)	"Son of the Village"	All Residents Linked in Multiplex Relationships
Clan	3 Clans: largest 786 smallest 359	The Clan (*Al-'Ashīra*)	Patrilineal Descent	Patrilineal Descent
Lineage	28 Lineages: largest 304 smallest 12	The Branch (*Al-Fandi*)	Patrilineal Descent	Patrilineal Descent
Close Consultation Group		Name of Group or ("Must" [Group]) (*Luzum*)	Patrilineal Descent	Patrilineal Descent, Matrilaterality, and Affinity
Household	ci. 250: largest 22 smallest 1	Family or House ('*Ayla* or *Dar*)	Both Patrilineal and Bilateral	Patrilineal Descent

possession of a common purse to which all members contribute. Approximately 74 percent of all households censused were nuclear families, while only 23 percent were extended families. Household size ranged from one to twenty-two persons with the modal number being seven.

The close consultation group contains a number of households—those that must be consulted in matters relating to land, marriage, and local politics. It is usually composed of several brothers and their families or of first patrilateral cousins and their families, but it may also include matrilateral relatives or affines. Quite often in the

Table 3
Composition of Local Descent Groups in Kufr al-Ma

Type of Descent Group	Name of Descent Group	Number of Households Counted by the Author	Total No. of Persons in Group Based on the Author's Census	Total No. of Persons in Group Based on Mukhtar's Census
Clan	Beni Yasin	76	493	786
Clan	Beni Dumi	50	338	548
Clan	Beni 'Amr	31	205	359
Lineage	Wazīr	9	46	46
Lineage	Shuqayrāt	10	71	124
Lineage	Rifā'iya	8	52	55
Lineage	Ikhtaba	7	42	51
Palestinian Refugee Families		4	28	28
Other Families		4	30	30
Village Totals		199	1305[1]	2027
Lineages of Yasin:	Massā'di	27	178	304
	Qar'oosh	15	101	151
	'Aqayli	10	59	143
	Shujūr	6	48	
	Sabbāh	10	55	94
	As'eed	8	52	94
Lineages of Dumi:	Basbūs	10	60	
	Diyāka	6	43	
	Khalaf	6	32	
	Husayn	5	35	
	Hasan	5	27	
	Qarāqzi	8	69	
	Al Hilu	4	29	
	Shehem	3	18	
	Kamal	3	25	
Lineages of 'Amr:	Sālim	7	45	
	Ghānim	5	40	
	'Ibādi	4	20	
	Jabāli	3	21	
	Al 'Asali	2	11	
	Daknoosh	3	19	
	'Udūl	2	12	
	Berek	2	13	
	Dhiyyabāt	3	24	

1. The author's household census covers 65 percent of the total population and over 75 percent of the households actually residing in the village. Due to the high incidence of rural-urban migration and the absence of many household heads in the village, I was not able to complete the household census even after a year's field work.

previous generation the group lived as one household under their grandfather or uncle in one big house. The close consultation group may be named or unnamed, usually is characterized by propinquity of land and houses and often holds land undivided among its members. Members are legally responsible for paying "truce money" in cases of honor.

The lineage includes patrilineally related men, their wives, and their children. Its size ranges from 12 to 304. Almost invariably it has a name and is usually characterized by spatial agglomeration of houses and land.[12] The lineage claims its own women in marriage, though it does not always enforce such claims. It aligns in disputes and expects representation on *ad hoc* village committees. It is sometimes difficult to distinguish between a close consultation group and a lineage both in terms of formal and functional criteria. The lineage is usually larger in numbers, has greater genealogical depth (usually at least five generations), and possesses a number of collateral segments and a name; it is itself incorporated in an over-arching social unit—the clan. However the close consultation group may also have a name and may be as large or larger than some lineages. Likewise in terms of functional attributes certain close consultation groups may possess more economic power and political influence than certain lineages. Due to their possession of important resources (e.g., key specialists, land) groups that do not qualify structurally as lineages (because they lack size, genealogical depth, or collateral segmentation) act as lineages. I have treated these consultation groups as lineages since they figure prominently in political competition for such prizes as influence over the mayor, membership on *ad hoc* committees, the largesse of the central government, and the location of the school or jobs.

Generally speaking while it may be true that what is being described is a continuum of formal attributes (size, point in the developmental cycle, genealogical depth, collateral segmentation) and functions (political, economic, and social), certain critical facts differentiate the lineage and close consultation group. Although certain social obligations are regarded as ethical at the lineage level, e.g., giving one's daughter in marriage to a lineage-mate rather than to an outsider, at the consultation group level these obligations are quasi-legal, resulting in estrangement of kinsmen when the norm is violated. Although many close consultation groups continue to hold land jointly, lineage-mates ceased to hold land jointly after registration by individual households in 1939. Although consultation is largely an ideal norm at the lineage level, it is a pragmatic norm at the consultation group level. And finally, although lineage-mates are expected to contribute to the eventual money compensation paid in a case of honor—and they usually do—close consultation group mates must contribute to it and, furthermore, must contribute to the initial truce-money payment.

There are three clans in Kufr al-Ma (see table 3). They are defined ideologically on a sliding scale by patrilineal descent. The largest (Beni Yasin) numbers 786 members and the smallest (Beni ʿAmr) numbers 359. Like the lineage and the close consultation group, the clan is characterized, with some exceptions, by spatial agglomeration of houses and land.[13] This agglomeration is remarkable in view of the fact that more than twenty years of a free market in land has prevailed, with land held in individual ownership and the buying and selling of land legally permissible to outsiders as well as nonclansmen within the village.[14] As is true of the close consultation group and the lineage, visiting is much more frequent between clan members than between them and other villagers. The clan, moreover, plays a key role in social control. Prominent clan elders act as self-appointed admonishers of clansmen who have violated fundamental norms of behavior, e.g., respect for the aged, modesty, and they help resolve disputes within the village so that resort to government agents is prevented. The clan also acts as a prestige unit, since villagers not of the clan may call in its elders to mediate a dispute. In addition the clan is an important political unit, for it can be represented by a formally recognized leader. This leader is the mayor (mukhtar), who is selected by his clansmen and confirmed by the government as their functionary in the village.[15] Local administrative policy allows one mayor for every thousand residents of a village, so Kufr al-Ma has two mayors. This means that one clan will not have direct representation through a mayor, although all villagers, willy-nilly, relate politically to one mayor or the other.

The Village as Community: The Process of Achieving Membership

In order to understand the process of coalition-formation and competition among the village clans, it is necessary first to discuss the ties that bind village members together and the process by which those ties are forged. Like other Jordanian villages, Kufr al-Ma can be distinguished by certain formal criteria: it is a nucleated village with its population clustered in a close-packed living area and surrounded by the cultivated lands that mark it off as a discrete unit, spatially separate from other villages; it is an administrative entity, the basis of government plans, estimates, and handouts and represented by an officially confirmed mayor or mayors. In some respects it is regarded as a legal corporation, for it is held responsible for damages done to government woodlands in its area. The village is also a locus of kinship ties, over 78 percent of all marriages being to mates within the village.

Certain functions also distinguish the village and set it off from other villages. It is a credit area in which debt can accumulate at village shops, usually for a year, without demand for payment. Kufr al-Ma is a framework for political competition—this in spite of the fact that it has no single political leader and no single political center. That is, members of clans and lineages vie for control of the prizes (e.g., land, jobs, money) made available within the village and not within some other unit. Moreover it is the village that is consciously regarded as the framework of status differentiation. Thus a former mayor belonging to the Beni 'Amr, a clan no longer represented by a mukhtar, commented on the plight of his clan by saying "We have no name in this village." Certain men are singled out as "curtaining the village," i.e., enhancing its prestige by offering hospitality on a regular basis in their own guest house. Men from other villages know that strangers passing through are always assured of finding food, lodgings, coffee, and good company. Above all the village is a unit of social control, that is, a common area of living where limits must be placed on the show of hostility and where men can be made to subordinate their own desires or interests to the interest of the larger unit.

Membership in a village "community" does not proceed automatically from residence within it or from formal connection to a representative of external authority (the mayor). It comes about by the gradual accumulation of interests, each constituting an additional strand to a relationship that becomes increasingly "multiplex."[16] Thus any individual who moves into a quarter of the village necessarily becomes involved with his neighbors in the giving and receiving of hospitality. The activities of planting, harvesting, building, and providing adequate drinking water for his family and his animals soon bring him into a relationship of day-to-day economic cooperation with many villagers. If he has nubile daughters, he marries them within the village either to kinsmen with whom he already has patrilineal ties or to other villagers, thereby establishing a tie of affinity to complement those already formed on the basis of neighborship and economic cooperation. In order to receive formal authorization for a marriage, he must solicit from a mayor of the village an official document that certifies the identities of the bride and bridegroom, their ages, and the lack of legal impediments to the marriage. The villager, whether he belongs to the mayor's clan or not, has now established a political connection in the village. The final stages of absorption into the community are marked by claiming to be a member of a particular patrilineal descent group, usually a clan, and finally, the actual representation of this claim on a genealogy. This last action is important because full-fledged community membership can only occur through the establishment of ties with a patrilineal descent group, and these ties are always described in a kinship idiom of descent ("my father's brothers," *'amāmi*), matrilaterality ("my mother's brothers," *akhwāli*), or marriage ("my affine," *nasībi*).

Some examples will demonstrate the particular strands that combine to establish village membership, but they will also show that the process is often incomplete to various degrees. The Ikhtaba, one of the independent lineages of the village (see table 3), live in the Dumi clan area, have adjacent land plots, pay the Dumi mukhtar for services rendered, and in the past they participated with Dumi in the *mushā'* system. Yet by and large they do not claim to be members of Dumi and they certainly make no genealogical claim to common descent. In addition a very high percentage of their marriages are endogamous to their own patrilineal descent group rather than dispersed over the lineages of Dumi.

Raji Wazir is another example of significant without complete absorption into a given group of kinsmen. Raji, a member of an independent lineage, lives in the Yasin clan quarter. Many years ago he married a Yasin woman, so that now he refers to Yasin members as his "mother's brothers" (*akhwali*). He transacts all his political business with the Yasin *mukhtār*, he frequents Yasin guest houses, and his daughter has just become engaged to the eldest son of the Yasin *mukhtar*. Moreover he participates in formal Yasin wedding deputations (*jahas*)—membership in such deputations is almost invariably reserved for *bona fide* representatives of the various lineages of the clan. Yet Raji does not claim to be of Yasin. Genealogically he is quite clearly tied to the Wazir family, and he will continue to claim this lineage because they are the most illustrious family in the area; formerly they served as semifeudal overlords and today they are represented by a member in the Jordanian Senate.

Anhar al-Ibrahim, a member of the As'eed lineage of Yasin is another interesting case. His attachment to his neighbors is much less advanced than Raji's, but in a sense his repudiation of his own clan is much more clear-cut. A few years ago, after a dispute with the Yasin mukhtar in which Anhar was fined by the government for animal depredation, Anhar moved from the Yasin quarter down to the lower quarter of town where he was surrounded mainly by Dumi members. He began frequenting Dumi guest houses, rarely appearing in the Yasin quarter. He does not pay the Dumi mukhtar for political services rendered, but on the other hand for the last five years he has not paid the Yasin mukhtar either. Recently he married his niece to the son of a prominent Dumi elder in spite of his own lineage-mates' claims of priority. Though he has reoriented his social and economic ties in the direction of Dumi, he still is clearly of Yasin and is represented on their genealogy.

The case of the Jabali lineage represents even further absorption into a descent group. The Jabali live in the ʿAmr clan area, they participated in the mushaʿ system with ʿAmr, they have married into ʿAmr lineages over successive generations, and they claim to be "of ʿAmr." Yet it is clear to all concerned that they have separate historical origins from ʿAmr, and when I collected the genealogy of ʿAmr, there was no attempt to attach the Jabali genealogy to that of ʿAmr, although they and others still insisted they were "of ʿAmr."

The final instance of absorption is the most advanced. The Majadbi, a close consultation group, live in the Massaʿdi section of the Yasin quarter and when I collected census data from one household head, he identified them as being Massaʿdi of Yasin. Several months later I discovered from others not only that they were not originally of Yasin but also that they were in fact Christians. This former identity was signified by the nickname given to their group, *al-majdūb*, or literally, "the one attracted." The group's ancestor had been a Christian who had been overcome by a vision (or alternatively swooned in an epileptic fit) which had resulted in his conversion ("attraction") to Islam. The group has married Yasin women through three generations, lives in the Yasin quarter, pays the Yasin mukhtar for services rendered, and is regarded by everyone including themselves as Yasin. If it were not for the tell-tale nickname, it would be impossible for any outsider to ferret out their true origins. The nickname's function as a reminder of their origins may explain the fact that the ideological identification of the Majadbi with the clan has not reached the final stage of genealogical attachment.

These examples indicate the inevitable process by which membership in the village community is forged. If some of these links are severed (for instance by Anhar al-Ibrahim with his own clan) they must be replaced by others. Wherever he moves within the village the individual establishes new links with new neighbors and friends and other kinsmen; in short, he establishes a new social network. Although an individual may reduce his ties with his patrilineal kinsmen—by marrying his daughter out of the lineage, refusing to give financial support to the clan's mukhtar, or moving out of the clan area—that reduction does not cut the bonds which bind them to the community as a "son of the village" (*ibn al-balad*).

Although all the instances suggest that the process of absorption into the village community is unilineal and inevitable, this is not so, for the individual can by choice refuse to take on additional strands of multiplexity or, having taken them on, can sever them. To do so, however, would deprive him of the rights of a son of the village— consultation with its elders and access to its resources, e.g., women, land, water, economic cooperation with neighbors and, not least of all, hospitality and good fellowship. I noted two instances of such behavior. One was the primary school teacher, posted in the village by the government. When he first arrived he rapidly began to accumulate strands of multiplexity. He rented a house in the village, established day-to-day relationships of economic cooperation with his neighbors (involving a regular supply of bread and water for his house), and regularly gave and received hospitality, entertaining villagers in his house and attending nightly sessions in the guest houses of the village. At the end of his first year he was forced to fail several students. The irate fathers came to him in a mood of righteous indignation, asking with astonishment how he could have failed their sons when they had shared bread and salt together many times in the past year. The schoolteacher decided that he could not, in our terms, increase the multiplexity of his relationship with the villagers; on the contrary if he was to maintain the universalistic criteria of evaluation established by the national educational bureaucracy, he had to sever some of the strands already forged and thus free himself of the ethical obligations such strands entailed. Thenceforth, although he continued to live in the village and to maintain day-to-day economic relationships with neighbors, he neither gave nor received hospitality. In the evening when he sought fellowship he walked to the next village, where the junior high school was located, and sought the fellowship of other schoolteachers—also strangers in the district. At this point he was compared invidiously with me, since while I continued to give and receive hospitality he did not. It was said of him that although he was in the village he was not "of it."

Of course three exceptional circumstances allowed the school-teacher to act in this way—circumstances that did not exist for nearly all other village residents. First, he was a Christian and could not look forward to marrying a daughter of the village, since this was proscribed by Islamic law. Therefore he was in no danger of forfeiting this potential resource by his actions. Second, he was posted in the village for a limited term; he could afford to alienate some individuals because he did not have to face the consequences of their enmity over a long period. Finally, he received a regular salary as a member of the national bureaucracy; therefore, he was economically independent of village members.

A final bit of evidence that village membership is achieved rather than ascribed by fact of residence is the widespread use of origin names. Men born and reared in other communities continue to carry as part of their surname the name of their village of origin. One villager who has lived in Kufr al-Ma many years is still called Mahmoud "al-Burqawi" (i.e., "Mahmoud, [the man] from Burqa"). The naming system reflects the fact that a man is chosen to be a villager or affirmed to be one by his covillagers in all the ways mentioned. His community membership is not contingent upon residence and is not, therefore, terminated by moving away. The fact that one can be a "son of the village" while living permanently away from it is the converse of the necessity to validate membership in a local unit through strands of interest.

There is an extended sense in which a significant part of the subdistrict, that part identified as "the peoples of Tibne," is also a community (see table 2 for the attributes of the "peoples of Tibne"). The ancestors of many Kufr al-Ma residents and those of other villages identified as "the peoples of Tibne" once lived together in Tibne, coming down seasonally to till the surrounding lands and to harvest them. Thus the ideology of subdistrict unity ("the peoples of Tibne") carries with it the ideology of common villageship. In this sense all "the peoples of Tibne" are "sons of the village." They say of themselves, "our ancestor is one, our attack is one, our genealogical tree is one" and they claim to have a common call of distress. But the solidarity of the peoples of Tibne has more than ideological significance. Collections of money are occasionally made from those so-designated in matters of common interest, e.g., to influence government officials to return land appropriated and set aside as a woodland preserve. More important, the peoples of Tibne still seek to coordinate actions in outstanding cases of honor. In 1960 they refused to give "protection" (*dakhl*) to some men (not of Tibne) who had impugned the honor of the group by taking sexual advantage of its women. In cases where an individual of the peoples of Tibne impugns the honor of other groups, the peoples of Tibne contribute to the compensation necessary for reconciliation and peacemaking (*SulHa*). To be sure, they do not contribute the same amount as the culprit's immediate patrilineal relatives, but however small, a sum is always expected and nearly always forthcoming. In addition the peoples of Tibne "rush to succor" (*yifza ʿū*) one another by a bodily and occasionally armed presence when they are threatened by others. Again, patrilineal kinsmen compose the core of the armed delegation dispatched, but it may include others. Finally there is a sense in which the peoples of Tibne offer one another "moral succor" (*faza ʿ ma ʿnawiya*). That is, they counsel and restrain one another and push each other toward reconciliation when that is clearly the reasonable and just solution.

In cases of honor social control can extend beyond the peoples of Tibne, although the ethical obligation is much weaker. Village members have been known to go as far as Kerak, a distance of one hundred miles, soliciting monetary contributions to provide the necessary compensation in a case of honor. This sort of obligation represents the furthest stretch of village involvement in social control and reveals the underlying reality of the phrase always heard among Transjordanians—"We are the children of tribes and clans" (*ihna awlād qabā ʿil wa ʿashā ʿir*).

Cases of honor have additional significance for the village as a community: the obligation of social control crosscuts political divisions. That is, a villager contributes to compensation solicited by a covillager regardless of the political faction to which that villager belongs. In like manner, members of one clan call upon elders of other, politically opposed, clans for counsel in mediating disputes. Since a significant percentage of marriages are out of the clan entirely, most villagers have affines who are members of clans and lineages opposed politically at any given moment. Thus numerous social ties crosscut the ties of political factionalism and reinforce the solidarity of the village.

The Comparative Strength of the Clans: Internal Resources

Before discussing competition for power among the clans of the village and analyzing the nature of core and support elements in each coalition, it is necessary to assess the internal resources available to the three clans and the independent lineages.[17]

As Table 4 shows, such resources fall into five general classes; numbers, social organization, key specialists, land ownership, and ideology. Beni Yasin is by far the largest clan and by far the richest in land. Although Yasin has nineteen men with over fifty dunums and thirty-four with over twenty dunums, Dumi, its chief competitor, has only seven and sixteen respectively.[18] Yasin leads not only absolutely in land ownership but also proportionately, since they compose only 38 percent of the population but own more than 50 percent of the land plots over twenty dunums and 60 percent of the land plots over fifty dunums. Dumi, although second in size, is the poorest in land; indeed, it is reputed to be a clan of "landless ones" (*fellawti*). The comparative size of the clans figures in political competitions, not for the number of men with guns who can turn out on a given occasion—the central government has kept tight control on guns available to the peasant population—but for the possibility of staging "passive confrontations."[19] One way of adding to clan prestige is to pack clan guest houses full of one's own clansmen on appropriate occasions—religious festivals, weddings, funerals, circumcision celebrations, etc. On these occasions not just anyone is invited; rather, the leading village elders and its key specialists as well as kinsmen and neighbors are invited. Yasin and Dumi have enough numbers and specialists to stage these passive confrontations, while 'Amr lacks numbers but, more important, key specialists; at present it has no mukhtar and no religious specialist. Although it has five elders who can mediate disputes, the clan is so riddled by grudges that each elder mediates only for his own lineage or for nonclansmen. When 'Amr members invite covillagers on special occasions, the guest houses are almost invariably crowded with as many or more non-'Amr as 'Amr members. Thus every such occasion publicizes the weakness of 'Amr vis-à-vis the other village clans. Dumi, on the other hand, although having far fewer knowledgeable elders to mediate disputes, has enough to reconcile differences among its own clansmen; in addition it has a mukhtar, a magician, and a religious chanter.

The focus and intensity of visiting relations further elucidates social organizational solidarity. Yasin clansmen visit one another far more than they visit other villagers and their visiting frequency is high. Dumi clansmen visit one another far more than they visit other villagers, but with less frequency than Yasin. Many 'Amr members, when they are not visiting their immediate lineage-mates, focus their visiting out of the clan, although even such visiting is relatively infrequent. Two of their most prominent men, their

Table 4
Internal Resources and Indices of Political Strength

	YASIN	DUMI
SIZE	786	548
SPECIALISTS		
Political	2	2
Economic (grocers)	3	3
Religious	1	2
Arbitral (Elders)	10	3
GUEST HOUSES		
of 1st Rank	6	1
of 2nd Rank	2	3
LAND OWNERSHIP		
over 50 Dunums	19	7
over 20 Dunums	34	16
Landless	34	23
JOINT ECONOMIC VENTURES	1	0
VISITING RELATIONS	INTRA-CLAN	INTRA-CLAN
Focus	HIGH	LOW
Number of Lineages[1] Having Patrilineal Ties in Other Villages		
4 Extra Village Ties	1	0
3 " " "	2	0
2 " " "	1	1
1 " " "	2	3
0 " " "	1	6
GENEALOGICAL DEPTH	9–11[2]	7–9
GENEALOGICAL AUTHENTICITY	GOOD	FAIR
SYMBOLIC GESTURES OF UNITY	3	1
SELF-IMAGE	"Yasin is all brothers and sons of brothers; there is no wrapping round it. The others are no-accounts." (1960 and 1966) (Yasin)	"We are two-thirds of the town" (1966) (Dumi)

'AMR 359	INDEPENDENT LINEAGES 286
0	0
3	1
0	0
5	1
3	1
1	1
6	
17	
12	
0	0
EXTRA-CLAN LOW	EXTRA-CLAN LOW
0	0
0	1
3	2
4	1
2	0
7–9 POOR	4–6 GOOD
(1)[3]	0
"Dumi and Yasin are very happy; They run things as they please; we have no name in this village any longer." (1960) ('Amr) "When the chips are down, we are relatives." ('Amr)	"We are as the scattered among the clans; we are a minority; no one listens to us." (Independents)

1. Actually it was named subsibs in the village that were calculated. This accounts for the discrepancy in numbers of lineages between this table and table 3.

2. Genealogical depth was calculated from the youngest living adult generation (age 15 and above) to the apical ancestor, thus the two-generation leeway in genealogical depth, a depth which varied with the particular branch calculated.

3. Gesture reported to the author but unwitnessed by him.

former mukhtar and their largest landowner, are often seen in the guest house of the Yasin mukhtar! Frequency of visiting in a community characterized by multiplex relationships increases social solidarity, particularly when such interaction takes place in a guest house, the appropriate arena to exchange information, to gossip, to make economic contracts, and to discuss and resolve intraclan disputes. The superiority of Yasin's social organizational solidarity was demonstrated a number of times. During the height of the summer drought the government brought water to the village in trucks, dumping one load in each clan quarter. While the Yasin mukhtar organized the distribution of water in his quarter efficiently, stipulating appropriate times for each lineage and its component families to draw water, neither of the other clans was able to arrange the distribution without a good deal of bickering.

Social organizational strength is also reflected in the column signifying the number of patrilineal descent ties each lineage has in other villages. Yasin is the only clan whose lineages boast patrilineal ties in four or three other villages. Eight of the nine Dumi lineages either have no extravillage descent ties or only one, while six of the nine 'Amr lineages either have no ties or only one. Thus Yasin is not only substantially larger and richer, with greater solidarity, it also has far more significant ties of descent in other villages. Put another way, although the sibs and subsibs of Yasin are potentially important resources for the clan, the sibs and subsibs of Dumi are not. The strength of such ties is reflected at funerals, when sibmates from other villages come during the mourning period to honor the deceased. Usually they bring goats that are slaughtered. A funeral of the Yasin clan was the only one I witnessed in which the mourning period went on for five days—two days longer than is considered appropriate by local Islamic jurists—in order to permit all families who had brought goats to honor the deceased by an appropriate ritual slaughtering and subsequent meal.

Although they possess a number of important men and substantial landowners, the independent lineages rank last in terms of nearly every index. They are by far the smallest in numbers, having many less than a hundred members and the grand total of all four coming only to 286. They are scattered spatially, they have little land and few elders, and they lack key political, arbitral, and religious specialists. They have only one shopkeeper. At the same time it must be mentioned that one independent lineage, the Wazirs, possesses some influence because of its former overlordship in the area and because one subsib member (residing in another village) sits in the Jordanian Senate.

It might be assumed that each clan has significant economic resources in the three grocery shops each possesses. Apart from the fact that shopkeepers must have capital, it is well known that they do much of their business on credit; therefore at any moment in time they have many individuals indebted to them, debts which conceivably could be converted into political support. However since each clan has shopkeepers, most debt remains within the clan and solidifies clan cohesion rather than creating cross-clan allegiances. Moreover shopkeeping is an extremely unstable enterprise in Kufr al-Ma. Since shopkeepers can seldom raise enough capital from their own agricultural earnings, someone usually has to bankroll them, producing a two- or three-way split in the profits. The most successful shopkeepers seemed to have at least one other source of income, e.g., land, magic, a tractor, army sons with regular stipends. Most shops are insubstantial enterprises that have precarious lives. When I returned to Kufr al-Ma in 1966 after a six-year absence, I found that six of the eleven shops had gone out of business or sold out and five new shops were open for business. Moreover I have no evidence that debt is converted into political support. Indeed the shopkeepers differ as to the degree to which debt is used for strictly economic profit (i.e., to charge interest for credit given). Some charge interest from the start for goods sold on credit, while others allow an interest-free grace period first. Still others do not charge interest at all. The Islamic prohibition on the taking of interest may explain such differences, for piety is not uniform within the community of believers.

Another indicator of economic resources are joint economic ventures sponsored by the clans. To the best of my knowledge only one was undertaken, and that by Yasin, whose members chipped in to help a clansmen open a shop in Irbid, a large market town fifteen miles away. I was told that fifty households invested from $1.00 to $3.00 in the shop. The shop only operated for about a year and the shopkeeper returned the money to his backers. I never heard of any other clan or independent lineage mounting any kind of joint economic venture.

The four political specialists mentioned on table 4 include the mayors of Dumi and Yasin (the subjects of chapter four), the schoolmaster of Kufr al-Ma, on the Dumi side, and the clerk of the local civil court, on the Yasin side. The political activity of these last two individuals merited their inclusion as specialists, although formally they held no political offices.[20] Although Dumi possesses two religious specialists and Yasin only one, the latter has by far the most prestige in the village and, more important, the most influence. He is the village's prayer-leader and preacher. In addition to his traditional duties he fulfills the general religious obligation of reconciling estranged Muslim brothers. At one time or another he has entered nearly every house in the village on peace-making missions, and he is present at almost all important attempts at mediation.

The dominance of Yasin in the arbitral aspect of politics is reflected not only in the larger number of Yasin mediators but also in their well-recognized skill. This dominance is reinforced by the preponderance of Yasin guest houses of first rank. A guest house of first rank can offer a guest a meal including meat (villagers rarely eat meat themselves), decent lodgings, and home-brewed coffee made from fresh-ground coffee beans. Guest houses of second rank can only provide coffee. It is the guest houses of first rank that, in the words of the village watchman, "curtain the village." That is, any stranger or guest can be sent to one of these guest houses with the assurance that the guest will have a host of ample resources and well-known hospitality. These guest houses preserve the village reputation for generosity and hospitality among neighboring villages and in the district at large. And it is Beni Yasin that curtains the village, since it has more guest houses of first rank than all the other lineages and clans combined.

Several columns in table 4 refer to ideological resources. Since the major ideology of the clans is patrilineal descent, the genealogical depth and authenticity of the patrilineal genealogy are major indices of ideological strength. Here Yasin is clearly superior, for it has deeper and more authentic genealogy. Authenticity and depth refer to the comprehensiveness of the genealogy and the ability of clan members to recount it. Although I was able to elicit from Yasin elders the complete Yasin genealogy, comprehending all lineages and linking them to an apical ancestor, I was not able to do so for the other clans. The Dumi elders linked up all but two lineages, one of which (Basbus) was the largest in the clan. When I commented on this fact, the elders quickly added an ancestor at the highest level of the genealogy and linked the smaller lineage to him, but the larger lineage was left unlinked, although the elders insisted that they too were Dumi. More than half the 'Amr lineages had no link to the apical ancestor and no one pretended that they were related by blood to the rest of the clan. However despite these acknowledged separate origins, all clansmen insisted that these lineages were "of ʿAmr." The differing authenticity of the claim of patrilineal descent is generally recognized; Yasin elders quite consciously assert the purity of their clan ties, as the quotation by a Yasin clansman in the column labeled self-image indicates. As a result of the greater purity of their descent, Yasin members regard their behavior as more ethical. Although thievery, they say, occurs in the other quarters of the village, it does not occur in theirs.

Each of the other clans and the independent lineages have a different self-image. Dumi, for instance, stresses numbers. This is a new basis of power, which assumes the establishment of a viable village council in which majority rule prevails. Patrilineal descent is not central to their self-image, since although they are of the "peoples of Tibne," they do not claim genealogical relationship to the founder of Tibne. Some clan members frankly declare that about two hundred years ago lineages formerly unrelated made a written or oral agreement to constitute a clan. ʿAmr's self-image is ambivalent. On the one hand they stress their weakness and lack of political representation (through a mayor); on the other, they stress their solidarity as part of an overarching sib when cases of honor occur requiring common action. "When the chips are down," they say, "we are relatives" (ʿenda l ijāb qarāʾib). "Relatives" refers here to the clan's patrilineal kinsmen, since these are the men who rush to succor beleaguered kinsmen or to pay compensation if these kinsmen are culpable according to tribal law. Thus, paradoxically, patrilineal descent constitutes a stronger element in their self-image than Dumi's, despite the fact that the latter's genealogical ties are more authentic. Although particular independent lineages (Wazir, Rifaʿiya) have inherited charisma and individuals from these lineages have played prominent roles in the Dumi-ʿAmr alliance (see chapter six) the independent lineages stress their small numbers and spatial dispersion as well as their lack of weight in village counsels.

Finally, considering ideological resources, symbolic gestures of unity must be taken into account. I witnessed three kinds of such gestures on the part of Yasin—on occasions of marriage, funerals, and cases of honor. That is, three times representatives from all the component lineages of Yasin attended these functions outside the village, in some instances at a considerable distance. In addition to fulfilling their individual obligations as kinsmen, their action was a symbolic gesture of unity. I witnessed only one such symbolic gesture on the part of Dumi, in a case of honor, and none on the part of 'Amr, although I was told that in the recent past 'Amr too had rushed to help kinsmen in cases of honor. The wedding was the most explicit gesture of symbolic unity, for each Yasin lineage in histrionic fashion made a public monetary contribution to the newly married couple in the name of the clan.

Movement and Machine

F. G. Bailey used the terms "movement" and "machine" to designate "two models for [political] ground organization."[21] In his study of Indian politics at the constituency level he was able to distinguish two means of persuading voters and recruiting workers. Movements base recruitment on loyalty and habit and a sense of the rightness of the cause; machines recruit on the basis of calculations of mutual advantage. Bailey holds that all political parties have elements of both models and implies that the elements are usually weighted to one side or the other.[22] More than a difference of motivation is involved in this distinction. Movements and machines also refer to different types of social relationships; the latter tending to be secret, individually tailored to suit local conditions, unstable in membership, of limited size, and focused on a single indispensable leader; the former tending to be open, mass-produced, stable in membership, larger in size, and characterized by substitutable leadership.[23] Since the primary aim of a movement is education and indoctrination of members, while the primary aim of a machine is to win votes, ideology is much more important in the former. Indeed, as I shall demonstrate, it is possible to identify a machine by the presence of ideological neutrals and renegades.

There is no question that the two models Bailey proposed present serious analytical problems. Different levels of the same organization may reflect quite different types of social relationships and motivation. A political party at the national level may stress ideology and the element of moral compulsion but at the local level it may stress material payoffs and recruit according to the principle of mutual advantage. It would simply be incorrect as a matter of fact to label a political party as either a movement or machine, and the mix of elements unless stipulated remains unclear. Moreover since the critical distinction between movement and machine is based on differences in motivation, considerable ambiguity arises in interpreting behavior unless these motivations are known. To give an example from Middle Eastern history: Muhammad entered into a series of treaties with various tribes of the Arabian peninsula in the latter part of his prophetic mission. Each tribe converted to Islam, swore allegiance to the Prophet, and promised to refrain from making war on fellow Muslims. From Muhammad's point of view and that of his intimate followers the political relationship thereby established was a movement, characterized by openness, unlimited potentiality for growth (through conversion), stability (since apostasy was both treason and a sin), moral compulsion, and unitary ideology. The tribesmen, on the other hand, clearly regarded the political relationship as that of a machine and, like all the other contracts between tribes, as temporary, limited in scope, and based on calculations of profit and advantage. When Muhammad died, the tribesmen were quick to rebel, setting off a two-year period of warfare labeled mistakenly (for them) but appropriately (for Muslims) the "Wars of Apostasy" (al-ridda)[24]. But this analysis is only from hindsight; at the time the tribes rebelled, it profoundly shocked the true believers who were Muhammad's early, fervent, and intimate followers. Likewise the unrelenting war to suppress the rebellion which Muhammad's pious successor, Abu Bakr, waged against the tribes shocked the tribesmen, versed as they were in a contractual theory of political obligation that automatically terminated with the death of one of the parties. It may not be clear, then, until some moment of truth arrives, what in fact the basic motivation for political support really is.

As we apply Bailey's two models to the political competition between clans in Kufr al-Ma, we shall come to understand such competition, to develop Bailey's conceptual framework, particularly the concept of partible allegiance, to stipulate refinements of concepts e.g., "muted" subversion, and to introduce additions e.g., "muted renegadism."

The Clan in Kufr al-Ma: From Movement to Machine or From Movement to Movement

In Kufr al-Ma the clan is a movement. Because relations between clansmen are multiplex, with disputes resulting in a review of grudge relationships and an assessment of ethical behavior, the element of moral compulsion is prominent. It is reflected in several ideologies, each of which reinforces and in part assumes the presence of the others. The ideology of patrilineality explicitly recognizes the right of clansmen to make ethical judgments of one another. Each clansman has "the right to [allocate] blame" (*haqq 'atab*) to other clansmen for violations of clan obligations. The ideology of patrilineality is reinforced by the ideology of common villageship in which all villagers are exorted to act with constraint and good will to fellow villagers, and this ideology in turn is reinforced by the ideology of common historical origin and propinquity which unites the peoples of Tibne. The fact that many of the moral obligations stipulated by these ideologies are violated does not negate them. On the contrary, the fact that the violations are recognized, commented upon, and often followed by estrangement stresses their continued viability as norms of behavior.

In Kufr al-Ma the mayor of the clan is a movement leader. His clansmen regard him primarily as a representative of his patrilineal kinsmen. He is selected even when he is personally disliked. In answer to my question of why this should be so, clansmen replied with the rhetorical question: "Shall we bring in someone from the outside?" Often the mayor is recruited against his will and at the expense of his own time, effort, wealth, and reputation. Aside from the meager monetary support his own clan offers, the mayorship has few tangible rewards: the mukhtar receives neither a government salary nor important perquisites, e.g., use of a telephone, automobile, office, uniform, etc. Why, then, does a man rarely refuse the commission? "Out of shame from his relatives" (*yikhjal min qarābtī*) is the reply clansmen give. He is expected to place the clan's work before his own (*byibaddi shughl al-'ashīra 'an shughlu*). As chapters four and seven demonstrate, there is a sizeable discrepancy between public expectations and the reality of the mayor's behavior. But without hesitation I can say that at least one of the mayors acted to a very large degree in accordance with the norms of the office. How can such behavior be explained? More specifically, why should an individual accept an office which requires considerable self-sacrifice and little tangible return? Such behavior can't be explained unless one assumes that the clan is a movement, that its moral compulsion is conveyed in an idiom of patrilineal kinship, and that the expediency of household economics is not the major motivation in determining political behavior.

The clan resembles a movement in other respects. The core of the mayor's following is composed of his patrilineal kinsmen, not renegades (from other clans) or ideological neutrals (from the independent lineages). Although the mayor is a leading political personality in the village, he is by no means necessarily the most influential or powerful clan member; his leadership is substitutable in the sense that other clansmen can represent the clan in his absence and even be decisive in formulating policy in his presence. To some degree the central government has recognized the movement basis of local-level politics in its regulations governing the constitution of village councils (see chapter four), regulations which provide for the recognition of kinship and confessional divisions.

But if the clan is a movement, it is a weak one, characterized by "muted renegadism," "muted subversion," incipient class fronts, social boycott, obstruction, and withdrawal. The strongest evidence of its weakness is "the gentleman's agreement." I use this phrase to designate the informal understanding between mayors that they will refuse to accept support from one another's clansmen. In watered-down versions of this agreement the mayor accepts the support of a nonclansman in the sense that he consents to prepare and sign official papers for him, but refuses to accept money payment or, alternatively, prepares the papers and accepts money but then passes the money on to the other mayor. The gentleman's agreement underlies the practice of muted subversion. If it were effective in its strict version, the gentleman's agreement would eliminate subversion between clans altogether (though the independent lineages would still be open to subversion) by defining all clansmen as permanent core members thus ruling out any support category.[25] In its watered-down version the gentleman's agreement allows muted subversion. That is, a mayor can render services for a nonclansman without officially gaining his support, thereby placing this nonclansman in his debt—a debt that increases the mayor's social credit, if not his political support in a strict sense. To be precise, this behavior is not muted subversion so much as "muted renegadism." Subversion implies that the leader, in this instance the mayor, initiates attempts to wean followers away from the competing coalition, but this is rarely, if ever, the case in Kufr al-Ma. It is the nonclansman who initiates the process by asking the mayor for his aid or services. Renegadism may not even go that far. A clan member may simply boycott his own mayor economically (by not paying dues), politically (by refusing to attend meetings of elders to discuss matters of clan interest), or socially (by not accepting invitations for meals or not visiting him). In addition the renegade usually engages in verbal aggression (petty gossip and backbiting) in the guest house. But renegadism may involve a blatant act of defiance; very occasionally, clansmen go so far as to petition the subdistrict officer to right a wrong they claim their own mayor had perpetrated. In all of these instances the renegadism is muted, for the followers of one mayor do not formally switch allegiance to the other.[26] The existence of muted subversion and/or muted renegadism is made possible by two other factors—partible allegiance and clan paternalism. Partible allegiance[27] can mean a number of things: that a man oscillates back and forth between opposing political leaders; that he supports both simultaneously in an overt political fashion; or that he splits his allegiance along lines of interest, e.g., supporting one leader socially and the other economically. In Kufr al-Ma all these forms of partible allegiance are practiced, and the next chapter describes and analyzes such behavior in detail. It suffices to say here that the clansman who does not pay dues to his own mayor while maintaining cordial social relations with him, or the nonclansman who pays nothing to the mayor while maintaining regular commensal and visiting relations with him, or the clansman who pays dues to the mayor while boycotting him socially all reflect major modes of political behavior in Kufr al-Ma rather than exceptions. Partible allegiance embraces a sizeable proportion of the population, although the identities of the individuals involved fluctuate, as does their degree of allegiance to one side or the other.

Partible allegiance reflects the multiplex relations linking villagers to one another and the cross-cutting ties that bring villagers separated by one set of affiliations together in another set. It is never to one's advantage to break off relations completely with the other coalition, since each individual has important social relations on both sides of the political fence. Thus subversion is muted on one side of the political relationship (the leader's, here, the mayor's) and renegadism is muted on the others side (the follower's). Even when economic boycott jeopardizes political relations, continued visiting and commensality preserve social relations and make possible the future rebuilding of political bridges.

Both muted subversion and muted renegadism are related to paternalism within the clan. A clansman can get so many services *gratis* from his own mayor or from the mayor of the opposing coalition that there is no reason for becoming a support element of the latter. By and large the mayor signs necessary documents, vouches for good character, offers hospitality, and mediates disputes for any son of the village. Clansmen are excused from payment of dues for reasons of poverty or physical disability or because of special kinship links with the mayor.

Furthermore the material rewards the mayor can offer for support are modest, since his office is poorly paid. If he is not wealthy, no substantial material inducements can be offered to potential renegades, even if the mayor breaks the gentleman's agreement and undertakes active subversion. And if the mayor lacks a carrot, he certainly cannot apply the stick in order to keep renegades in line. He cannot apply penal sanctions against renegades, nor can he himself apply economic sanctions. He cannot expel a renegade for disobedience and, although he has limited police powers within his local jurisdiction, he seldom exercises physical coercion against those who are disloyal and blatantly defiant for all the sociological, spatial, and ideological reasons cited above. It is significant that the one instance of physical coercion by the mayor I recorded was against a stranger—a bogus magician practicing his magic clandestinely within the village (see chapter six). This man was a stranger of farthest degree, not only was he from out of the village but he was from outside the area occupied by the peoples of Tibne as well.

Nevertheless certain events have occurred in the last fifteen years that indicate a trend from movement toward machine politics. This trend was partially inspired by events outside the village in the capital of Amman. Beginning as early as 1954 certain ministries in the government began to foster a policy of establishing village councils.[28] An attempt to apply this policy to Kufr al-Ma was made in 1964, and much of the local-level politicking of 1965, 1966, and 1967 concerned the council's composition.[29] In 1964 a new regulation was introduced by the central government also revising the basis of remuneration for mukhtars. These two government policies have encouraged the development of machine politics because the first called for selection of village council members in rough proportion to the size of the significant social units in the village. Since these units were patrilineal descent groups in Kufr al-Ma, the representatives of Dumi and ʿAmr in alliance could outweigh Yasin representatives on the council if they voted as a bloc. Decisions on the council were by majority vote. Sheer numbers could have become the single most important political resource—more important than land, money, ideological claims of superiority, or key specialists, which were the traditional resources. Moreover the new regulation meant that the mayor could now recruit supporters from the whole village, since remuneration was no longer limited to his own clansmen but expected from every villager for whom he performed a service. The basis for the mayorship ceased to be moral and became transactional, a basis which allowed for more free-wheeling competition between mayors, implied the discarding of the gentleman's agreement, and, consequently, a more abrasive political competition between the clans.[30]

Several events within the village also reflected the trend from movement to machine politics. In 1960 a number of villagers from different clans, including Yasin, presented a formal petition to the subdistrict officer complaining about the Yasin mukhtar's unfairness in the distribution of government grain. In 1965 an unprecedented and, as far as I know, unique event occurred. One lineage of Yasin (Shujur) went so far as to withdraw formally from the clan by proclaiming such action publicly to the subdistrict officer in his office. They further indicated that they had attached themselves to the mukhtar of Beni Dumi. The mukhtar of Dumi was present on this occasion and accepted their allegiance. Shortly after this, a lineage of Dumi (Khalaf) went to the mukhtar of Yasin and told him that they were willing to attach themselves to his mayorship. Unlike the mayor of Dumi, however, the mayor of Yasin observed the gentleman's agreement, thanking Khalaf for their support but refusing to accept it. After all that has been said about the clan as a movement recruited on an ascriptive basis once and for all by patrilineal descent and united by an ideology of blood relationship, such events are astonishing. However this is not the end of the story.

By the end of 1966 some members of Shujur had resumed commensal relations with the Yasin mukhtar, one member had contracted to rebuild his house, and another paid the festival visit to him at the end of Ramadan. By the spring of 1967 the mayor of Yasin claimed that Shujur had always remained loyal (in 1966 he had insisted that they would come back), the members of Shujur denied they had ever seceded, and the mayor of Dumi said that he had never needed them in any case.[31] Thus the evidence for cumulative change in the village's political processes must be weighed against the evidence for cyclical change.

More important for the present discussion is the fact that these events demonstrate the existence of certain built-in limits to the trend toward machine, or what some students of politics would describe as "factional," politics.[32] That is, the mayors, particularly the Yasin mayor, find it difficult to set aside the gentleman's agreement and to conduct their political business on the strictly contractual basis now provided for by the law. These built-in limits to cumulative change in the direction of machine politics include some of the factors already discussed: the fact that all potential machines or factions are embraced and united by movements of wider scope—the village and the peoples of Tibne; the fact that ties of patrilineal descent and affinity cross-cut machines; the fact that the clan itself is a movement that claims its prodigal sons and treats them with benevolent paternalism when they err. In addition, the fact that the mayorship is a permanent office terminated only by resignation or government displeasure limits the development of contractual politics. Such politics tend to flourish when contests for political offices and other resources occur at regular intervals, and there is the possibility of unseating the leader by subverting or otherwise winning over his supporters. Finally the factor of "model character" is important; the village's image of "the good man" restrains active subversion and active renegadism. Chapters three and four examine some of these built-in limits to machine politics in relation to the strategy and tactics of the two mayors and chapter seven analyzes the influence of individual character, in both its model and idiosyncratic aspects, on local-level politics.

Two main conclusions emerge from this chapter. The politics described in the following chapters is "low-key"; that is, competition takes place mainly by withdrawal, obstruction, avoidance, boycott, muted renegadism, passive confrontation, backbiting, and acts of omission—and only infrequently by subversion and active, abrasive confrontation. Second, rather than viewing "machine politics" as a linear, evolutionary development out of "movement politics," it is more useful and also more realistic to view them as two simultaneous, opposed processes and trends: the trend for ideological neutrals (strangers, members of independent lineages, and unrepresented clans, i.e., 'Amr) to be incorporated into movements (the clans and their component lineages) and the trend for all followers of movements (clan members) to be incorporated as "supporters" in machines. Thus there is the constant pressure to join a movement—by taking a woman in marriage, giving a woman in marriage, registering land together, living in a particular quarter, giving and receiving hospitality, etc.—and at the same time the constant temptation to leave it, that is, to transact business with a leader (mayor) on the basis of calculations of mutual advantage and profit. The leader feels the constant pressure to restrict the search for political support to his own movement (i.e., clan) and to focus his efforts on curbing (clan) renegadism; yet at the same time he is constantly tempted to extend the scope of his political support to the whole village and in so doing work in terms of political contracts rather than kinship obligations. This simultaneous, and opposite process, pressure, temptation, or opportunity—depending on the point of view of the actor and/or observer—underlies the analysis of the mayor's strategy, tactics, and intercalary leadership presented in chapter four.

The Development of Criteria
for Distinguishing Core and
Support: Four Points of View

In a number of essays and addresses on local-level politics Frederick G. Bailey has developed the concepts of "core" and "support." In a paper written in 1965[1] he distinguished them by their mode of recruitment—groups with large cores are recruited on the basis of a common moral purpose or ideology and groups with large support elements are recruited on the basis of calculations of mutual advantage. However this paper and one that followed[2] introduced or at least implied a second criterion, that of continued loyalty through successive encounters—"the hard core" as opposed to support elements which are unstable and recruited for particular contests. In his book on the social anthropology of politics, *Stratagems and Spoils* (1969), Bailey contrasted "contract teams" with "moral teams" and the "transactional principle" with the "moral principle," again mainly on the basis of the individual's motivation for following a leader.[3] This distinction is in line with the dichotomy propounded in *Politics and Social Change* (1963) between political groups that are "machines" and those that are "movements." But even in *Stratagems and Spoils*, the last full statement of Bailey's conceptual framework, core continues to imply constancy through successive encounters, since in addition to being based on an ideology and love for the leader, "it is based upon long-term political credit given by the supporters to the leader."[4] What appear to be separate strands in distinguishing core and support are nearly always fused in his writings. Bailey has changed and somewhat refined his terminology, for at first a coalition was composed simply of a core element and a support element.[5] In his latest work he distinguishes between the core (based on moral attachment) and a "following" (based on a transaction), with "supporters" as a general cover term including both.[6] Apparently he has discarded the term "dependent," which he used in earlier works to identify those recruited on a transactional basis.

If one considers the concepts of core and support from the standpoint of content, ambiguity also arises because "support" may refer to resources, e.g., money, land, personnel, or even administrative principles (see table 4) or to the action of supporters, e.g., paying taxes, bullying, offering hospitality, or deferential behavior (see table 5 and chart 1). Bailey is aware of this ambiguity,[7] but has not dealt with it at any length.

It is clear, then, that despite Bailey's pioneering work, refinements of these concepts are needed to deal with the ambiguities that arise in analysis. In the remainder of this chapter, taking the data I have collected on local-level politics in Jordan and the data Alan Horton gathered in a north Syrian village, I shall argue that at least four separate points of view with their appropriate criteria are available for distinguishing and analyzing core and support elements.[8] No point of view contradicts the others, but rather each complements them, contributing insights into the political process lacking in the other views. The four points of view are the processual, the ideological, the economic, and the ethical.

In his analysis of disputes in a Syrian village Horton recorded four separate coalitions between clans beginning in 1900.[9] The village, Atareb, has a population of approximately 4,500 and is composed of nine patriclans. The clans have formed two opposing clan alliances that occupy opposite sides of the village. Each clan (the largest of which, Ahmed, has 343 members) is composed of lineages that vary from about 23 to 133 members.[10] In addition to the nine clans, there are politically minor segments—lineages of clan status as well as unattached families that are genealogical and political neutrals. Each clan alliance selects its own mayor (mukhtar), there being two for the village. No panvillage council exists, although there is an *ad hoc* committee composed of the leading families of the seven largest clans. In map 3 Horton indicates the location of the clans in the village together with the number of fighting men each possessed at the time he conducted his field research. The four sets of opposing coalitions Horton reported are as follows:

Alliance One		Alliance Two
Round 1, 1900 Ahmed, Mir'i, Sulayman	vs.	Gibran, Hasan, Obeid
Round 2, 1914 Ahmed, Hasan	vs.	Gibran, Sulayman, Obeid, Mir'i
Round 3, 1944 Ahmed, Hasan, Obeid	vs.	Gibran, Sulayman, Mir'i
Round 4, 1949 Ahmed, Hasan	vs.	Gibran, Sulayman, Obeid, Mir'i

Map 3
Spatial Distribution of Clans in Atareb

North

Cemetery   School

BEIT AHMED
75

Beit Shilo*   BEIT MIR ʿI
10   50

BEIT SULAYMAN
40

Beit Aʿoub
20

West   *East*

BEIT HASAN
50

Beit Akkash
15

BEIT OBEID
30

BEIT GIBRAN
40
South
Cemetery

* Clans represented in small letters are politically subordinate to the closest capitalized clan.

If one applies the first point of view, that a core element is defined by temporal constancy, that is, that the core is the relatively permanent element which persists through a number of contests, then in the last three rounds Ahmed and Hasan can be construed as the core elements of alliance one, the "support" elements being composed of the unattached families and lineages of clan status; the same would be true of Gibran, Sulayman and Mir'i in alliance two. If, on the other hand, one took all four rounds into consideration, then Ahmed would be core for alliance one and Gibran core for alliance two, since they alone manifested temporal constancy. If one wished to make further distinctions from this point of view, Ahmed could be designated as the primary core in alliance one, (present through all four rounds) and Hasan as secondary core (present through three rounds). In alliance two Gibran is the primary core and Sulayman and Mir'i the secondary core.

If one takes into account size of group as well as constancy, then in round three Obeid might be viewed as primary "support" for alliance one, the lineages of clan status as secondary "support," and the unattached families as tertiary "support." In this instance temporal constancy determines the difference between core and support elements, but size of group determines the degree of support. If one departs again from a strict application of the criterion of temporal constancy and takes wealth into account as well as number of fighting men, then Ahmed would be designated as core for alliance one through all four rounds, but Gibran would not be so designated for alliance two, since it was dominant neither in numbers nor in wealth. Thus departure from a strict application of the criterion of temporal constancy introduces substantive differences in the content of core and support.

A number of interesting observations can be made as a result of applying the criterion of temporal constancy in this case. Ahmed and Gibran have never participated in the same coalition; the same is true of Sulayman and Hasan. Moreover every coalition has been composed of spatially adjacent units, while the two "primary cores" of the alliances (Ahmed and Gibran) are spatially the most distant. And after one case of honor between two clans of opposite alliances, a stipulation of the reconciliation was the removal of two families of one clan living in the quarter of a clan of the opposite alliance. To call the area of the opposite alliance the "quarter of the enemy" is not metaphorical but reflects real spatial segregation. The criterion of temporal constancy taken in conjunction with the necessity of spatial contiguity suggests a good deal about the political process.

Second, shifts in coalitions do not coincide with cases of honor involving the killing of clan members from opposite alliances. The periods Horton identifies as those of "corruption" (*fasād*), when relations between alliances are broken and alliance areas become truly enemy territory, are 1904–06, 1916, 1948, and 1949. Only in the last instance was the "corruption" related to a shift or threat of shift in a political alliance. Thus the political process, in which the clans seek to preserve their own security in a situation of opposing alliances within the village, seems to run a separate course from the process of social control, in which gross violations of village mores (including murder, rape and elopement) are followed by revenge and eventual reconciliation. The insulation is not complete, as the 1949 case demonstrates, but is nevertheless substantial.

Third, as I have argued in "Pertinent Variables," the presence of two separate arenas of social control (here, the two clan alliances) which coincide with two separate political arenas (the two clan alliances) within a single community restricts competition at the village level, with spatial separation and mutual avoidance characterizing the relationship of the clan alliances. In Atareb the insulation of the two political arenas over the past fifty years has been rather thorough and effective; they have separate mosques, cemeteries, and living quarters and endogamous patterns of marriage. However when that insulation has broken down over cases of honor involving members of opposite alliances, encounters become violent. When accounts are squared, the village lapses into its traditional but precarious *modus vivendi*, each alliance practicing strict separation and avoidance and each reasserting its resolution not to interfere in the political affairs of the opposite alliance. The important fact here is that the type of political competition is very much related to the phase of conflict development. During Horton's "time of peace" or his "time of corruption" it is inappropriate and perhaps impossible to seek to subvert clans and lineages from the opposite alliance. However during the intermediate "time of dispute," pragmatic rules allow such subversion, although normative rules (the gentlemen's agreement to refrain from interfering in the opposite alliance's affairs) forbid it.[11]

The second point of view for distinguishing core and support is ideological.[12] Core members are defined by adherence to a particular ideology and "by a sense of moral dedication to a common purpose."[13] Here I am deliberately twisting Bailey's usage, for the quotation applies to certain elements characterizing political parties recruited on a voluntary basis, whereas I have applied such criteria to kinship groups recruited on an ascribed basis, that is, to patrilineal descent groups. Bailey emphasizes ideology and moral compulsion as tendencies characteristic of all political parties to one degree to another, whereas I emphasize them to distinguish core from support elements. Bailey uses the term movement to summarize such tendencies, e.g., the focus on a unitary ideology, the element of moral compulsion, the substitutability of leadership, the stability of membership, and the mass-produced nature of the ties between followers and leader, due to communication through the mass media.[14] In chapter two I argued that the clan in Kufr al-Ma is a movement, albeit a weak one, by focussing on such factors as multiplexity, the gentlemen's agreement, the mayor's leadership role within the clan, muted subversion/renegadism, and the over-arching movement embracing the clan. But it is also a movement with respect to ideology and moral compulsion, a point that must be restated and elaborated here in order to forward the argument regarding core and support.

In Kufr al-Ma each member of a patrilineal descent group (clan, lineage, or close consultation group) believes in the ideology of patrilineality and this in several senses. The group itself is defined genealogically, actually or putatively, by patrilineal descent. Those so related are *ipso facto* members of the group and those not so related are *ipso facto* not members of the group. Members of patrilineal descent groups must aid one another in cases of honor, that is, they are morally obligated to pay compensation in such cases, although only the members of the close consultation group are legally bound. From the ideology of patrilineality are derived norms that stipulate a very wide range of acts between kinsmen as insults, e.g., neglect of various kinship obligations, miserliness in hospitality, manifest anger, or nicknaming.[15] Reinforcing the ideology of patrilineality is the ideology of common villageship. The village is regarded as a common area of living and toleration, where limits must be placed on the show of overt hostility. As one villager said on the occasion of a dispute, "We must allow one another room in this village." This ideology, too, entails specific norms. Hospitality is a village-wide expectation, and neighbors are expected to treat one another with civility and politeness. Of course in Kufr al-Ma neighbors are usually patrilineal kinsmen. Filial piety is a norm applicable not only to close family members but, in an extended sense, to clansmen and covillagers. The young of the village must respect all the village elders. Thus ideology and moral compulsion are important attributes of the village and the clans, as well as of their component patrilineal descent groups.

Although many of the norms described are village-wide in their scope, the economic and social sanctions which make them effective are applied by the elders of the patrilineal descent groups. Thus although the label movement can be affixed to the whole village and even to the whole complex of villages that compose the peoples of Tibne, the clan is the widest effective unit of social control and the unit of widest scope having political representation (the mukhtars).

All clan members are expected to support the mayorship of their own clan—but not that of other clans—whether they do so or not. Conversely, nonclan members are not expected to support the clan's mayorship, although they may very well do so. Thus, from the ideological point of view clan members are core members and nonclansmen are supporters, if they conduct political business with a mukhtar of a clan other than their own. From this point of view, the core elements of a coalition are stable and unvarying, since membership in a patrilineal descent group is defined at birth for life. Although long association and/or marriage make the eventual forging of spurious genealogical links possible, it is a long-term process irrelevant to the formation of particular coalitions at particular moments in time.

There is one final respect in which the clan in Kufr al-Ma is a movement: leadership in the group is "substitutable." Any elder of the clan can act in its name in an unofficial but nevertheless effective capacity. Indeed this often occurs; the mukhtar is by no means always the most influential figure in the clan, there being a number of clan elders who mediate and have the ability to forge a consensus in a moment of crisis. The most important difference, then, between Bailey's movement-as-political-party and the Jordanian movement-as-clan is in the mode of recruitment—the former being achieved on a mass basis through the media, the latter being ascribed individually at birth. In both instances, however, a "platform" for action exists; in the former there is a particular political ideology, in the latter a genealogical charter.

The clan, then, is a movement rooted in moral compulsion and defined by a particular ideology. It is the strength of this ideology that renders an ideological point of view of core and support not only possible but also useful, as the discussion of the mayors' strategy and tactics demonstrates. If one accepts the ideological point of view, core elements are defined once and for all and hold for every round of competition, although support elements can vary; if, on the

Table 5
Socioeconomic Backing of Village Mayors in Kufr al-Ma

| | Contributions to the Dumi Mukhtar | | | |
	Dumi	Amr	Independent Families	Y
Annual Payment in Kind (*Makhtara*)	2	0	0	
Annual Payment in Cash (*Makhtara*)	1	0	0	
Ad hoc Payment for Service Rendered (*Mathbata*)	31	28	31	
In-and-Outers	1	0	5	
Nonpaying Supporters	0	0	4	
Nonpaying Cooperators	10	2	0	

other hand, one accepts the view stressing temporal constancy, both core and support elements can only be determined by observing the coalitions formed through several rounds.

A third point of view from which to distinguish core and support is the economic. Here regular economic contributors to the group, in this instance, the patriclan, form its core, and irregular contributors or noncontributors form support elements. The socioeconomic support for the Yasin mayorship (makhtara) and the Dumi mayorship in Kufr al-Ma are indicated in table 5. Historically the makhtara was the traditional annual payment in kind made to the mayors on the threshing ground on the occasion of the harvest (horizontal column 1). It was made only by those owning land and in proportion to the size of their holdings. Thus the term of reference for the basic economic contribution to the mayor and the term for the mayorship itself are identical. Seventeen households still make such payments, although only two are to the Dumi mukhtar. More recently this

Contributions to the Yasin Mukhtar

asin	'Amr	Independent Families		
12	1	2		
19	2	1	CORE	
3	2	3		
4	9	8		
31	13	22	SUPPORT	
0	3	6		

same regular annual payment has been made in cash (see horizontal column 2). In 1964 the central government passed a law stipulating that remuneration of the mukhtar would be according to services rendered; for each document (*mathbata*) he drew up and stamped he was entitled to $.28, except documents of marriage, for which he was entitled to $1.40. This change represented in microcosm a dramatic example of one aspect of what Sir Henry Maine has referred to in social evolution as the shift from a society based on status to one based on contract.[16] Although the law broke sharply from previous legislation and administrative fiat, it did not produce a sudden radical shift in the mukhtar's political support; it did, however, bring about a gradual and cumulative change. Even though the overwhelming majority of the followers of the Dumi mukhtar now make *ad hoc* payments on a contractual basis for services rendered, a few (three) continue to pay the makhtara. On the other hand, most of the Yasin mukhtar's economic support comes from those who continue to pay the makhtara on an annual basis; only eight pay on an *ad hoc* basis for services rendered. Generally as one proceeds from the top of table 5 towards the bottom, one moves from core elements (strong and/or regular economic contributors) to support elements (weak and/or sporadic economic contributors). Those designated as "in-and-outers" oscillate in payment of the mathbata between the Dumi and Yasin mukhtar; those designated as "nonpaying supporters" come to the given mukhtar when they wish official papers to be drawn up and stamped, but they do not offer payment for such services.[17] The designation "nonpaying cooperators," the most amorphous of the categories, refers to those who pay the mukhtar for documents drawn up but in services rather than cash, to poor men of the clan who are excused from payment but come to the mukhtar for documents, to nonclansmen who come for advice or mediation of disputes but not necessarily for documents, or to patrilineal kinsmen or other relatives who are excused from payment entirely for various reasons.

What is demonstrated clearly in table 5 are the different breaking points between core and support elements for the Dumi as opposed to the Yasin mayor. The breaking point for the Dumi mayor is below the line separating payers for *ad hoc* services from "in-and-outers," since the great bulk of economic aid (from 90 of 121 households) comes in the former category. The breaking point for the Yasin mayor is below the line separating annual payers in cash from *ad hoc* payers in services; it is the 37 households who make regular makhtara payments in kind or cash that allows the Yasin mayorship to carry along the 66 households who are nonpaying supporters. The direct inference that can be made from these figures is that whereas the locus of politicoeconomic strength for the Dumi mukhtar lies more in "machine politics" (*ad hoc* transactions voluntarily entered into for mutual advantage—the mathbata), the locus of politico-economic strength for the Yasin mukhtar lies in "movement politics" (regular annual aid given on the basis of ideological identification with the clan and moral obligation to its present leaders—the makhtara).

The significance of the economic point of view for core and support can now be assessed. Considered strictly along a continuum measuring size and regularity of economic contributors, the first two horizontal columns in table 5, the makhtara (regular and substantial payments), constitute the core or perhaps primary core; the third horizontal column, the *mathbata*, secondary core or perhaps support; and the remaining columns degrees of secondary or tertiary

Chart 1
Degrees of Socioeconomic Backing for Mayors in Kufr al-Ma

ECONOMIC
CONTRIBUTIONS

1. Pay the makhtara annually in kind or cash.
2. Pay the mathbata in cash voluntarily at the time of the transaction.
3. Pay the mathbata later by service or granting of privileges.
4. Pay the mathbata in cash later under pressure.
5. Pay the mathbata but boycott socially.
6. Oscillate in payment of the mathbata between the Dumi and Yasin mayor.
7a. Wish to pay the makhtara or mathbata but are not allowed to do so due to matrilateral or affinal ties.
   b. Wish to pay the mathbata but are refused due to the gentlemens' agreement.
   c. Wish to pay the mathbata but are not allowed to, due to poverty or physical disability.
   d. Wish to pay the mathbata but are not allowed to, due to official position.
8. Always come to the mayor for documents but do not pay.
9. Give commensal support only (invitations to meals).
10. Give voluntary contributions on the occasion of special collections only.
11. Regular visitor at mayor's guest house only.
12. Come for advice and mediation only.
13. Clansmen who do not pay mathbata or makhtara (i.e. who are politically estranged but renew commensal relations).
14. Make the annual festival visit only.

SOCIAL
ACTIONS

support. And because the clustering of contributions for Dumi and Yasin differs, core and support elements, however determined, will differ in form and content for the two sides.

In fact table 5 grossly simplifies the degrees of backing given to a mukhtar by those who favor him. Chart 1 is a more detailed and accurate account of the continuum. It stipulates fourteen degrees of backing.[18] As one moves from the top of the chart to the bottom, one moves from core to support, and also one moves away from the economic aspect of the relationship between leader and follower and towards the social aspect. Of the fourteen categories only seven involve payments in cash, kind, or service; clearly payment is not necessary to indicate political backing. Indeed by far the largest number of those backing the Yasin mukhtar, sixty-six, were "non-paying" supporters. Thus a number of acts that American society would not necessarily construe as political acts are so considered in Jordanian society. For instance, a regular visitor to the mukhtar's guest house is in some sense a backer. An individual from one's own or another clan who comes to the mukhtar to seek advice or mediation in a dispute is in some sense lending his support. Even a clansman who pays neither makhtara nor mathbata but after estrangement renews commensal relations by either offering or accepting hospitality is regarded as a backer. At the end of Ramadan villagers customarily visit one another on the first day of the festival of breaking the fast. Indeed among patrilineally related men such visits are obligatory. The mukhtar himself makes the rounds of his kinsmen and neighbors while others are visiting his own guest house. He posts his eldest son there to receive the visitors and on his return is quick to ask his son, who came and, more important, who did not come, for the feast visit is the most appropriate time for estranged kinsmen and friends to terminate "their anger" (za'al). Failure of a clansman to visit indicates continued nonsupport and hard feelings. Payment of the festival visit, on the other hand, indicates not only the cooling of anger but also the expectation that the individual will soon back the mukhtar by more substantial acts.

Chart 1 also shows, however, that political and social relations are not always in *tandem*. Thus, as category 5 shows, an individual may back the mukhtar economically but boycott him socially, or as category 11 shows, he may back him socially on a regular basis but not at all economically. Category 7 is interesting, for the mukhtar sometimes refuses individuals who are willing and/or able to make economic contributions; this comes about because clans are movements in which moral compulsion plays an important role. Thus the poor of the clan and its disabled are exempted from payment. Since a considerable percentage of marriages are endogamous to the clan, a number of patrilineal clansmen will also be matrilateral relatives, and the tie of matrilaterality is an affective one; thus matrilateral relatives within or outside the clan are often exempted from payment; in addition, affines are also sometimes exempted.

These instances highlight another point. Although this discussion has focussed on analyzing core and support from an economic point of view, the analysis has led to a consideration of ideological factors. It is no accident that in Table 5 the mukhtar of Yasin did not designate a single member of his clan as a "cooperator"; rather all were called nonpaying "supporters," the reason being that he quite clearly exposed an ideological view of core and support in which all clansmen *ipso facto* are core members. The analysis has also had to take into account temporal constancy, since the continuum referred to in both Table 5 and Chart 1 is a rough measure of regularity of economic contributions as well as size of contributions. Indeed by combining these three points of view, it is possible to arrive at a fourth view of core and support. The primary core of the Yasin mayorship is composed of regular landowning, dues-paying (makhtara) clansmen as defined by the economic point of view; the secondary core is composed of all other clansmen as defined by the ideological point of view; and support elements are all others who contribute in the variety of ways indicated by the categories toward the bottom of Chart 1—but always in an unstable fashion as defined by the criterion of temporal constancy.

The fourth point of view by which to distinguish core and support is the ethical point of view. Thus far I have omitted how the leaders evaluate the degrees of political succor their backers provide. However, leaders do make such evaluations and do rank contributors along a continuum that stretches from honor at one end to invidiuum at the other. The propensity not only to attribute political significance to a wide variety of social acts but also to make ethical evaluations of such acts arises in part from the movement character of descent groups and the village itself. But this propensity also arises from the multiplexity of relationships characterizing clan members. Although I have discussed the significance of multiplexity, its implications for ethical evaluations must be elaborated further here. Clansmen are also coreligionists, neighbors, affines, land partners, and covillagers. That is, every relationship between two clansmen cuts across many interests. This being so, every interaction has an import far beyond its immediate context. Thus individual acts, far from being considered in relation to a given set of goals in a given context, are constantly reviewed and evaluated in terms of the widest possible context—the context of the whole man and the morality of his behavior. It is not happenstance that only the mukhtar of Yasin provided me with a full set of such ethical evaluations, for Beni Yasin is much more multiplex in its social relations and much more oriented toward the movement type of politics than the other clans of the village.

Chart 2 records the Yasin mukhtar's ethical evaluations of his backing. As one moves from the top to the bottom of the chart, one moves by degrees from the most laudatory category to the most disapproved.

Individuals named in category 1 were always from the mukhtar's own clan and referred mainly to the members of its poorest lineage (Aqayli), the implication being that those who could least afford to give were most honorable in giving. The second category referred to

Chart 2
Ethical Evaluations of His Own Backing by the Mayor of Beni Yasin

1. "The people who always give."

2. "The people who are not constant in support but have principle."

3. "The people about whom I know nothing."

4. "The sometimes here, sometimes there people."

5. "The people without principle."

nonclansmen who backed the mayor though not necessarily by economic contributions; when a quarrel occurred and economic contributions lapsed, these individuals did not rush to support the other mukhtar and they did not backbite; they merely remained aloof until the period of estrangement ended. Category 3 was in an evaluatory sense neutral; it referred mainly to most members of Beni Dumi, from whom the mukhtar could not expect support, he made no ethical evaluation of their behavior—simply a statement of unconcern and ignorance. Category 4 referred to both clansmen and nonclansmen; the mukhtar stressed the inconstancy of support of these individuals and further stated, "They soothe with false promises" or "They talk a lot" or "They are apple-polishers" (*byarūhu byamallsin*). Category 5 included both clansmen and nonclansmen; an example of the former is a man who goes to the mukhtar of the opposite clan for documents, thus, by implication, betraying his own mukhtar; an example of the latter is a man "who leaves you over the slightest difference." Attention should be paid to the ethical importance of constancy in these evaluations. Those who are inconstant are criticized most severely and those who are constant are lauded most. From the ethical point of view constancy is more important than the presence or size of economic contributions. Thus category 6 on Chart 1 (oscillators in mathbata payments) would be ranked near the very bottom from an ethical point of view, even though their annual economic contribution would be much greater than the eight categories ranked below them from an economic point of view. Most of these eight categories include villagers who are REGULAR in their social support (e.g., commensal support, visiting, mediation requests) and, therefore, laudable. What I have just argued seems to be contradicted by category 2 in Chart 2, since people who are "inconstant" are rated high. In fact, the people designated in category 2 are constant both in principle and social support, and their economic inconstancy is relatively unimportant since they are not clansmen. But economic inconstancy by clansmen is not excused ethically and accounts for the very low rating given to category 13 in Chart 1. Ethical evaluations have, of course, to some degree influenced my informant's and therefore my own rankings in a chart that purports to be a continuum of socioeconomic support.

Again, it is obvious that any point of view implies or alludes to the others. Categories 1, 2, and 4 in Chart 2 include not only temporal constancy and economic aid but also the ideological point of view, since condemnation for not giving or giving sporadically is always greater for a clansman than for a nonclansman. Nonclansmen in category 2 did not make regular contributions but were still praised.

I said at the beginning of this chapter that from the standpoint of content the terms core and support are ambiguous, particularly with regard to whether they refer to resources, e.g., money, land, personnel, or to the actions of individuals, e.g., paying dues, offering hospitality, bullying. From the ethical point of view, core and support elements clearly relate to the acts of individuals and not to resources as such. From the ideological point of view, on the other hand, the acts of individuals are irrelevant, since members of the patriclan are *ipso facto* core and nonclan members are *ipso facto* support; the resource involved here, if any, is the principle of patrilineal descent. From the point of view of temporal constancy, the focus is on the single resource of personnel with the added implication that the personnel have arms of one kind or another and, further, that in a crisis they will rush with them to help their comrades. On the other hand, from the economic point of view it is both the resources committed—money, crops, services, time—and the act of commitment that is important in discriminating core and support.

All four points of view focus on recruitment, but whether the additional backing is defined by actions or resources depends on the point of view taken. At one extreme the ideological view regards actions as irrelevant, while at the other the ethical view regards actions as all-important. Temporal constancy focuses on personnel and on other resources only by implication, with actions important in the forming of coalitions, but not in their definition. Paradoxically, it is the economic point of view, which ostensibly must focus on resources, that most emphasizes both actions *and* resources. Chart 1 and Table 5 demonstrate that at the upper end of the continuum economic contributions are stressed, but at the lower end social actions are what count.

What was said at the beginning of the chapter about the complementary nature of each point of view for the other can now be restated with a greater degree of understanding. The different points of view highlight different aspects of political action—the processual, the ethical, the economic, the ideological. However each point of view, even stated in its own terms, almost always takes into account, explicitly or implicitly, some aspects of the others. The fullest understanding of the process of coalition-formation, then, requires taking into account all four points of view and their conjunction rather than any single one in isolation from or in preference to the others.

The Mayors: Strategy,
Tactics, and Intercalary
Leadership

Since the turn of the century local-level leadership in Kufr al-Ma seems to have passed through four phases: the shaykhdom; the period of the single long-term mayorship (*makhtara*); the period of multiple short-term mayors; and the period of multiple long-term mayors. In the past the Shaykh of Tibne traditionally controlled the twelve villages populated by "the peoples of Tibne." This control often extended to the whole of the Al-Kura subdistrict and included the power to collect taxes, demand economic contributions, and raise paramilitary forces.[1] The key political role of the Shaykh in this period can only be understood in the context of the villagers' political and military position vis à vis the Bedouins on the one hand and the Turkish authorities on the other.

Although the Bedouins did not subjugate the Ajlun district, of which Al-Kura was a part, as they did surrounding districts, it was sometimes the object of their raids. In 1918, when Turkish defenses had collapsed, one of these infrequent raids occurred; Bedouins occupied Kufr al-Ma, most of whose able-bodied men had been conscripted into the Ottoman army. The Bedouin ate all the stores, appropriated the animals, and shot villagers who resisted them. Logistically villagers were always at a disadvantage because of their sedentary occupations. If a Bedouin killed a villager he fled to a nomadic tribal area and was seldom apprehended; indeed, according to the villagers, the government seldom pursued him. However if a villager killed a Bedouin, he was always pursued and usually caught.

The relations between the Bedouins, the villagers, and the Turkish authorities were complicated by certain cultural factors. In ad-

dition to being inaccessible physically, the Bedouins had the reputation of being difficult to discipline; therefore army recruiters focused
on the peasants, who were regarded as more pliable human material.
Many older villagers recalled serving with the Ottoman army in
such farflung places as Serbia, Greece, and Egypt. Typifying the view
of Bedouin unfitness for military service was the anecdote recounted
in the village about the Bedouin conscripted into the army who
when ordered to stand at attention replied to the officer in charge,
"Do you mean me, lieutenant, or my comrade [standing alongside]?"
By contrast, the peasant replied immediately to the Turkish recruiting officer's announcement of conscription, "I am at your service,
sir!"[2]

In spite of taxation and forced conscription by Turks and depredation by Bedouins, the villagers' attitude toward both groups was ambivalent rather than completely hostile. The Turks were fellow
Muslims and the sultan was the defender of the faith against European unbelievers. One villager explicitly excused the Turks for "not
building up our land and protecting us from Bedouins" because he
said "they were busy fighting Europeans." Moreover the sultan's
representative in the area—the *wali* or governor—was the only
court of appeal from injustices wrought by local tyrants. Although
they constantly threatened the villagers' security, the Bedouins
shared a culture with the peasants—hospitality, valor, and addic-
tion to poetry and coffee were also prized by villagers; indeed many
villagers in east Jordan were recently settled nomads who still traced
relations to their nomadic cousins.

Aside from Bedouins and Turks, brigandage and theft were common in the area. Theft was a mark of valor: "In those days if you
didn't steal, your wife wouldn't accept you," remarked a villager.
Before the turn of the century one small patrilineage with a saintly
reputation was living in Kufr al-Ma among the "peoples of Tibne,"
to whom it was unrelated genealogically. Repeatedly robbed by its
stronger, more aggressive neighbors, the lineage elders finally complained to the Shaykh of Tibne that his relatives were oppressing the
group. He suggested that they move to a nearby village, then in ruins
and uninhabited, which they did. Villagers from Kufr al-Ma often
swapped stories about raids to plunder sheep which they conducted
into the Jordan Valley. Of course retaliatory raids followed. Not
necessarily or even usually the work of Bedouins, these raids were
made by other tribally organized villages who formed another "people" (*gawm*). The district of Ajlun was broken up into a number of
territories, each of which was regarded as the home of a potential

enemy—another tribe. Thus the problem of security involved groups of villages with one another as well as Bedouins and Turks, and the Shaykh's principal political function was to provide protection against these threats and to mediate between the villagers and hostile outside forces.

The Shaykh could demand economic contributions from villagers as a mark of their allegiance, and he could make war and peace and raise a military following when the occasion demanded. Often, he placed members of his family—usually his sons—in various villages as deputies and later as *mukhtars;* these men were often welcomed by the villagers and sometimes given grants of land as an inducement to settle there. To have a member of the Shaykh's family in residence was the best insurance possible against external threats and was, moreover, cheap, for agricultural land was plentiful. It goes without saying that establishing law and order in such a situation was not easy. As villagers said about the political leadership of the Wazir family, "They paid for it with their heads." But, once having achieved the shaykhdom, the Shaykh "could loose and bind" (*kan yafiq wa yirbuT*). Although he usually took council with leading elders, "the owners of opinion" (*SaHbīn al-ra'i*), his word was the last.

The Shaykh also played an important role in social control and in redistributing economic surplus. His guest house was the final court of appeal and the fount of generosity. This was so because of the Shaykh's power and his control of tribute but also because of transportation and the Transjordanian way of life. A person could not travel from 'Ajlun to Irbid to attend court in a single day. He broke the trip in a village of Al-Kura, where he would receive hospitality from the leading personalities, of whom the Wazirs were the most prominent. Hospitality included not only lodgings for the night and appropriate food (a sheep was slaughtered for honored guests) but also fodder for the horses. Since men sometimes moved in mounted groups, the expense of offering such hospitality was great. Only the Shaykhs of Tibne could provide on such a lavish scale, so only they achieved the reputation of being "good men" par excellence since valor and generosity were the model acts of manliness. Economic surplus was converted into "value power," which, in turn could be converted into political support when the Shaykh required arms and men in an emergency: "rushing to succor" is still the term used to indicate response to calls of distress among the peoples of Tibne.

Justice was also rendered in the Shaykh's guest house. Men came from throughout the district with their disputes, asking the Shaykh to arbitrate. It was not only his power that made him the supreme arbitrator but also logistics and local custom. Before World War One and to some extent until World War Two, the Shaykh's guest house was much more than the locus of hospitality, gossip, and entertainment; it was a semisacrosanct house of justice where strict rules of decorum were applied: only one man spoke at a time, and then only with permission; silence was observed while each person spoke; formal politeness formulas regarding greetings, departures, sneezing, prayer, and seating were observed; young men and women were barred from the guest house. Various ploys were available to pressure villagers to accede to the Shaykh's wishes, e.g., the Shaykh might take the initiative and visit a recalcitrant villager, but refuse to drink the tea or coffee of his host until the villager had acceded to the Shaykh's request. A violator of village mores was "called to justice" (*kañu yiTlabū lil Haqq*) in the Shaykh's guest house. If at first he did not accede to this request, he was insulted, boycotted, and finally compelled to go—and the same pressures were placed on the individual to accept the decision. Of course, the threat of being blacklisted by the Shaykh was not the least effective sanction in these situations.

The Shaykh's power and influence in social control must be considered in relation to available alternatives—there were none. Ottoman rule in Jordan was ineffective and, at best, sporadic. There was no local police post, and the Ottoman governor, located in Der'a in Syria, was far too distant to provide practical justice for a peasant. The Ottomans for their part preferred to rely on an effective local leader who could at least maintain some semblance of order and perhaps collect token taxes. The peasants much preferred the arbitrary rule of a culturally familiar figure with whom they identified—they were all "peoples of Tibne"—and the protection he offered than the arbitrary rule of the Turks who, despite religious affinity, were still foreigners. Only such circumstances can explain why the Shaykhs of Tibne were able to maintain their power and influence in Al-Kura until 1922, when British planes flying for Amir Abdullah bombed Tibne and reduced it to submission.

After 1922 the Shaykhdom in its traditional sense ceased to exist, although the Wazir family continues to exert an inordinate influence. Those members of the lineage who had not already done so moved out of Tibne into the new subdistrict capital, Deir Abu Said, or its surrounding villages, where they would have greater access to government offices and the amenities, including secular education, that the central government eventually provided. By 1950 the son of the Shaykh who had resisted Amir Abdullah had been appointed to the Jordanian Senate and grandsons of the Shaykh, benefitting from their secular education, had received posts in the local bureaucracies. The adversity of surrender to the central government and imprisonment had been converted into the sweetness of official government positions.

Despite the establishment of central government authority in Al-Kura, the break between the Shaykhdom and the period of single long-term mayors (mukhtars) was not all that clear. Since at the beginning members of the Shaykh's family served as mukhtars in many villages, it was not always clear whether they were acting as official government representatives or as the Shaykh's deputies.[3] The Shaykh continued to possess considerable prestige not now as the result of his political services (protection) but because he remained the leading agent of social control in the subdistrict; the residents of the area still asked him to arbitrate disputes; and, to a lesser degree, because he continued to carry out economic redistribution. As an example of this useful ambiguity of roles, which smoothed the transition to central government control, the favored son of the Shaykh, who is even today addressed as "Pasha," served as mukhtar of Kufr al-Ma three times in the period between 1916 and 1928. During these times he was the sole official spokesman for the village. Intermittently and subsequently other prominent elders served as sole mukhtars for the whole village for periods varying between two and nine years.

In this period of single mukhtars the man selected was almost invariably an elder, a leading personality in the community usually noted for his skill in arbitration, an illiterate, a relatively wealthy man, and an individual known for his generosity and courtesy. The single known exception to this list of attributes was the son of the Shaykh, the Pasha. One of the first, if not the first, in the subdistrict to receive a secular education, he was at the time of World War One in his first term as mukhtar only twenty-two; however filiation more than made up for his age, and his literacy was by no means regarded as a handicap. Wealth and generosity were perhaps the key attributes for a successful mukhtar during this period, since a man's reputation depended on the adequate display of hospitality. By noon the mayor always had fresh-brewed coffee available in his guest house for his friends, neighbors, kinsmen, and supporters; and he always had to have a plentiful supply of fodder for the horses of out-of-town visitors. Obviously the *mukhtar* had to have a spacious guest house, sufficient mattresses and pillows to outfit it, and the wherewithal to purchase coffee and the implements to make it—a carved wooden coffee mortar and pestle, numerous brass coffee pots and cups. In this post-World War One period there were very few government officials at the local level—a corporal was in charge of the police post and the highest administrative official in the subdistrict, the *mudir al-nahiya*, was the lowest order of official in the Transjordanian administrative hierarchy. There were two factors working for the maintenance of the single mayorship during this period. Often a single leading personality in the community was recognized as the natural political leader by consensus; this was particularly so when members of the Wazir family happened to be residents. And second, the government always preferred to deal with a single leader at the local level.

It is unclear precisely what factors accounted for the shift from a single long-term mayor to multiple short-term mayors. Population growth was probably one—as the three clans in the village grew, each probably felt that one of its own members would more adequately defend clan interests. It is possible when bureaucrats detected irreconcilable divisions within the local community that the central administration may have favored such a policy. Or some other factor may have been responsible. Whatever the cause, several years before World War Two at least two mukhtars were regularly representing Kufr al-Ma to the outside world. Usually each mukhtar represented his own clan and was supported by it with an annual levy collected from the prominent landowning members on the threshing ground immediately after the harvest. However there is a great deal of evidence to suggest that competition even during this period was not strictly between clans; rather support for particular mukhtars often cut across clans. The most pronounced case of such incipient "factionalism," if it can be called that, was in 1956, at the beginning of phase four, when two prominent members of Yasin ran against one another on slates in which they were teamed up with members of other clans. According to village informants, during this period the mukhtar had to be officially reconfirmed at the end of each year or else another mukhtar had to be selected. The clan had to formally nominate the mukhtar by forwarding to the subdistrict officer (*qāʾimaqām*—Al-Kura had been elevated in the administrative hierarchy by this time) a petition signed by about twenty of his backers. This petition was sent to the local public defender, who determined whether there were any outstanding legal claims against the nominee, such as nonpayment of taxes or pending lawsuits. If there were none and opposition to his nomination was absent or weak, he was confirmed as mayor for the coming year. During this period informants recalled only one election (in 1942); otherwise, mayors were always selected by this process of informal consensus by elders, formal petition, and confirmation by the local bureaucracy.

The fourth phase in the development of the mayorship—the period of multiple long-term mukhtars—began in 1956 with a unique event—a hotly contested election which badly split Beni Yasin, hitherto the most solidary clan in the village. Several factors accounted for this notable departure from "low-key politics." First, the central administration announced that the next duly chosen mayor or mayors would serve till they resigned, i.e., the mayorship was to become a permanent office. Furthermore, by fiat it was ruled that villages could have not more than one mukhtar for every thousand persons; since Kufr al-Ma had about two thousand, two mukhtars might be selected. A number of rumors (all of which turned out to be false) circulated to the effect that henceforth the mukhtar would (1) have a salary, (2) have a car at his disposal, (3) be more than a functionary, i.e., have executive power, and (4) have a telephone. A slate with one nominee from Yasin and one from 'Amr defeated a slate with one nominee from Yasin and another from Dumi. Two months later members of Beni Dumi formally protested their lack of representation to the subdistrict officer and to the Pasha, who was now living in the subdistrict capital, Deir Abu Said. Shortly thereafter a mayor from Dumi was appointed; he was still mayor in 1967 when I left the village. This appointment was facilitated when shortly after the elections the Beni 'Amr mayor resigned over a quarrel involving a marriage internal to his own clan. The Beni Yasin mayor possessed all the traditional attributes of leadership—including illiteracy. The local bureaucracy and perhaps many villagers now considered his election inappropriate to the needs of the time. A precedent for a new type of mukhtar had been set many years earlier, in 1945, when a member of Yasin had been elected mayor at the age of seventeen—his outstanding qualification was having completed eight years of schooling. So in 1957 the members of Yasin retired the elected mayor (who was an elder and a pilgrim) and selected another, who combined the traditional qualities of leadership (e.g., age, piety, skill at mediation) with the new ones (literacy, knowledge of town ways, and dedication to local improvement). This mayor was also still in office when I left the village in 1967.

A fifth phase in the development of the mayorship may or may not have taken place (as indicated in chapters two and three) when in 1964 the central government reorganized the basis for the remuneration of village mukhtars.

The phases in the development of the mayorship were accompanied by certain trends in fiscal support and the extension of hospitality. The Shaykhdom served as the model through the first three periods: clansmen with land were expected to make the regular annual contribution (makhtara) in kind on the threshing ground. This basis of fiscal support tended to accentuate the division in the clan between those who had land and those who did not and made the distinction between core and support (or, from an ideological point of view, between primary and secondary core) fairly precise economically. The mayor, in return, was expected to offer regular hospitality to his clansmen, to visiting officials, and to strangers. He was expected to be on hand at all times to deal with all visitors, and although his powers were not nearly as great as the Shaykh, his guest house, along with those of the other prominent men of the clan, was a forum where pressure could be exerted on men to reconcile their differences. Gradually, even for men like the mayor of Beni Yasin who fully accepted the traditional model as an ethical norm, the fiscal basis of the mayorship changed. Regular annual contributions in kind by clansmen have declined so that even for the clan that most resembles a movement, Beni Yasin, only twelve households paid on that basis in 1966. One can still refer to the fiscal basis of the Yasin mayorship as traditional in the sense that the great bulk of economic support comes from men who have land or regular monetary income from employment outside the village (as soldiers or clerks), which allows them to make regular annual contributions. But the income has diminished considerably: in 1960 the mayor of Yasin received seven sacks of wheat and seven sacks of barley worth a total of £42 sterling; in 1965 he received grain (three sacks of wheat and two sacks of barley) valued at £14 sterling;[4] and this must be compared with the ten to twelve sacks of wheat and the ten sacks of barley he used to get in the immediate postwar period. The Dumi mayor told me that his father, who had been mayor between the two World Wars, had received twenty-five sacks of grain and five sacks of barley a year. In 1965 the mayor of Yasin told me that he had received less of a makhtara each year for the last five years. In view of this "diminished mayorship," it was not surprising that the mayor of Yasin, who continued to operate in terms of the traditional model of a "full-blown mayorship," sought by various means to strengthen his fiscal base. In 1957 he entered into an oral agreement with his clansmen which stipulated that for every kirat of land held, a clansman would pay a *rub'iyāt* (a quarter of a measure) of wheat and a rub'iyat of barley. Clansmen who did not own land promised to pay 25 piastres ($.70). Soldiers were exempted from payment. He said that if everyone had paid him on the basis of the agreement, he would have received seventy measures (*mud*) of wheat and seventy measures of barley; actually he received only forty measures of each. In 1966, perhaps recognizing that a majority of the men of the clan were engaged in nonagricultural employment for wages or salaries, the mayor sought to establish a regular but "limited" mayorship; i.e., he and his clansmen now agreed orally to abandon the old division between landed and nonlanded members and to stipulate that every household, excluding the poor, contribute 50 piastres ($1.40) annually. At this same time another, wealthier elder of the clan who was employed as a clerk of court in the subdistrict center actually took the responsibility for offering clan hospitality on himself by serving coffee in his guest house every evening thereby relieving the impoverished mayor of an important obligation. By the beginning of the fifth phase even the Yasin mayor's fiscal basis had shifted considerably. Thus in 1965, although he received the equivalent of £14 sterling in makhtara payments in kind, he received £12 sterling in contractual (mathbata) payments. This statement of total income suggests that the totals given me by the Yasin mayor regarding the number of men who made *ad hoc* payments for services rendered (mathbata) in table 5, only eight men, underweights the contractual sources of the mayor's income. However it does reflect the Yasin mayor's continued ideological commitment to a full-blown mayorship and the sources of income appropriate to it.

By contrast, the mayor of Beni Dumi, at least as early as 1960 and probably from the very beginning of his mayorship in 1956, has consciously operated a "watered-down" mayorship. He did not expect anyone to pay him the makhtara (only three still do), and he collected from his own clansmen only on the basis of services rendered, anticipating the change in government policy by several years. There is another side of the coin; since collections were limited, services were limited. Often the Dumi mayor was not present in the village when needed, for he operated as a medic in the surrounding villages much of the time. When he did provide a service, it was to his own clansmen or to members of 'Amr and the independent lineages who supported him unambiguously; he did not offer any hospitality at all—if he could possibly get out of it—either to clansmen, government officials, or strangers. He closed the guest

house for which his father had been the renowned host; and, following as a logical consequence, he did not seek to build a reputation as
a skilled mediator in his own or any other guest house. The implications of this explicit rejection of the shaykhly model of the mayorship will be examined in chapter seven.

The Official Duties of the Mayor

The official duties of the mayor have been stipulated, reaffirmed,
and slightly modified in a series of laws promulgated in 1954, 1958,
1959 and 1964.[5] The following discussion is based on the 1954 law,
except where that law was amended by later laws or regulations, and
on the substantive practice of mayors in Kufr al-Ma. According to
the 1954 law the electors of the mayor are males above the age of
eighteen permanently residing in the village. To be eligible for the
office, the individual must be twenty-one, a permanent resident of
the village, and not convicted or charged with criminal or moral
offenses. The 1958 law added that the nominee had to be literate, a
permanent resident of the quarter or tribe he represented (the term
village was not used in this context), and a taxpayer of at least one
Jordanian dinar (£1 sterling)—this last a very minimal property-
ownership requirement. A directive issued by the Minister of Interior in 1959 stated that nominees having "political party inclina-
tions" were barred from seeking the office. All three laws stipulate
that the mayor can be removed by the provincial governor for any
neglect of obligations, wrongdoing, or other sufficient cause and that
the governor can appoint a replacement. The mayor is expected to
select a deputy to act as mayor in his absence.

The procedures for selecting the mayor are stipulated in the 1954
law as follows: the governor, after setting the date of the election,
appoints an electoral committee of not fewer than three members,
one of whom is the district officer or his deputy and the others notables from the village. This committee draws up a list of eligible candidates from whom nominees can be drawn. Any man so named can
nominate himself as mayor during the three-day period during
which the list is posted in the village. The committee must also
arrange for voting and the counting of ballots. Any citizen can protest the absence of his name from the list of eligible candidates or
protest the appearance of a name to the governor or district officer
within five days of the list's posting. Since I was not present during
any mayoral election I cannot assert one way or the other that these

electoral procedures were carried out in the village. As noted above only one election has taken place in the village's recent history and the current administrative practice of permanent incumbency makes elections unlikely. The powers granted to the governor with regard to the selection and incumbency of mayors were considerable; he sets the date of election, recommends the number of slates, appoints the electoral committee, removes mayors considered negligent, and appoints others. The significance of this authority will be examined in the next chapter. The 1958 law amended the mayor's powers by giving him the authority to appoint two "members," who were required to assist him in his duties.

The duties of the mayor are to preserve law and order; to inform the police of violations or threatened violations of law, of suspicious characters, and of deaths from unnatural causes; to aid all government representatives coming to the village, including the tax collector. In Kufr al-Ma the tax collector, the agricultural inspector, the police, and most other government officials come directly to the mayor in order to dispatch their business, much of which takes place in the mayor's guest house to which the relevant parties are summoned; in Kufr al-Ma the mayor is also called upon to organize official greetings for members of the royal family who passed through the district. The 1954 law stipulates that the mayor must publicize all official government pronouncements and regulations and to keep the official stamp of the mayor and to stamp all documents brought to him for certification. In Kufr al-Ma such documents include divisions of inheritance, wives' requests for conjugal maintenance from the Islamic court, marriage documents (in which the mayor certifies that there are no legal impediments to the marriage, such as age, previous marriage, or milk siblingship), divorce petitions (in which the mayor certifies that the woman is not capable of bearing children), documents certifying the birth date of children (so their fathers may receive stipends for them from the army), and statements certifying the imminent death of a family member (in order for soldiers and police to receive furloughs). The 1954 law also stipulates that the mayor is expected to inform local authorities of the death of an individual with property and without heirs, and to inform them of the use of false weights and measures. The mayor is expected to safeguard railroad lines and telegraphic and telephonic communications within his jurisdiction and to safeguard public ways and forests and other government property. He has the duty of reporting all archeological finds to the authorities and of protecting historical sites; he also must notify the authorities when any plague or disease appears among the crops. He also gathers and preserves statistical records; in Kufr al-Ma these include records of birth and death and rosters for the distribution of government largesse, e.g., wheat.

The 1954 law also grants the mayor certain rights and powers: he may exercise all the powers and privileges granted to the police within his area of jurisdiction (the village). Any person who refuses to aid the mayor in matters relating to public security is to be fined not more than five Jordanian dinars. The mayor has the right to exact fees determined by the Ministry of the Interior or by other laws—but only these fees and no others. Mayors guilty of collecting fees in excess of what is allowed or of falsely certifying documents can be fined up to ten Jordanian dinars. In Kufr al-Ma no official fees were collected from villagers for whom the mayor performed services—at least not until after 1964. However the Dumi mayor collected very small unofficial fees beginning in 1960. Mayors received financial support on the customary basis of an annual payment in kind or in coin at the time of the harvest (see chapter three). The official regulation of 1964 set rates of remuneration for particular services. Henceforth the mayor was empowered to collect 10 piastres ($.28) for certifying any document to be handed to the government for examination and 50 piastres ($1.40) for any marriage document. The significance of this change for the strategy and tactics of the mayors in Kufr al-Ma will be discussed below.

Intercalary Leader or Power Holder

In his discussions of the village headmanship in Central Africa Max Gluckman pointed out that the headman was inserted (like an intercalary number) at the intersection of two hierarchies—administrative and domestic-kinship, that he was subject to sanctions of different kinds (diffuse and moral as opposed to legal and organized), that he was "closely involved in every matter over which he should preside impartially," and that as a result his position was difficult pragmatically (in terms of getting things done) and psychologically (in terms of his own peace of mind).[6] In some respects Gluckman's analysis applies to the position of mayor in Kufr al-Ma. The mayor is the lowest-level functionary in the national administrative system, as indicated by the enumeration of his duties and by the fact that he is held legally responsible for certain acts which take place within its boundaries. He is also a *bona fide* representative of the village: he bears its official stamp, acts in its name, and is regarded by the villagers as its spokesman and defender of its interests. If a significant proportion of the village's population believes that he has violated its best interests, they will take action against him—in 1960 villagers in Kufr al-Ma sent a petition to the subdistrict officer which accused the mukhtar of favoring the rich in a distribution of fodder. In addition, the mayor represents his clan; he is selected by it, receives the bulk of his financial support from it, and is regarded as working primarily for its interests. Indeed many men consent to serve in a position of such low rewards only out of a sense of loyalty to the movement—the clan. From the mayor's point of view each social unit—the administration, the village, the clan—exerts some degree of moral compulsion; the first appeals to his patriotism, the others to the loyalties of propinquity, descent, kinship, and marriage. However since village and particularly clan members enmesh the mayor in a web of multiplex relationships, while the local administration does not, the moral compulsion of the clan is most persuasive, of the village somewhat less, and of the local administration far less. This should not be construed as indicating relative weakness on the part of the administration, for it possesses political power and legal sanctions. Since the interests of these three social units sometimes conflict, the mayor must subordinate some loyalties to others and thereby court the displeasure of the offended unit. If a robbery occurs in his own clan quarter, the mayor must identify possible suspects to the police even though they may be his own clansmen. Often he must act as an official witness to customary practice in the village in the civil or religious court or before the subdistrict officer, even when such action discredits his fellow villagers or clansmen in the eyes of law. Thus certain exchanges of property are customary on the occasion of marriage and validate or invalidate subsequent claims by either spouse; since the mayor must testify as to the passage or nonpassage of the property involved from the family of one spouse to the family of the other, his testimony affronts one of the parties, particularly when that party is from his own clan. Even apart from any formal duties attached to his office, the mayor, like any elder of the clan or village, suffers certain role conflicts which result from the fact that he himself is caught up in a whole range of inter- and intraclan grudges at the same time that he is called upon to mediate disputes involving the parties to those grudges.

This situation conforms fairly well with Gluckman's analysis of intercalary or, as he has termed it more recently, "inter-hierarchi-

cal" leadership. However in Kufr al-Ma the mayor's position is complicated by an additional factor—ideological ambiguity as to his
proper role or, stated in another way, ambiguity as to the relationship his politicoadministrative roles have to one another. At one and
the same time the mayor represents the clan, the village, and the
government, but the members of each unit see him as primarily representing that unit in particular situations. Moreover although the
clan and village are forced to recognize the claims of the government, because of its authority and power, they do not always regard
such claims as legitimate. While local government officials regard
the collection of taxes as their right and payment the duty of every
citizen, many peasants not only seek to evade taxes out of self-interest but also deny their moral validity. And the government on its
side is often unwilling to recognize the legitimacy of pleas based on
clanship and kinship. When one mayor told the subdistrict officer
that the new school could not be located at a particular place in the
village because it would result in dissension among the clans, he was
chided by the subdistrict officer, who told him he did not want to
hear about clans and tribes—only about progess in the village. Interestingly enough, this view was also propounded by one of the
most traditional villagers—the preacher—who stated that such allegiances were irrelevant, since all Muslims were cobelievers. The
fact remains that not only the overwhelming majority of villagers
regard such allegiances as compelling, but even the government officials do too; this fact is officially recognized in the laws governing
the composition of village councils, which stipulate that traditional
kinship and sectarian divisions are to be considered when determining representation.[7] However the reality of power relationships inside the village is captured neither by the ideology of clanship, nor
by the ideology of government officials (in its *de jure* or *de facto*
version), for the social units that compose various coalitions or incipient factions are much smaller ones—the lineages and close consultation groups.

As an intercalary leader, then, the mayor faces a nearly impossible
task: he must get the most out of the government "gravy train" for
his clansmen and village mates, while warding off the unpleasant
consequences of government action; at the same time he must
cooperate fully with government officials and carry out their directives at the local level. His difficult social structural position, together with the related ideological ambiguities, may be largely responsible for the high mayoral turnover rate in Kufr al-Ma during

period three in the development of the mayorship (before 1956). Although many "good men" were willing to serve the movement (the clan), they were not willing to persevere against such great odds.

The mayor's position was also inherently weak because he had neither force nor effective sanctions to help resolve the contradictions in his position. One day an old woman who often saw me accompanying the mayor in his rounds about the village, asked, "Why are you paling around with him all the time? He's of the peasants, from the weak; he cannot loose and bind." Then she went on to describe by contrast the old-time Shaykh, who had not only force and an honorable pedigree but also charisma. Even with respect to his own clansmen, not to mention other villagers, the mayor's sanctions are feeble. If his clansmen refuse to pay their annual dues, he cannot force them to do so; as the last chapter pointed out, a significant number do not pay dues. Although clansmen are supposed to remain loyal to their own clan's mayor, the gentlemen's agreement signifies the possibility of disloyalty. When disloyalty does occur, the mayor cannot expel the renegade. Even outright acts of disloyalty and defiance, such as signing a petition against him or officially siding with the other clan's mayor (see chapter six), do not result in expulsion, ostracism, or any other effective economic or social sanction. The mayor cannot levy fines, and although he has police powers within the village, I myself never witnessed and only once heard of him using physical force against a villager. That villager was publicly pummeled by the mayor and his son, after which he was so shamed that he shortly moved out of the village. However, the resulting scandal—it was revealed in the course of the incident that a bogus magician was operating in the village—brought village condemnation down on the mayor for his behavior. In fact the mayor very seldom calls for the support of government officials, such as the civil judge and the subdistrict officer, against recalcitrant villagers although his office gives him authority to do so. During the first twelve months of my stay in the village the mayor called on the police only twice; on one of those occasions he apologized profusely when they arrived, told them that the parties had been reconciled, fed them, and sent them back to the police post. The mayor also lacks the sanctions associated, for instance, with "headmen" in central Africa: he has no ritual functions and therefore no ritual sanctions; he cannot grant rights in land; he does not supervise cultivation, and he cannot force payment of taxes. The ultimate power of the village and clan—the power of ostracism—can only be wielded in the rather infrequent instances when the elders of these social units are practically unanimous in their support.

The problem with applying Gluckman's analysis of Central Africa to Jordan and in general is that by stressing the "burdens" of leadership and the predicament of the interhierarchical leader, he overlooks the possibilities of choice and manipulation and thus the possibilities for the accumulation and exercise of power and influence.[8] When looked at from this point of view, the same factors we discussed lead to another analysis and other conclusions. It is certainly true that the mayor is reluctant to use local government authorities against the villagers; nevertheless he does have that power and has sometimes exercised it. The mayor caused one man to be fined $35 for collecting the fruit of an olive tree that was not on his land; another villager was jailed fifteen days for harboring a bogus magician; five suspects named by the mayor in a robbery case were jailed for periods varying between seven and seventeen days for giving false testimony to the police—the mayor refused to bail several of them out (see chapter six for an analysis of the case). Thus although the mayor himself does not have the power to fine or imprison, his role as key witness to village events can lead to such action. He also witnesses to economic condition and legal status. In cases where wives claim support from their husbands, in the Islamic court, the mayor will testify as to the woman's economic status and whether adequate provisions exist in the house. When a man or woman seek to marry the mayor must certify that they are of eligible age and and marital status. When a soldier applies for a family-maintenance stipend, the mayor must certify that he has a certain number of children born on certain dates. In all of these situations the mayor has the leeway to certify or not to certify and, more important, to certify in one manner or another. Since peasants frequently attempt to evade the law, for example by contracting marriages for spouses not quite of legal age, the mayor is usually justified in refusing the service, but he can render a favor by performing it. In the case of the man seeking family maintenance, the size of the stipend will vary slightly depending on whether the birth is recorded at the beginning or the end of the month; such slight increments in income are often critical for peasants so the mayor again performs a favor by registering the birth at the earlier time. Of course if the mayor flagrantly abuses his authority, he is subject to checks both on the part of the villagers and the government. One mayor was finally removed by the government at the behest of his clan when he refused to certify marriage papers for a clansman—he wanted the girl in question to marry his own son. Villagers were so upset with another mayor for his alleged bias in distributing wheat that they petitioned the subdistrict officer. Just as important is the mayor's role as a morals witness. When the mayor named suspects in the robbery case, it was tantamount to a statement of bad character; such evaluations carry weight in local government offices, for government officials recognize that villagers "know their own." Every villager who applies for a government office for a job must produce a statement of good character, which is usually provided by his mayor.

Another view of the mayor's position must be considered which also stresses choice, but not manipulation. The law is hard. Any rule, even the most specific, cannot cover every contingency; uninterpreted, it strikes persons of different status and circumstance with uniform indifference. Of course all individuals in an administrative hierarchy must interpret the rules, but the mayor's interhierarchical position puts him in a unique position to soften the law. There is, for example, a regulation that any person owning any land in any village must pay the village improvement tax. Many villagers own land in more than one village; to enforce the law strictly would amount to double taxation. The respective mayors, therefore, only count such individuals every other year for taxation purposes. Or, alternatively, they pay a reduced tax in each village, or the extended family household is split in two, with each half paying in a single village. The mayor can soften the law in another way since it is village custom—custom accepted by the local government officials—to exempt the poor and needy from payment of such taxes. It is the mayor who identifies those eligible so that the subdistrict officer may officially strike them from the tax list. The mayor also sees to it that the tax burden falls heaviest on those most able to pay; this is done by singling out the village's salaried employees and making sure they pay their just share. The mayor, then, can be viewed as a power-holder and as the occupier of a strategic position which can be manipulated to build up his own following or to soften the hard law just as much as he can be regarded the victim of his intercalary position and the carrier of the burdens of leadership.

The Arena

Before discussing the mayors' strategy and tactics, however one construes their powers or burdens, it is necessary to clarify the "arena" in which they operate. Do the mayors compete primarily within a village arena, within some arena internal to the village, such as the clan, or within a more comprehensive arena such as the subdistrict or even the kingdom? Bailey has defined arena as the locus of conflict-interaction for the gaining of a given "prize."[9] In *Politics and Social Change: Orissa in 1959* he was concerned with the circumstances in which arenas were transformed into "groups" or, to use a later term, "teams" and vice versa. He was also concerned with distinguishing arenas in which political and social relations overlapped (that is, in which social relations were multiplex) from those in which there was no such overlap.[10] He distinguished three separate arenas—the elite arena, the village arena, and the constituency arena—with the former two being alike in multiplexity, while the last was not. Thus the arenas of the widest and the narrowest geographical scope had similar social relationships and contrasted with the arena of middling geographical scope—the constituency arena—where relationships tended to follow a line of single interests.

In Kufr al-Ma the political arenas of narrowest scope—the clan and the village—have similar (multiplex) types of social relations and contrast with the more comprehensive political arena, the subdistrict. However since Kufr al-Ma is not a (single) clan-community, it is possible to weigh the relative importance of arenas whether of like or unlike social relations. One could argue that the clan is the *de facto* political arena, because in the overwhelming majority of instances, the man selected by the clan automatically becomes the village's mayor. I know of only one case when the subdistrict officer refused to certify a clan nominee. Village elections between different slates of nominated candidates are very rare. Thus one can argue that competition for the mayorship, in so far as it exists, takes place within the clan—or within two of the clans if one takes into account the one-nominee-per-thousand-of-the-population administrative rule. What seems to be, on the face of it, a two-stage competition is in fact only a one-stage competition. On the other hand, one can also argue that the clan's main importance is as a team rather than as an arena. Every villager must affiliate with a mayor to compete for the prizes made available at the village level, including jobs, grain, and water. He must also affiliate with a mayor to benefit from his role as key witness and morals witness in efforts to register land, pay taxes, and get married. Since local administrative policy follows the one-nominee-per-thousand-of-the-population rule, only two teams (clans) are allowed to compete within the village arena.

To argue that the clan is more significant as a team than as an arena does not deny the clan its important role in social control—that is, it still can bring effective pressure to bear on its members when they violate clan and village mores.

If Bailey's view that the arena is defined by competition for a given prize is accepted, then a comparison of prizes available at the clan and village level ought to clarify the problem of the relative importance of the clan and village arenas. A number of institutions which are potential foci for competition and attempted control exist at the village but not at the clan level e.g., the school, the mosque, and the incipient village council. In addition the village, and not the clan, is the framework of competition for prestige and status. Whether the comparison is of individuals or groups (e.g., lineages or clans), the context of comparison is almost always the village. The statements of villagers make this fact clear: "We [the clan] have no name in this village" or "There are fifteen [men] who curtain the village [by maintaining open guest rooms where visitors can always be entertained thereby preserving the village's reputation for hospitality]." The clan has resources at its disposal—the services of its key specialists, land under its control, and the good will, charity, and fellowship of its members, but clan paternalism makes most of these resources available to all members and in any case they are not prizes won in political competition. Of course the mayorship itself is a prize, but whether one considers it a prize of a village arena or a clan arena or both, it must be remembered that substantial material rewards or perquisites do not attach to the office; therefore the intensity of competition within the arena is not great.

Another index for identifying arenas besides that suggested by Bailey (i.e., the prize that is the focus for competition) is available, namely, the scope of recruitment for core and support. According to the gentleman's agreement such recruitment should only occur within the clan. But as the last chapter demonstrated, support for a mayor comes from clans other than his own and, conversely, not all his own clansmen provide backing either from the economic, ethical, or processual points of view. Even if the gentlemen's agreement were kept, each mayor would still recruit support elements from ʿAmr and the independent lineages. Using this second index, it is clearly the village and not the clan that constitutes the arena; the administrative ruling of 1964 that changed the basis of the mayor's economic support gave official confirmation to this view.

What of the third arena—the subdistrict? If prizes define the arena, then there is no doubt that a most-favored-person relationship with the subdistrict officer is a prize, for he has access to substantial central government resources, such as wheat, water (in time of drought), and the wherewithal of modernization—school buildings, school teachers, electricity, and financial aid for village improvement projects. He distributes most of the resources originating at the state and even the international level. Although the next chapter will be devoted entirely to the subdistrict arena, it may be said here that whether the subdistrict officer and other bureaucrats really control state and international resources is a matter of question. In 1959 grain was sent to villages in Jordan as part of an AID international loan program. Charges of speculation and unfairness in its distribution were brought not against the subdistrict officer but against the mayors of villages by their own constituents. One possible explanation of this is that the national-level authorities handed the resources over in a fairly direct manner according to universalistic standards to village-level authorities. Whatever inequities of distribution to individual peasants occurred at the village level, not the subdistrict level, the subdistrict officer merely acting as a transmitter. If such is generally the case—and I am not arguing that it is, merely suggesting the possibility—then the subdistrict arena may not be as important as it seems.

One final point should be made about the subdistrict arena in Jordan as compared to the situation Bailey analyzed in Orissa. The alternative for Indian peasants who reject the village arena and wish to draw on resources and supporters from the more comprehensive constituency or even national arena are either bureaucrats or political party members or representatives—e.g., the police, judges in the courts, Congress Party members—men who at least in the context of their occupational activity represent the modern world and its values. In Jordan the subdistrict arena is usually bifurcated both in respect to authority and values. In the case of a land dispute a villager of Kufr al-Ma may go to the subdistrict officer, to the land registry officer, or in the event of an altercation to the civil court or the police in the subdistrict capital—which happens to be the next village. But he may also go in the same village to the Pasha, the descendant of the Shaykhs of Tibne. This man views the dispute and mediates it according to a very different set of values—a set of tribal values—than those held by any of the above bureaucrats. The implications of this option will be examined in the next chapter.

The Strategy and Tactics of the Mayors

Before discussing the strategy and tactics of the mayors in Kufr al-Ma, the environmental and demographic circumstances limiting the competition and the basic unstated assumptions regarding it must be mentioned. To sharpen perception of these circumstances in Kufr al-Ma, it will be useful to examine a situation where precisely the opposite circumstances hold and where the opposite assumptions are made: the situation Turner describes in his classic study of competition among the Ndembu in a Central African village.[11] Ndembu society is one of a class which can be characterized as societies "of perpetual politics": every decision affects the constitution of the competing teams, if not the entire community.[12] The Ndembu were traditionally a society of shifting hoe cultivators and hunters who abandoned the land after one or two plantings of cassava, allowing the bush to regenerate; after thirty years this process of regeneration was complete, and the land became suitable for exploitation once again. Since the land could only carry between seventeen and thirty-eight persons per square mile, villages that grew beyond a certain size were forced to relocate on the average of every five years. The holdings of a single village were scattered in discrete plots over a wide area, usually between five and eight miles. According to Turner, in villages containing about twenty huts (about fifty people) powerful social tensions existed. The building up and maintaining of a village was always hazardous and depended on the ability of the village headman to keep his following together and to maintain good relations not only among the men of his matrilineal core but also with his brothers-in-law and classificatory cross-cousins. In the absence of ecologically constraining conditions, the maintenance of a village depended upon the quality of social relations, upon the ability and personality of the leader, and upon chance.

In Kufr al-Ma, on the other hand, ecological constraints on village fission do exist. The agricultural regime is based upon sedentary dry farming of wheat and barley. Each village settlement in the area is nucleated and located permanently in the center of its lands. Even villagers employed outside the village, a considerable portion of the male labor force, maintain their homes and families in the village, either because they have land in the village—and not elsewhere—or because they have patrilineal kinsmen in the village—kinsmen who are willing to support them in times of economic difficulty or personal crisis. At least since World War Two a shortage of land has characterized the district in which Kufr al-Ma lies; the best evidence of this is the very high percentage (about 60 percent) of the labor force that must engage in nonagricultural occupations some part of the year. In contrast to the traditional situation of the Ndembu, whose access to land was almost unlimited, the residents of Kufr al-Ma are surrounded by other villages fully exploiting their own lands. Since the towns of Transjordan lack large-scale industries and most of the villagers employed there are low-paid, unskilled labor, villagers must maintain a base in their own village regardless of where they work in order to safeguard their own economic and social security. These environmental, economic, and social constraints make the village community a stable social structure in which the decisions of particular village or clan leaders do not threaten fundamentally the village or its constituent social units. Although individuals and individual households may make a temporary or even, rarely, permanent move to town, large kinship groups (close consultation groups, lineages, clans) do not and cannot, since they cannot earn enough to sustain themselves in the new locale. This set of constraints, far from conducing to "perpetual politics," reinforces the tendencies towards "low-key politics"; the decisions of mayors in Kufr al-Ma, then, do not threaten the existence of the village or the integrity of its constituent groups, and the building up and maintaining of a political following is not a frantic and abrasive competition between resolute adversaries. Although the competition is real, it is often passive and fraught with ambiguities regarding the nature of core and support, as the last chapter indicated.

In some respects the assumptions Turner makes about political motivation among the Ndembu stand directly opposed to those that can be made about political motivation in Kufr al-Ma. Turner assumes that most prominent men in the Ndembu village are political entrepreneurs, that they aspire to the headmanship. Even if they do not want it, their comrades who stand to gain by their candidacy will force them to try. To quote Turner:

> A person who endeavours to avoid pressing his claim to office when the position of headman falls vacant is subject to intense pressure from his uterine kin and from his children to put it forward. If he fails to do so, there occurs a displacement of the locus of the conflict, not a resolution or bypassing of conflict. Instead of leading a group of kin against the representatives of

other pressure groups, he becomes the target of criticism from members of his own group.[13]

If one individual can't be forced, the pressure to compete will merely shift to a stand-in.

In Kufr al-Ma the burdens of intercalary leadership, the lack of important prizes attached to the mayorship, and the demands of the model personality keep most men from political entrepreneurship. Those that compete nearly always do so in a low-key manner as a result of factors already mentioned: multiplexity of social relations, cross-cutting ties, propinquity of lands and houses, mutually reinforcing ideologies of descent, common villageship and common historical origin, and the expectations of the culture regarding the behavior of the model personality (see chapter seven).

Until quite recently the men involved in public village affairs took a static view of village politics. They assumed that cores (of clans) were large and unchanging; clans held true whether viewed ideologically, economically, or processually. The taking-on of support was regarded as a temporary act in which one mayor simply acted as a ward for the other until the clansman in question, realizing the natural order of things, returned to his own mayor. The strongest evidence of this static view is the gentlemen's agreement. Even at the height of the estrangement between the two mayors, which resulted from the Dumi mayor's blatant violation of the gentlemen's agreement—he officially took on a Yasin lineage (Shujur) as support, the Dumi mayor told me, "It can happen that one mayor takes on the adherents of the other until they are reconciled." And in fact several months later he allowed Shujur to return to Yasin without challenge, although earlier he had flatly denied the possibility of such a return. This mayor, on the face of it, had abandoned a static view of politics for a contractual view by his violation of the agreement. But his explanation of his action affirmed the existence of the agreement rather than its obsolescence. The view that clan cores (ideologically defined) held true was a keystone of his own strategy, not merely lipservice. His strategy depended on the superior numbers an alliance of Dumi and 'Amr would have in the newly formed village council. Since the council representatives were selected on a democratic basis, Dumi and 'Amr could dominate Yasin and any other independent lineages allied with it in any council vote. But this would be so only if the clans actually voted as ideological blocs. The Dumi mayor, like the Yasin mayor, assumed not only that they should, but that they would. Thus although we

should not minimize the significance of this violation of the gentlemen's agreement (discussed at greater length in chapter six) its
continued acceptance as general principle reflected not only the
continuation of low-key politics but its strategic implications as
well. Such an agreement allowed each mayor to solidify his own
secondary core (economically defined in categories 2, 3, 4, and 5 in
chart 1, by restricting the range of his own support. The gentlemen's
agreement ruled out subversion as a tactic for either mayor, but a
watered-down version allowed muted renegadism: support could be
accepted in a minimal sense without involving a change of allegiance. It also established one's own clan rather than the village at
large as the proper locus of team recruitment.

To understand the strategy and tactics of each mayor it is necessary to review and elaborate their resources. Beni Yasin is much
stronger in terms of total numbers, landed wealth, and number of
key specialists—in fact it leads with respect to practically every
index of strength recorded in table 4. Its wealth is enhanced by a
large number of men who draw regular salaries outside the village
either as soldiers or government employees. This wealth, old and
new, has made possible and encouraged "the full-blown mayorship," a mayorship which gives maximum services in terms of hospitality, mediation, arbitration, and the mayor's full-time presence
in the village. Maximum services, however, demand maximum
financial support, especially since Beni Yasin, while possessing the
largest number of wealthy men, also includes the most poor men
(see the "landless" category in table 4). The key Yasin strategy has
been to maintain the distinction between the primary (makhtara-
paying) and secondary (non-makhtara-paying or nonpaying) core.
The former used to be pressed to pay in full their annual contribution, but the most recent revisions of this obligation (1957 and 1966)
have considerably obscured the original distinction. The fact remains that the clan must raise a substantial sum (in village terms)
on a regular basis in order to maintain the magnitude of the operation. The most recent attempt (1966) of the Yasin mayor to establish
a "limited mayorship"—a regular contribution of $1.40 from every
clan household—had the same purpose as the original bifurcate distinction. As the original primary economic core diminishes, the
Yasin mayor has also begun to press the support category to pay for
contractual services rendered. I once saw him berate a nonclansman
for never having compensated him for a mathbata after he had promised to do so. Since contributions have steadily declined and the
Yasin mayor is personally impoverished, maintenance of the full-

blown mayorship has required other clansmen to furnish its socio-economic basis. From 1965 to 1967 the local clerk of court, Abu Fayid, served coffee nightly in his guest house in the middle of the clan quarter. His guest house became the principal meeting place for clansmen during this period. Before him, from 1960–1965, the clerk-usher of the local religious court, Abu Kamil, performed the same function. On the ideological side, the strategy of the full-blown mayorship now demands the attempted repression of muted renegadism, for the mayorship cannot be maintained at its present level without active economic and social contributions from many clansmen.

As table 4 indicates, Beni Yasin also has considerable social organizational and ideological resources: it has greater social solidarity, whether measured in terms of visiting, spatial agglomeration, number of guest houses, or joint economic ventures, and it has a stronger sense of ideological identity, whether measured in terms of genealogical depth and authenticity, patrilineal ties in other villages, symbolic gestures of unity, or self-image. It is this stronger sense of identity that requires the Yasin mayor to reject nonpaying cooperators (see table 5), since the term suggests that clansmen are not integral members of the group. It also accounts for his rejection of renegadism and his adherence to the gentlemen's agreement, both with respect to his own clansmen and those of the competing clan: he never admitted that Shujur had left his clan and he did not entertain the offers of two Beni Dumi lineages to support him politically. The larger size of the Yasin lineages, their greater social solidarity, and their stronger sense of identity all combined to make renegadism and subversion a much greater threat to Beni Yasin than Beni Dumi. The subversion or renegadism of any single Yasin household was likely to lead to mass renegadism, since the lineages of Yasin acted much more like corporate groups (though they were not) than the smaller, less solidary Dumi lineages. Thus the basic strategy of the Yasin mayor was to play movement politics to the hilt: to stress the idiom of corporate clan unity and to make ethical evaluations in terms of departures from that unity (see chapter three); to martial the resources of the clan through the operation of the full-blown mayorship and through the definition of and reliance upon a primary economic core; never to practice the discard ploy with respect to clansmen (since core was ideologically defined in terms of patrilineality); to reject subversion and even muted renegadism; to adhere to the gentlemen's agreement (since given the superior numbers and resources of Yasin, dominance would be safeguarded); to practice clan paternalism (thereby distributing the resources of the full-blown mayorship over a wide social structural range); and finally to exploit clanship, kinship, and quasi-kinship ties for all they were worth. This final tactic had many variations, of which only a few can be mentioned. The system of Arabic kinship terminology allows an individual to use the term "mother's brother" (*khāli*) in address and reference for any person belonging to a group into which one's own clanswomen have married. The use of this term converts the relationship into an affective one; it is often the prelude to asking a favor, which because of the affective context is less likely to be refused. The mayor of Yasin had expert knowledge of marriage ties several generations back and could manipulate the idiom of kinship skillfully. He also utilized visiting to strengthen and renew relationships—he was always visiting one family or another. For instance, at the end of Ramadan he made it a practice to visit clanswomen who had married into other quarters of the village or into other villages. By doing so he not only renewed relationships with these women—and provided the basis of future hospitality—but he also interacted with their husbands, who might provide future political support. The extension of generosity in a quasi-kinship context often created personal ties that had potential political significance. At the time Shujur withdrew their support from the Yasin mayor, a member of another Yasin lineage, Khalil Marwan also withdrew his support. When Khalil's nephew returned to the village after spending several months working in town, Khalil informed him that he was boycotting the Yasin mayor and he advised his nephew to do the same. However the nephew had previously worked for the mayor as a sharecropper and had been housed and fed by him during the agricultural season; this extended period of common residence and commensality converted the contractual relationship into something more. Refusing to boycott the mayor, the nephew came to him a few days later to register the name of his newborn daughter. Finally, the mayor extended the policy of clan paternalism beyond corporate clan contexts into a personal sphere. He did numerous unremunerated favors for many villagers, regardless of kinship affiliation: he was an amateur carpenter and fixed plough handles; he was an expert on arborculture and gave villagers advice about when to prune and in what manner; his skill in mediation was often called upon to resolve the most picayune matters; and villagers invited him constantly to their *soirees*, where they knew he would regale them in his usual gregarious manner regarding his previous experiences in Palestine working with the

Jews, fighting against the British, and smuggling guns or, alternatively, regarding such diverse matters as plant folklore, agricultural conditions in the valley, the necessity for progress, the relative merits of achieved as opposed to ascribed status, and the improper ritual divergencies of the Shiites. The assumption behind these actions was that ties of clanship and, to a somewhat lesser degree the ties of kinship, marriage, and quasi-kinship were continuing debt relationships—one helped kinsmen build their houses, meet their water requirements, and resolve their disputes without requesting or expecting either short-term or long-term compensation. The mayor was investing in a lifetime social insurance policy with lifetime neighbors; the good will which was the dividend would inevitably translate into future social support, which given the cultural framework would be construed as a measure of political backing.

Because Dumi has fewer internal resources than Yasin in almost all respects—size, landholdings, arbitral specialists, extravillage ties, social solidarity, ideology (and fewer than ʿAmr with respect to landholdings and extravillage ties)—it has operated a "watered-down mayorship" at least since the accession of its latest mukhtar in 1957. Extension of hospitality to government officials, clansmen, and strangers has been minimal, as have the traditional services of mediation and advice. The Dumi mayor could not even be depended upon to be on hand in the village to take care of day-to-day affairs. For Dumi, therefore, the distinction between a primary and a secondary core within the clan was unimportant and practically nonexistent, since there were few landowners who could have made a regular annual payment and the watered-down operation required less regular substantial contributions. Moreover while the Yasin mayor was forced increasingly to expect, if not solicit, contributions from supporters outside the clan, the Dumi mayor had no such expectation and did not do so. The Dumi mayor told me, and my own observations support the claim, that beginning around 1960 he relied almost exclusively on the small payments made to him when he performed a service. Table 5, reflecting the situation in 1965, certainly gives credence to this view. The basic strategy of playing contractual politics had certain consequences and implications. It left the way open for breaking the gentleman's agreement, although it did not necessarily lead to such an act. More important, it repudiated much of the substance, as well as the technique and idiom, of movement politics.[14] Thus, the Dumi mayor was not often found visiting other families; he did not manipulate the idiom of kinship with aplomb; he did not freely give advice or mediation either to kinsmen or other villagers. He was much too wrapped up in his own affairs to give that much attention to those of others. Far from employing the idiom of clanship or kinship, the Dumi mayor often spoke in a mode antithetical to them—the idiom of individualization. When told of a clan elder's pronouncements on various subjects, he would often say, "Who is so-and-so [name of elder]? Don't pay him any attention" or literally, "Don't [bother to] reply to his talk" (*lat ridd 'ala l hakki*). The implication was not only that what he had to say wasn't worth listening to but also that he had no power or authority or influence to get the individual to do what he wanted.

Although Dumi lagged behind Yasin in almost all the resources, they were much larger than 'Amr, spatially more concentrated, had more focused visiting relations, more political and religious specialists, and a more positive self-image. When a kind of Dumi-'Amr coalition formed in 1965, Dumi, through its mayor, came to lead it. However this leadership was not entirely or perhaps even mainly a result of Dumi's dominant resources, it was also the result of the internal divisions of the component 'Amr lineages, many of whose members were hardly on speaking terms with one another due to past grudges. While 'Amr might have held the balance of power (they had land, arbitrators, ties in other villages, and guest houses of first rank), they became simply the tail of the coalition and not one that wagged the dog.

With the introduction in 1965 of a village council that was to reflect the proportionate numbers of descent groups and that was to decide by majority vote, numbers came to be the key Dumi-'Amr resource and the factor that guided their strategy. This strategy also had certain implications. It required little or no subversion, since the Dumi-'Amr coalition could dominate Yasin in the village council without incremental support from the independents or renegadism from Yasin.[15] This explains why the Dumi mayor invoked the discard ploy when Shujur decided to return to Yasin. Assuming he had a majority also led the Dumi mayor to make increasing use of confrontations and encounters (which had been rare) and a decreasing use of the bye (letting the challenge pass without response). As chapter six will outline in detail, on four separate occasions the Dumi mayor challenged the traditional hegemony of Yasin and asserted the principle of the contractual mayorship (by taking on Shujur) and the dominance of numbers (by insisting that Yasin was a minority in the village and deserved minority representation on the council)—to assembled village elders, to the subdistrict officer, and finally to the district officer).

It might be asked at this point what the members of Dumi (or 'Amr) got from their mayor besides the signing of official papers and the witnessing of good character. The answer is that among other things he got the most important political plums for poor peasants—jobs—not many, to be sure, but more than his competitor, the mayor of Yasin. The headmaster of the village school was from Beni Dumi, as was its janitor. When the annual recruitment of men into the army took place in the subdistrict center (recruitment is not the proper word, since young peasants compete intensely to enlist in order to receive the regular army stipend), the Dumi mayor managed to sign up five villagers, all from Dumi, 'Amr, and an independent lineage allied with them—none from Yasin. The ability to deal effectively with government officials and to "deliver the goods" is an essential part of the Dumi mayor's strategy, since the watered-down mayorship demands it (lest all substantive services disappear) and the contractual mayorship assumes it (since real services rather than loyalty are required).

Yasin's reaction to this strategy was twofold. First, they resorted to a discard ploy, or at least attempted one. Rather than discarding support elements, they discarded or attempted to discard the arena itself—the village council. They suggested that Kufr al-Ma attach itself to the municipality of Deir Abu Said, the next village and subdistrict center, and passed around a petition to this effect among the villagers. By operating in a larger arena where they would have allies—many clans in Deir Abu Said were "peoples of Tibne" and had kinship or quasi-kinship ties with Yasin—they would avoid majority dominance. Yasin's second reaction was to argue in terms of the "idiom of discrepancy" in order to safeguard the basic element in their broad strategy of movement politics—the politics of hospitality.

In order to understand this reaction a brief discussion of hospitality and its relationship to the "idiom of discrepancy" is required. When the government began to institutionalize the new village council and the Dumi-'Amr alliance threatened to relegate Yasin to a permanent minority position, Yasin men argued both to government officials and to the other villagers that proportional representation according to the size of clans and lineages was extremely unfair. "We curtain the village and you wish to rule us," they said. As the Yasin mayor told me, "When a guest comes to the village, no one tells him, 'The lower [Dumi] quarter is better'; we always receive him here [in the guest houses of the Yasin quarter]." This argument had some merit. Government officials and strangers passing through expected to receive hospitality from the village and, in the case of the former, were frequently insulted if they did not. Since the richest men, with the guest houses of first rank, were mainly from Yasin, they bore the brunt of such hospitality. Indeed guests were often directed to Yasin guest houses by members of other clans. Yasin's conversion of wealth into "value power" (in terms of building up the reputation of its elders for hospitality) and political influence was jeopardized by the new turn of events. While still being asked "to curtain the village," they could no longer expect the appropriate political rewards of such expenditure.

The Yasin clan's consistent commitment to "curtaining the village" relates to its pursuit of the politics of hospitality as a key strategy. In Kufr al-Ma hospitality is a "cultural focus," embracing a wide variety of highly valued activities in many different contexts. Certain basic assumptions are made about its significance and, particularly, about the consequences that follow from its offer and acceptance. One such assumption has political significance and is epitomized in the folk saying,[16] "A taste in the mouth causes the eye to be modest" or rendered another way, "When the mouth feeds, the eye feels shame (yiT'am al-timm, tastaha al-'ayn)." That is, accepting hospitality from another limits one's ability to act with complete freedom toward him or, more specifically, against him in the future. In addition to establishing social credit, hospitality shuts up criticism. Beni Yasin's relatively lavish extension of hospitality to government officials in the past had been a key political strategy—one that was perfectly suited to their resource base. It was not strange, then, that they vigorously objected to a new arrangement which jeopardized that strategy and cancelled out some (certainly political influence), if not all (possibly status and prestige), of its benefits.

On the other hand, Dumi and 'Amr had clearly to reject both the argument based on the idiom of discrepancy and the appeal for attachment to the municipality of Deir Abu Said, for in doing so they undermined the politics of hospitality, safeguarded the village arena, strengthened the contractual mayorship, and bound the ring of numbers more tightly around their opponent.

The External Arena:
Its Roles and Resources

Although previous chapters have mentioned the administrative integration of the village into the state political structure, the posting of bureaucrats at the local level, and the existence and growth of long-distance mobility and occupational differentiation and even though the last chapter traced a few of the implications of an external arena for local-level politics, the discussion so far has proceeded without part of the vital evidence. That evidence relates to the political and economic changes which have taken place since World War Two, and it will be the aim of this chapter to examine the implications of these changes, first generally and then specifically, for local-level politics.[1]

Many changes have occurred in transportation and communication. The first bus to the nearest large market town, Irbid, was introduced in 1947. In 1952 a macadamized road by way of the Jordan valley reduced the bus ride from the village to town from more than two-and-a-half hours to one hour. Although taxis were available sporadically before then, in 1963 the first taxi office was established in Deir Abu Said, making taxis available all day every day for transport to Irbid (and thence, if desired, to Amman); by 1967 two taxi offices had been established. Today a macadamized road runs from the bottom of the village to Irbid, and four or five buses go by every day. By 1967 one of the buses "slept" in the village, its terminus in the evening and its starting point in the morning. By 1965 a telephone was installed in the village post office—which had been established in 1962—permitting immediate communication with the subdistrict officer in the next village or the governor of the region in the market town.

Direct links with the outside world have come through employment in the army. In 1965 at least nine retired soldiers, including three officers, were living in the village on pensions. As table 1 indicates, about a third of the village's employed men are in military occupations. After 1964 an accelerated recruitment drive absorbed an even larger number. Two men are studying at the Islamic University in Riyadh, a third is studying medicine in Izmir, Turkey, and two others are studying medicine in Germany. By 1966 eight young men from the village had worked in Kuwait (for periods from seven months to four years) and more than twenty-two had worked in Beirut (for periods varying between three weeks and one year). Within Jordan the generation of sons working outside the village is engaged in a variety of occupations including: typist, clerk for a road gang, barber, road-gang laborer, presser (of pants), gas station attendant, primary school teacher, janitor, clerk of court, construction laborer, malaria unit employee, forestry department employee, watchman, stonecutter, ditch-digger, painter's assistant.

The siphoning off of many young men into extravillage occupations and the new money it has brought in have had a number of consequences, only a few of which will be mentioned here. First, there has been a general reduction in the keeping of livestock, for the young men are not available to act as full-time or part-time shepherds for their own households and the cost is too much for other households who might want to hire them. Reduction in livestock has in turn reduced the hospitality offered on traditional occasions, since such occasions require the slaughtering of a sheep or goat. Second, agriculture has been affected. Because the cost of agricultural labor increased, for the first time four men in the village have invested in tractors, which they hire out to villagers in the area. At least one of these men took out a bank loan to buy the tractor, and he is now paying interest on the loan. Five years earlier a number of village elders refused to support the village improvement program (*taHsīn al-qarya*) because it entailed the taking out of loans and the payment of interest (proscribed by Islamic law). In addition the labor shortage has caused the amount of fallow land in the village to increase substantially. Third, occupational mobility and new money has altered the mode of marriage, collapsing marriage stages. Whereas before, the events marking the contraction of marriage were often spread out over a period of months or years, today it may be a matter of days. Soldiers home on furlough sometimes betroth, make full marriage payment, make the religious contract, and celebrate the wedding within a matter of two weeks. The traditional three-day wedding celebration is often reduced to one day (since the soldier must return to camp), and the girl, instead of being placed, veiled, on a horse at sunset and sent on to her bridegroom's house accompanied by a throng of wellwishers, is now often packed into a taxi which takes her directly to her husband's house in the village where the consummation takes place early in the evening or is taken with her husband directly to the army camp where the couple may plan to live. A direct economic consequence of new money is the inflation of marriage payments. In 1966 one worker just returned from Kuwait offered a village girl £350 sterling as a marriage payment, £100 more than usual. These young men often neglect to give traditional items (such as Bedouin cloaks) to the appropriate members of the bride's family because they consider the gifts old-fashioned.

The increasing impact of a money economy is evident in the growing number of village shops. In 1925 only one existed. By 1960 there were eleven. Although many of the shops are unstable ventures, the variety of goods has increased substantially. Many items were sold in 1965 that were not sold five years earlier: boots, galoshes, western-style shirts, plastic water cans, colored thread, toffee candy, oranges, apples, and vegetables. A number of individuals have furnished their guest rooms with chairs, tables, glass cupboards, and one villager even has a stove. This "diwan," so-called, is in stark contrast to the traditional guest house, which is devoid of furniture and has only straw mats and pillows for those who recline against the walls. A few individuals have begun to paint the interior walls, the grilles of the windows, and even the exterior walls of the house. Some houses are now being built with cement walls, rather than the traditional stone adobe-covered walls, and a few even have cement roofs.

The implications of all these changes for the social structure are numerous, but only three will be mentioned here. First, the young men who have made good in nonagricultural employment outside the village together with the sons of the relatively few prosperous landowning peasants are achieving the status markers of the life cycle at a much earlier age than the other young men of the village—they are betrothing, marrying, and fathering children in their late teens or early twenties. Because they can afford to, they move out of their father's house and establish a nuclear family household usually in a separate house on the outskirts of the village; the sons of poorer peasants, on the other hand, live unmarried in larger households located in the village center under the authority of their father and/or their elder brothers. Second, in cases where men making a substantial income in nonagricultural employment continue to live with fathers or brothers still engaged in agriculture, tensions are created that did not exist before, at least not to the same degree. Some fathers are now beholden to their sons economically since the latter often have regular monthly stipends (if they are in the army or bureaucracy); over the long run they may not be in a position to block their son's wishes regarding the timing or arrangement of marriage or the choice of bride. Many fathers have taken their sons to court claiming that the sons have not contributed to their maintenance. Third, strains have increased within the nuclear family between husbands and wives, as evidenced by the increasing number of "cleavage and contention" cases (*shiqaq wa nizāʿ*) taken to the Islamic court.[2] One solution for a man who has taken up a town way of life to which his wife cannot adapt is divorce, but more usually it is polygyny, with the first wife remaining in the village and the second accompanying the man to town.

For the purposes of this analysis, however, aside from the introduction of new wealth into the community the most significant change has been the integration of the village into the state administrative structure. This integration has been indexed by the continuing addition of government offices and functions in the neighboring subdistrict center of Deir Abu Said: forest ranger (1938); enlarged police post (1941); health officer (1950); subdistrict officer (1951); religious court (1953); agricultural inspector (1954). By 1960 the subdistrict center included a land registry officer, a tax agent, and a civil court judge.

To understand what this means for local-level politics, it is necessary to briefly describe the administrative structure of the kingdom.[3] Before World War One the northwestern part of Transjordan, later established as the governate of Ajlun, was superficially incorporated into the Ottoman Empire as a subdistrict of the sanjak of Hauran, whose capital was in Der'a, Syria. Although the final years of the Ottoman Empire witnessed an attempt to provide greater local autonomy—indeed, legislation was passed to further that goal—highly centralized local administration prevailed, although the task of maintaining order remained in the hands of prominent Shaykhs. The government of Amir Abdullah, established under British tutelage in 1921, accepted the Ottoman system, which recognized three levels of administration: the district (*liwā*), governed by a *mutasarrif* (later termed *muHāfiTh* or governor); the subdistrict (*qaDā*), governed by a *qāʾimaqām*; and the subsubdistrict (*nāhiyah*), governed by a mudir nahiyah.[4] Within his district the

Chart 3
Dispersion of Functions over the Administrative Hierarchy

Area Larger Than the Muhafatha	The Entire Muhafatha	The Mahafatha Through Its Subdivisions	Subdivisions Basis Only
Lands and Survey	Income Tax Public	Public Security	Finance
Urban Assessment	Public Works	Health	Customs
Audit	Passports	Welfare	Post, telephones, and telegraph
Information	Education	Agriculture	Lands and Survey registration
Civil Aviation	Supply, Import and Export	Veterinary	
Tourism	Reconstruction and Development	Forests	
Antiquities			

mutasarrif had responsibility for neither justice nor security, security being vested in the army (Arab Legion) from the early 1920s.

At the present time administrative functions, which have proliferated since World War Two, are dispersed over four levels.[5] Some serve an area larger than the muhafatha or district (formerly termed liwa); some serve the muhafatha; some serve the muhafatha through offices in each of its subdivisions (i.e., in each qada or subdistrict); and some serve the subdistrict or subsubdistrict directly through independent offices. Chart 3 traces the distribution of functions over the administrative hierarchy.

The Ideology of Central Government Officers

During the early and mid-1960s the Jordanian government resumed with greater vigor the enunciation and application of two policies to which the state had already been formally committed—local participation and decentralization. The first policy was begun in the 1954 "Law for the Administration of Villages," which established the new village councils, while the second policy had originated long before, first in the office of the Ottoman governor (wali), then in the post of the British district officer, and finally in the office of the mutasarrif, established under the amirate of Transjordan. The central government agency created to encourage local participation was the Ministry of Interior for Municipal and Rural (Village) Affairs; the first minister of the new department, Dr. Qassim Rimawi, was appointed in 1965. According to Grassmuck, Rimawi saw "local government and local elections as the best machinery for establishing understanding and consensus at the local level and thus creating the ability to perceive problems, plan solutions, and combine citizens to form the power to solve them."[6] In a speech delivered March 1966 Rimawi declared that it was the right of each individual citizen to elect and be elected to village councils and to give his individual opinion about plans. He urged citizens to pay attention to the execution of programs and to participate in their consequences. He stated that citizens had the right to call these councils to account for their actions.[7] Citizens on village councils were regarded as the best guardians of village welfare; they would make sure that contracts were fulfilled and roads were built. Rimawi did not regard the establishment of village councils as undermining tradition; rather, he saw them "as a means of enabling the citizen to preserve traditions and his primary groups in the face of and while accepting an advancing technology."[8] Rimawi regarded the local councils as having great authority and flexibility even under existing legislation; they had "from force of habit" allowed the police and the district officer to handle many matters that were their own responsibility.[9] The power of the ministry vis-à-vis the councils was the power of the purse; the ministry released or withheld funds according to how well the community conformed to central government regulations.

The basic law governing village administration provided for a council made up of the village mukhtars plus three to twelve other male inhabitants, who were elected for three-year terms. The mutasarrif or muhafith set the date of the election and its mode, and all the council actions were subject to his approval. The council had a corporate identity, could sue or be sued, sign contracts, levy taxes, and borrow money. It was charged with meeting local needs relating to education, sanitation, transportation, water, marketing, public areas, and general welfare matters. A law promulgated in 1957 allowed the council to collect taxes on land and buildings, on the sale of agricultural products, and (a head tax) on male adult residents. By November 1965 only 36 of 511 East Bank villages had councils.[10] On 29 August 1965 the Ministry renewed its effort to establish councils in villages of more than 800 inhabitants. But when I left Kufr al-Ma in 1967 the overwhelming majority of villages in the Ajlun district did not have councils.[11]

There is no doubt that central government officials wished to encourage local participation, create a new ethos of independent problem-solving, and achieve a consensus at the local level. However the government's main ideological commitment was to change, more specifically to development, which meant substantive changes—water, roads, electricity, buses, increased grain production, afforestation. Its commitment to elections, village councils, majority rule, single-function jurisdictions, fundamental education, and a problem-solving ethos remained strong only as long as those things furthered development. Thus the governor or the subdistrict officer determined how the village council was selected depending on what brought results: these officers often appointed the first council members; if elections promised to exacerbate divisions among village kin groups, as they often did, selection of clan representatives by clan consensus occurred. The law specifically recognized sectarian divisions as a basis of representation; if such divisions made the election or selection of a council chairman impossible, the chairmanship was left vacant and the administration provided leadership. If selection of the council itself provoked dissension (as it did in Kufr al-Ma), officials simply tabled any attempts to implement the council and ran things themselves or worked through the village improvement committee, which was closely tied and subservient to administrative officials.[12] When recalcitrant individuals were selected or elected to the council (including mukhtars), officials could often nullify their selection by one means or another. When the aims of development and local representative government coincided, both could be encouraged, but when they conflicted, the latter was sacrificed. Indeed, from the point of view of many administrators, local participation and decentralization (strengthening the rights and responsibilities of regional and district officials) were alternative means to the same end. If village councils did not work they were simply shelved and the district or subdistrict officer took things in hand, often through the local village improvement committee.

Aside from the ideology that motivates and/or justifies their policies, officials also have their own conceptions about the character and ideology of the peasants and pashas (local elites) with whom they have to deal. On the one hand they recognize the reality and legitimacy of peasant social organization and culture; on the other hand, they deride and manipulate them. High-ranking local government officials sometimes become upset if villagers are not on hand to greet them and offer hospitality—normatively, the slaughter

Table 6
Composition of Local Committees

Text Reference	Name of Committee	Membership representation (x) - - - - -														Footnote Reference
		Muhafith	Public Security	Public Works	Finance	Education	Health	Justice	Agriculture	Supply	Land and Survey	P.T.T.	Mayor (of municipality)	Mukhtar	
MINISTRY OF INTERIOR COMMITTEES:															
1	Objection on Voters Registration	x			x										2
2	Traffic and Transportation	x	x												1
3	Civil Defense	x	x	x											3
4	District Relief	x	x				x								1
5	Village Development Projects	x							x	x					2
6	Village Roads	x		x											1
7	Planning and Zoning	xa		x	x		x	x							1
OTHER MINISTRIES' COMMITTEES:															
1	Local Education	x				x									2
2	Education Tax	x				x							xc		2
3	Tax Collection	x			x										2
4	Property Rentals	x		x	x										2
5	Procurement	x		x	x		x								1
6	Trades and Industries Classification	x		x	x			x					xb		2
7	Objection on Levied Tax				x								x	x	
8	Distribution on Unsettled Lands	x			x	x			x			x	xd		3
9	State Domain Administration	x			x		x			x	x	x	x	x	2

1 — Committee headed by either a muhafith or a mutasarrif.
2 — Committee headed by either a muhafith, a mutasarrif, or a qaimaqam.
3 — Committee headed by either a muhafith, a mutasarrif, a qaimaqam, or a mudir.
xa — Administration is represented by the muhafith and the planning and zoning inspector.
xb — Municipality is represented by all its council members, such members being different for each municipality.
xc — Municipality is represented by three of its council members, such members being different for each municipality.
xd — A qualified unofficial member selected by the muhafith, mutasarrif, or qaimaqam.

Source: Griffenhagen-Kroeger Inc., "An Administrative Review," Appendix.

of a goat or sheep; but yet they ridicule peasants for extreme shows of hospitality. Some lower-ranking officials pick the fruit off a peasant's tree without asking permission and scrounge meals. Although ties of kinship, more specifically, of descent, are recognized as important for local-level administration and political representation, such ties are often derided as holding back the welfare of the village and the nation. The recalcitrance of villagers to accept programs associated with development readily is blamed on the existence of such ties rather than on the multiplex nature of social relations or the low-key type of politics. Alternatively, officials blame opposition to government plans and programs on individuals such as the mukhtar or the pasha, who are regarded as selfish and/or reactionary rather than representative of local opinion.

The other policy embraced at the ministerial level is decentralization. This policy attempts to place the activity of an office located in Amman in the local area.[13] It could be argued that decentralization has assumed special urgency recently due to work-load limits rather than ideological considerations, but the policy does go back to Ottoman times. The new impetus for decentralization in the middle sixties has come with the appearance of salaried and educated class in the village and it has focused on the office of the muhafith.

The muhafith is the highest government official in the region. Most central government ministries and departments are represented in his jurisdiction.[14] He supervises activities in his region either directly or through many special-purpose committees. The degree to which he dominates regional activities is reflected in his membership on these local committees as compared with other members of the bureaucracy.

The muhafith helps mayors and village heads to enforce their laws and decisions; he supervises elections and approves village ordinances and budgets. The muhafith directly or through the subdistrict officer keeps in touch with the mukhtar and village notables regarding village development projects, and he decides the order of priority among such projects. He also decides the amount of head tax to be levied on village inhabitants and he initiates action to collect the funds for these projects. He also has the power to exempt people from taxation if he finds them poor or handicapped. The muhafith supervises the construction and maintenance of village roads. Although the decisions of the committees (table 6) are by majority vote, the muhafith usually executes their decisions. Laws and regulations authorize the muhafith (or the mutasarrif) to hold hearings and to look into cases relating to state security, public safety, border

incidents, smuggling, crime, revenge prevention, and forest maintenance. He is charged with supervising processes of mediation and
reconciliation in order to prevent crime and disorder. He has the
official power of appointment over all mukhtars and village councils
in his region. The muhafith (or mutasarrif) has long had overriding
power in emergencies and over particular administrative questions,
but the law of 20 December 1965 increased his powers substantially
by giving him control over all public security forces in the region.

Although this would seem to demonstrate that decentralization,
at least with respect to the muhafith, has been carried out, the
reality is otherwise, since practice often deviates from the intent of
current laws and regulations. Much local service to the communities is in fact administered nationally.[15] My own observation in the
subdistrict of Al-Kura in 1967 indicated that the police still operated
independently of the muhafith. Local communities are dominated
by government employees and officers, and citizens with a grievance
still bypass the committees and the muhafith to go directly to Amman for redress.

If the governor is limited, so to speak, from above, he is also limited from below. That is, governors are never recognized as the real
leaders of particular districts. The leaders are notables from particular families, and they must be accommodated if effective local government is to take place.

A fundamental assumption about the policies of decentralization
and local participation (in village councils) is that regional officials
and villagers will assume the independence of action the law now
not only allows but actually requires. There is no doubt that governors have been given more power, but they have not used it or have
used it only spottily. How can this Machiavellian paradox be explained? In part it can be explained, as Grassmuck has stressed, by
the continuing fact of highly centralized government. Power remains in the capital,[16] which finances development and distributes
international aid. But the paradox can be explained more satisfactorily by the ethos of an insecure centralized government and a society
in which nepotism and bribery (construed in noninvidious terms
from the point of view of local custom, bribery is helping one's
needy kinsmen and friends) have been accepted norms of political
behavior.[17] Thus local foci of power, whether regional or local government officials or village councils, are viewed with distrust and
apprehension. Some of the checks created to control them include
the frequent rotation of local government officials, the stationing of
officials outside their home districts, and the close supervision of

village councils by governors and subdistrict officers. This system generates superiors who resent initiative taken by subordinates; the subordinates in turn recognize these attitudes as a fact of life. Since governors are the highest appointive positions in the kingdom and since many have ambitions of climbing up to the ministerial rung, few wish to antagonize their superiors or jeopardize their political futures. There is the added fact that summary acts at the local level may bring down severe reprimands, if they do not turn out well.

The peasants at the village level are peculiar victims of the Machiavellian paradox. Before World War Two any increased responsibility or even contact with the government usually meant increased taxes, increased conscription, and increased interference in village affairs. Until recently the peasant's whole training has been learning how to avoid responsibility through duplicity, circumlocution, secrecy, and regulation of consumption. The place for rendering justice was the village and resort to extravillage institutions was considered unethical.[18] Peasants moreover, were quick to recognize that, when all was said and done, power remained in the capital, which would initiate the important changes that would affect their lives. This recognition is most clearly reflected in their attitude toward the Program for Village Improvement (*tahsin al qarya*), especially the drive to establish village councils.

The program for village improvement was initiated under the "Village Projects and Services Law" (Law no. 27, 1957).[19] It provided for the mukhtars and village notables to make annual project proposals to the governor (through the subdistrict office where he existed) before a certain date. The proposals would stipulate where the new projects would be located, the kinds and quantities of material necessary, the approximate starting date of the project, the number of laborers necessary and the kinds of services the project would afford. Projects regarded as suitable included road building, cleaning of channels, digging of ponds and wells, other projects improving village health, and anything the governor thought would benefit the village. The governor or mutasarrif (as he was then termed) was to supervise the execution of projects and the management of village services directly. However a "committee for village improvement" (*lajnat taHsīn al-qarya*) composed of representatives from the Department of Public Works, the Department of Health, and the Department of Finances was to help the governor carry out the projects, and any project costing over £20 sterling had to receive their approval. The powers given to the governor (and to a lesser degree, the subdistrict officer) under this law were considerable. If the village notables did not present a project for consideration according to the schedule, the governor could set up a schedule and execute a project in accordance with it. He could also postpone any project on the schedule. The governor could hire any number of employees to carry out the projects stipulated. He had the power to decide upon, impose, and collect the head tax, which varied between one half and two pounds sterling depending on the agricultural year; he had the power to exempt anyone from the tax on grounds of poverty, disability, or inability to pay. (The tax was collected from all healthy males between the ages of sixteen and sixty who owned immovable properties within the boundaries of the village, regardless of residence.) If a dispute arose between two villages on which should collect money from particular individuals (who might own property in several villages), the governor arbitrated the dispute. The head tax was collected by the tax collector, usually posted in the subdistrict town, and kept by the local accountant of the governate in the name of the governor.

In Kufr al-Ma the head tax imposed in 1963 was £1½, in 1964 £1, in 1965 £½, and in 1966 £1 pound. According to village informants the amount levied varied with the number of projects undertaken as well as the kind of agricultural year; they also noted that about thirty families considered "poor" were exempted from the tax in 1965. Government employees and soldiers not in the village on the day of tax collection had their names recorded and sent to the subdistrict officer, who in turn informed the army or the pertinent government departments, which deducted the tax out of their pay. Recent village improvement projects carried out in Kufr al-Ma include the widening of the main village way, the building of a new school (which cost over £400), the hiring of an additional school teacher (paid by the village the first year and subsequently by the central government), and the payment of an annual stipend to the village preacher and muezzin. £300 was also borrowed and spent for agricultural purposes.

The program for village improvement reflects in several respects the points made regarding decentralization and local participation. In it the village saw the power of the central government, since villagers who did not pay their taxes were warned, given twenty days to pay, and then visited by the police, who, in the case of continued nonpayment, jailed them. If after a month in jail they or one of their relatives did not pay, the government was empowered to appropriate their property. The program also reflected the weakness of local participation. Although villagers (particularly notables and the mayor) were asked to advise the Committee for Village Improvement (*laj-nat taHsīn al-qarya*), they were often reluctant to do so or did so unenthusiastically, for it was clear that the governor's (and in lieu of him the subdistrict officer's) power of initiation, execution, and termination of projects reduced their autonomy to a minimum.[20] One mayor in Kufr al-Ma was particularly unhappy with this situation, but to my knowledge he made no formal representation of dissatisfaction to the authorities. When the new drive to establish village councils was undertaken in 1965, therefore, a drive that would have increased local autonomy not only with regard to initiation and execution of projects but also with regard to collection and dispersal of funds, one might have expected the villagers to welcome it wholeheartedly. Of course some did so. However others, perhaps the majority, preferred to continue with the Village Improvement Program, in which their participation was minimal. Although this preference can in part be explained by local political events and the nature of incipient village factions (to be discussed in the next chapter), it is also an aspect of the Machiavellian paradox. Peasants argue with a great deal of cogency that the government has developed the district in the past, is developing it now, and will continue to develop it in the future. Roads, water, afforestation, schools, grain, electricity—all have been introduced in the past or will be introduced in the future without the necessity and the added responsibility that comes with a village council—and also without the squabbles that such a council has and will engender. The villagers have correctly assessed the central government's primary commitment to development, the concentration of power and money that enables it to carry out its policies, and the burdens and contingencies that accompany genuine local autonomy. Thus in Kufr al-Ma and elsewhere peasants have opted to follow a course that is not only congenial to their own ethos (an ethos in which the burdens of leadership are more to be feared than the rewards of manipulation) but also consistent with the actual priorities of the central government and its regional officials, priorities in which representative government is a distant second to technological change and material progress.

External Roles

Before examining the values of the external arena, the factors encouraging and preventing competition in that arena, and the cost of utilizing external resources, a brief discussion of external roles is necessary. Many of these have already been mentioned: policeman, subdistrict officer, tribal leader, migrant laborer, governor, religious court judge, civil court judge, citizen (of Jordan), land registration officer, tax collector, teacher, political party member. Here I shall focus on the first four in order to bring out some of the very different implications these roles have for villager-nonvillager relations.[21]

The local police post is a half hour's walk from the village. However villagers rarely make use of the police on their own initiative. If the police are called to the village, it is usually at the behest of the mukhtar. Sometimes they are called in to investigate routine violations, such as land trespass, death of animals, or petty theft. In most such cases an attempt is made to resolve the difficulty without resorting to the police or other outside authorities. Even more rarely the police are called on in the case of extreme emergencies, such as threatened mayhem, or after flagrant violations of critical norms of behavior, such as respect for the aged or the modesty of women (including elopement, rape, and fornication)—violations that threaten to become cases of honor and result in violence. Even though as late as 1935 this was not so, today the police are given full cooperation in their efforts to perform their official duties in the village.[22] The police are in the most prominent position to enforce the disabilities of "citizenship" or, stated another way, the norms of "legality," since they are charged with acting against violators of national and local laws and regulations, including the nonpayment of taxes. Although the police are formally acceptable outsiders, they are generally disliked. This is only partly because their official duties penalize residents for their actions. It proceeds more from a value gap between peasants and some lower-echelon bureaucrats. In the summer of 1966 a donkey was found dead on the land of one villager. By following its bloody track, the donkey was traced to the land of another villager. The local police post was contacted and a mounted policeman came to investigate. The concerned villagers soon realized that the policeman didn't care about the donkey—to him it was a trivial matter. One villager said later that if it had been an ox (worth almost a hundred dollars), they would have brought a committee to investigate and bloodhounds; he further stated that if the police had investigated properly and found the culprit, further incidents would be avoided—now, more would follow. All the policeman cared about, he said, was breakfasting in the village; he picked out the best fig tree and started eating its fruit, then went home with the owner of the donkey to get breakfast—on his way he yelled to another policeman who had arrived in the village, "Come on, we'll breakfast on honey and clarified butter."[23] The villager ended with the exclamation, freely translated, "Woe be to us when the police arrive" (*ya wayli bil junud*). Although the service of rendering security is not unappreciated, villagers think many policemen fail to recognize the importance of basic village values and processes—social harmony, justice (according to local norms), hospitality, and reciprocity—or, if they recognize them, merely manipulate them for their own purposes. To ask for hospitality before being invited, particularly when future reciprocity is foreclosed, certainly violates an important village norm, whether deliberately or not. Even if the policeman had recognized the appropriate village norms and had acted in accordance with them, rather than in terms of manipulation, the value gap could not have been closed very much, for closing it depends on a certain sociological state: the cultivation of multiplex ties with members of the community. Since this policeman and others acted in terms of single interests vis-à-vis villagers—providing security, apprehending malefactors, enforcing laws—yet seldom visited particular communities, not to speak of establishing other ties of interest (e.g., marriage, propinquity, economic relations), the value gap and the attitudes and social relations built on it have remained.

The subdistrict officer (qaimaqam) is a second external role/resource available to villagers. The duties that bring him into contact with villagers or their representatives include his cooperation with the agricultural agent in evaluating the dearth or bounty of crops (as a basis of requests for government grain allotments), the distribution of wheat, the evaluation of the degree of water shortage in each village and the distribution of water, and the investigation of damage done to crops or trees when such damage is by persons unknown. He also works with the agricultural agent and the village guidance officer (*murshid rīfī*) and mukhtars in planning community development schemes. The villagers use him, like the police, as a counterforce against their opponents. In Kufr al-Ma villagers complained to him that the mukhtar had distributed grain unfairly; others complained that the proposed village council was unrepresentative. The subdistrict officer, being closer to the scene, often carries out responsibilities officially the governor's. Although the governor has the ultimate say on projects under the Village Improvement Law, the subdistrict officer's recommendation is usually accepted; although the governor is supposed to determine the mode of selection of the village council, it is the subdistrict officer in consultation with the villagers who does so; although the governor has the right to exempt individuals from the head tax, it is actually the subdistrict officer in consultation with the mukhtars who does so; although it is the governor who is vested with the power to act in emergencies to prevent damage or injury, it is the subdistrict officer who is first privy to such threats. As a result of his proximity to village affairs (Kufr al-Ma is a twenty-minute walk from the subdistrict officer, the governor is an hour's ride by taxi or a two hour's ride by bus), the subdistrict officer actually mediates and arbitrates in cases of potential threat to good order. Thus one villager went to the village post office and wrote out a telegram to the governor accusing the local schoolmaster of violating government regulations and working against the best interests of the village. The village postmaster notified the mukhtar (without sending the telegram), who in turn notified the subdistrict officer, who called the sender in to reprimand him for stirring up dissension (*fasad*) in the village. Just as he is the first official contact, the first focus of petitions, and in a sense the first ally outside the village, so also the subdistrict officer is the first object of the villagers' resentment. Villagers said that he was slow-witted—one stated that he didn't even know what place the village notables were to occupy in the parade on the occasion of the visit of the king's brother. He bore the brunt of their anger when he did not agree to the building of extra schoolrooms— there was talk of going over his head and petitioning the governor directly. As will become apparent in the next chapter, although the subdistrict officer is regarded as a potential ally in many situations, he is also thought to be both a cultural and social outsider and therefore fair game: to deceive the subdistrict officer by padding the grain rolls so the village would receive more than its fair share of wheat was expected behavior, applauded within the village.

The subdistrict officer's position in the administrative hierarchy, the norms governing his appointment, and considerations of security all made it impossible for him to cultivate really close and firm ties with the villagers in his district. Gubser has spelled out some of these factors in his discussion of the composition of administrative councils in the Jordanian town of Al-Karak.[24] He points out that the criteria for recruitment of senior officials in the local departments differs from those in lower levels of the civil service. The positions of governor and police chief—and in the Ajlun district of subdistrict officer and mudir al-nahiya—were filled by men from outside the district in order to assure their neutrality. Lower-level positions that required special technical skills were mainly recruited on the basis of technical criteria (e.g., veterinary services, accountancy, health), while other positions were mainly recruited on the basis of kinship and friendship (e.g., social affairs, education, post office, and telegraph). Due to underemployment most lower-echelon bureaus are overstaffed. Moreover high-echelon officers, such as the subdistrict officer, are shifted frequently from one district to another to insure that their initial neutrality does not become dissipated with the establishment of friendships and other social or economic ties. In Kufr al-Ma I cannot recall that a subdistrict officer ever served more than a year; during a total of more than sixteen months of field work in 1959–60, 1966, and 1967 four separate judges presided in the subdistrict religious court. Deliberate rotation and recruitment of political neutrals have not only discouraged the possibility of top-level local bureaucrats becoming "insiders" from a village perspective, they have guaranteed their remaining cultural and social structural "outsiders."

A third external role/resource is the tribal leader, to be more accurate the former tribal leader, the Pasha. Since 1922, it has not been correct to label the Wazir family's leadership as tribal: although most subdistrict residents continue to identify themselves as the peoples of Tibne, any semblance of a tribal political hierarchy was dismantled. Through its mutasarrifs and police posts the central government established control over an area that had formerly given its military support and economic contributions to the leader of the Wazir family. However the heritage of past domination continues to give certain segments of the Wazir family political power and influence: since the Wazirs were placed as mukhtars in various villages and since marriages tied the Wazirs living in these villages to other descent groups, a quasi patron-client relationship developed. Since the Wazirs and particularly the Pasha's family had more land and more flocks, they have been able to display more hospitality than other families. The Pasha began a family tradition of higher education by being the first in the subdistrict to go beyond a sixth-grade education. Education in turn opened up positions in the bureaucracy for members of the family. The Pasha himself was appointed to the Jordanian Senate, where he continues to serve. Ordinary peasants, village mayors, and others still seek his advice and mediation and still solicit his influence in a wide variety of matters: contraction of marriage, divorce, village factional quarrels, land boundary disputes, cases of honor (assault, elopement, fornication, rape, burglary, violations of tribal reconciliation), and elections. Because of this constant parade of visitors seeking advice and favors, not only local bureaucrats but even other members of the Wazir family have accused the Pasha of being or seeking to be a *za'īm*, a local political boss. The Pasha denies both the fact and the aspiration, declaring that people come to him out of habit and tradition. He does not encourage either their visits or their deference—indeed he immediately withdraws his hand when peasants seek to kiss it on entering his guest room. All this notwithstanding, the Pasha does exercise great influence, not because he sits in the Senate, which only affirms his status, but as a result of his inherited charisma and, perhaps more important, his ability to achieve results—whether in the contraction of a marriage, the reconciliation of estranged neighbors, the provision of a job, or the warding off of the consequences of governmental policy. It is not surprising that local bureaucrats often seek the Pasha's advice and counsel before proceeding on certain matters. His knowledge, his wealth, his continuous residence in the district, and his renowned skill in mediation and arbitration are valuable resources for government employees as well as peasants. At the same time, the Pasha takes the other external agents of the bureaucracy into account. He has no formal office at the local level and he often declines to interfere or even offer advice on matters that he knows lie fully within the province of a local bureaucrat. Peasants from one clan of Kufr al-Ma asked him if they could use his uninhabited house in the village for the new school. The Pasha said that he would be delighted to donate his house for the school but that since some other villagers had made various proposals regarding the school's location, all such proposals should be taken to the subdistrict officer, who would investigate their suitability. On another occasion the Pasha accepted the commission to arbitrate a dispute in which one party sought divorce and the other consummation of the marriage. But only after consulting the judge of the religious court as to the possibilities of settlement according to religious law—the case had already been in court, did he arbitrate the dispute, and then within the limitations set by religious law. Be this as it may, the Pasha not only wields great influence in the subdistrict as a result of his widespread consanguineal and affinal ties, his wealth and the hospitality it makes possible, his inherited charisma, and the contacts that open up job possibilities, but also because local-level bureaucrats both seek his advice and usually accept it.

At the root of his leadership position among the peasants is the fact that he reflects their basic values, in fact acts as a model for their realization; in addition, he communicates in a culturally fa-

miliar idiom. As a mediator par excellence he epitomizes their concept of the wise man. As the most munificent provider of hospitality, he epitomizes their concept of the good man. Like them, and
unlike many local bureaucrats, he frequents their houses, sits on the
floor, patiently hears their complaints and problems, endures their
bickering and the endless give-and-take of argumentation in the
guest house, and finally offers a resolution—a resolution that may
be vociferously argued against but is nearly always accepted in the
end. The Pasha was one of the first in the subdistrict to buy a televi-
sion set; he placed it in his guest house, expecting bureaucrats in
the subdistrict center, neighbors, and fellow-villagers to come
frequently, watch it, drink tea, and share his company. They did not
come, because they had not received a special invitation; instead,
the peasants from surrounding villages came, for in their subculture,
which the Pasha shares, invitations for social visits are never extended but always implied between friends, quarter residents, former neighbors, kinsmen, and quasi-kinsmen (the peoples of Tibne).
On one occasion Kufr al-Ma was fined £330 sterling for damage the
village's shepherds had done to hundreds of trees the government
had newly planted on the Pasha's land; the shepherds had trespassed
on the land, broken down tree limbs, and fed them to their flocks.
After the village mayors collected the amount—a levy was placed on
each household—the Pasha forgave the villagers and refused to accept the money; there was a reconciliation (*sulha*) between the
shepherds and the Pasha in the best traditional manner, including
the slaughtering of a goat, a mutual bussing by all parties concerned,
and the eating of a common meal. Forgiveness is not only a running
theme in Islamic law and ethics but also in tribal law and ethics; the
gesture was completely understood and greatly appreciated. But the
government, in the person of the subdistrict officer, did not relent
regarding the trees and the remaining hundred pounds was collected
and paid over.[25] In more technical terms the Pasha's power and
influence was founded in his mastery of the basic form of communication and means of social control—"encounter through mediation"—as well as the traditional mode of establishing political influence—the politics of hospitality—and the values that underlay
both: generosity, hospitality, social equality, long-term reciprocity,
patience, eloquence, and honor.

The critical significance of the Pasha as an external role/resource
is simply that he offers villagers a choice—a choice between value
systems as well as between social processes and political mentors.
The degree to which so-called "modern" and "traditional" values

and processes are merged, accommodated, accepted as mutually viable alternatives, or rejected out of hand often depends on the presence or absence of men like the Pasha (linkers-with-the-past) at high levels in the hierarchy of power and influence. Bailey's description in *Caste and the Economic Frontier* (1957) of the situation in Bisipara, India was notable for the absence of such a linker in the external arena; within the village such linkers abounded, but outside it the men with the resources and power—the Congress party politicians, the police, the judges—all represented, at least in the context of their occupational activity, the values of the external arena. The villagers in Bisipara had no choice in values or social processes if they wished to tap the resources of that arena. In *Politics and Social Change* (1963) Bailey suggested that the larger feudatory states of Orissa had witnessed a rapid decline in the power of the rajas after 1948 but that local chiefs continued to control "small vote banks"—men who gave their vote according to their chief's choice, out of sentiment and from a habit of allegiance.[26] At the same time, however, he suggested that such vote banks would soon disappear unless traditional leaders such as chiefs and zemindars performed practical services for their former subjects and clients. In other words here too the choice between values and processes would soon disappear, for the cost of survival for traditional leaders in the external arena was conversion from movement-like politics to machine-like politics. The situation Fallers described for Uganda presents still another possibility.[27] Due to a colonial policy that emphasized gradual but steady change and with few open conflicts between the two social systems, Africans came to accept many aspects of European culture. Both cultures focused on the chief, who acted or, to be more precise, was expected to act in terms of particularistic values in the fields of kinship and clientship and in terms of universalistic criteria in "official matters." In fact, according to Fallers, the chief internalized both sets of values and symbols into his personality at considerable psychic cost to himself. Here there is a possible choice in the external arena, but from the point of view of the chief's clients, it is an ambiguous and uncertain choice, since the chief can act on the basis of either set of values in any given situation, and that set may not be the one on the basis of which the client expects action.

In the Pasha's case, no such ambiguity exists. This is not to say that in every respect the Pasha's style of life and values are those of the peasants. He lives in a different style house, possesses more education, land, and wealth and has the prerogatives and burdens that power, office, and inherited charisma entail. However his food and dress are not different in kind from those of the peasants, though they may be different in quantity and quality, his piety and sobriety follow the peasant pattern, and his language is the peasant's own. Moreover his family has both given and taken women in marriage from a large number of descent groups in surrounding villages. He is nearly as entwined in the peasant's social structure as he is partial to their values. For the villager, then, the choice is genuine: although his pleas may not be heeded, his case not be accepted, or the Pasha's decision go against him, the villager knows that the decision will be made in a way that he can understand and on the basis of values he accepts as his own.

Although almost all peasants among the peoples of Tibne consult the Pasha in matters related to social control (mediation and arbitration), in more strictly political contexts, such as regional or parliamentary elections or the "spoils system" (obtaining jobs through government influence), some peasants prefer to support the head of the municipality of Deir Abu Said—also a member of the Wazir family and in many contexts the Pasha's competitor. In Kufr al-Ma the members of Beni Yasin overwhelmingly back the Pasha, but Beni Dumi and the independent families back the head of the municipality; the members of Beni ʿAmr are divided. The success of the Dumi mayor (and the failure of the Yasin mayor) in getting his candidates into the army largely reflected Dumi's backing (and Yasin's long-time opposition) to the head of the municipality. When the king visited the area, the Dumi mayor's contacts with the head of the municipality enabled him to get many more tickets for the reception tent than the Yasin mayor could get for his following. On the religious festival days following the fast of Ramadan and the end of the pilgrimage, the Dumi mayor and notables always visited the head of the municipality; the Yasin mayor and notables never did, but instead paid a visit to the Pasha. Thus politically the Wazir family was split into factions with each leader drawing on separate vote banks.[28] Both sides recruited these vote banks with practical payoffs, but the Pasha had also built up good will through more than a half century of the politics of hospitality and successful encounter-through-mediation. The muffled competition between the Pasha and the head of the municipality, not for office or specific rewards but for influence within the subdistrict, reflected to a large degree the difference in values discussed above. Some local government officials interpreted the Pasha's mode of encounter as evidence of what they termed his "feudal" control over the peasants. Some accused his family of "not caring for the interests of the people" and "of helping only those who would help them maintain their position." One charged that "they eat the people's wealth." They held them, the Pasha and his family, responsible for blocking "progress," and they interpreted the Pasha's role in the subdistrict as self-serving and reactionary. Those who supported the Pasha among both peasants and government employees contrasted the Pasha's piety and sobriety with the municipality head's fondness for drink and, by implication, women, the Pasha's munificent hospitality with the municipality head's miserliness, the Pasha's honesty with the municipality head's alleged readiness to offer money for votes. In fact in the 1967 parliamentary election, although the Pasha in a loose sense of the term "campaigned" for office by visiting other villages, he refused to form alliances with other politicians outside his own subdistrict. They had offered to trade off votes, that is, to encourage their supporters to vote for him if he did likewise, but he replied that such trading of votes resulted in "blocs" and hard feelings when the leader could not or did not deliver on his promises. The Pasha, then, explicitly repudiated machine politics. Thus the choice of political mentors in the external arena involved the same value dichotomies as the choice of social processes: social control in the give-and-take manner in the guest house vs. ajudication in the courts; enforcement by gossip, avoidance, and social sanctions vs. enforcement by police; and decision-making through consensus and for harmony vs. decision-making by election and for victory.

The fourth role/resource, the migrant-laborer, differs from the first three in that the roles are mutual. That is, villagers who interact with migrant laborers from outside the village are usually themselves sometime migrant laborers. Since a very sizeable percentage of the village's men did or do engage in migrant labor, one might expect that such migration has brought important changes in the traditional culture and/or social structure of the village.[29] I have recorded a number of changes in economic patterns and style-of-life at the beginning of this chapter, but in general the village has remained traditional. This fact requires some explanation. Some migrants, particularly those who have worked in Beirut (a small minority), say that life there is much better than the village; in the words of one, "He who has tasted the meat and fat does not tire of it." But the majority preferred life in the village. They contrasted the fresh air of the countryside with the city's filth and congestion. Most in fact spend only about a month in the city, return to the village for one or two months, and then go back to the city. They desire to visit wife and family (almost all migrants leave them behind in the village), need to work their own land, or require rest after their strenuous work as unskilled construction labor, which is paid for on a piecework (producing so much cement or cutting so many stones) basis. Some of the reasons that migrant labor makes a relatively small impact on the social structure and culture of the village are revealed by examining the immediate milieu in which the large majority of migrant laborers live (the quarter above the vegetable market, *Hisba*, in the capital city, Amman). A month of labor at unskilled construction jobs, usually on the basis of a seven-day week, allows the village migrant to save between £10 and £12 sterling, enough to support a period of rest and relaxation combined with agricultural work back in the village for a month or two, but not enough to encourage prolonged residence and work in the city. Second, the social relations and pattern of residence of villagers in the city resemble those of the village. Village migrants often share a room with kinsmen or fellow-villagers, and though it would be inaccurate to say that everyone is related to everyone else in these neighborhoods, everyone is related to somebody. Often they live with other villagers, but almost invariably with villagers from villages surrounding their own. To a large degree they live an insulated social life, gathering in their rooms, in shops run by villagers-come-to-town, or in a restaurant with other villagers-come-to-town rather than with long-time urbanites. Thus, paradoxically, their city experience increases their knowledge about and intensifies their interaction with villagers of their own district, but does not serve a similar purpose with regard to the city, at least not to the same degree. Although cinemas and (in Beirut) bars abound, village migrants do not attend them very often. On rainy winter days when work was not possible, by their own account, they sat in their rooms, listened to the radio and visited their friends; others washed their clothes and took sponge baths. Many said they could not afford to go to the cinema, which cost $.15–.22 (the daily wage of construction laborer was between $2.00 and $3.75), or to the bathhouse, which cost $.45. Others said that while they would have liked to go to the cinema on days off, they were too tired and welcomed a day of rest. These migrants simulated the village life style. All wore the Bedouin shawl and headband at work or in any other public place. In their cramped quarters—one small room often housed four or five migrants—they tended to recreate the decor and atmosphere of the village guest house: they spread out pillows and mattresses along the walls, sat on the floor, drank tea, discussed cases of honor, and visited one another. Although they relaxed the code of modesty somewhat inside their rooms—when the heat was insufferable, they doffed their shawls—outside they were strict in their observance—I was chastized for sitting on the edge of a roof because there were women below (the quarter was located on a steep hill) and they would resent it. A number of these small one-room housing units resembled nuclear families in some respects, since they lived together, shared good company, often visited together, shared the rent, and ate together. Although financial stringency obviously prevents many village migrants from enjoying the amenities of urban life, evidence indicates that the villager's worldview also closes off many opportunities. One villager who joked about it back in the village was obviously taken aback in Beirut when a pimp repeatedly encouraged him to "cool his ardor" and promised him an opportunity to "raise his pecker." Another responded to an advertisement to apply in person for a job as lifeguard at a first-class Amman hotel swimming pool; he later described the scene he witnessed around the pool (western women sitting around in their bathing suits) as "nakedness, only nakedness." He said that he felt like a monkey walking through the hotel—everybody stared at him, for he was the only one wearing a shawl and headband. Although the manager asked him to return for another interview the next day, he did not. When I asked others why he had not returned, they said, "He will become corrupted (*byif-sad*)." A third villager got a job as watchman in an orchard in a village outside of the city of Tripoli in Lebanon. The owner's family made wine for home consumption; they also cooked with wine, stated the informant. One day after the grape harvest, they began making wine at about twelve noon—the villager was assisting in the process—and continued for twenty straight hours. The villager stated that he went home to sleep that night and passed out. Later in the night he began sleepwalking. Although he had not touched a drop, he said that he had got drunk from the aroma of the wine. The next day, although he was being given room and board in addition to $20. a month, he quit and returned to Jordan. The fact that this villager was a pious Muslim for whom drunkenness was a gross violation of religious norms is very much the point of the story. When I asked another migrant laborer from the village how social life was in Beirut, he replied in an obviously deprecatory tone, "Social life is the glass and the bottle."

Most village migrants, then, because of the nature of their work, its low rewards, its day-to-day (since most laborers rehire on a day-to-day basis) or week-to-week uncertainty, their ties with their fam-

ily and land back in the village and their own world-view do not
urbanize; they remain sporadic migrants. Those men who make
large salaries (in the army or the bureaucracy) often move out of the
village permanently or only return to the village to retire. They usually invest their savings in their sons' education, so very little remains to finance a new or lavish style of life that would contrast
with that of most villagers. Their food, their clothing, their housing,
and their hospitality more or less resemble those of other villagers—
it is their sons who will reap the benefits of their high incomes,
become professionals, and settle in the towns. The present-day,
run-of-the-mill migrant laborer simply raids the city for additional
income—to keep alive, to marry, to open a shop, to build a house.
These men are young, of low economic status, and consequently of
little political influence. They are unnoticed in the village guest
houses or absent, preferring to hang around the grocery shops when
they are in the village. Even if they had internalized different models
of behavior based upon their urban experiences (which with very
few exceptions they have not), they would not have been able to
effect changes in the mode of political action or its substantive
results.

Encapsulation of migrant labor preserves traditional village values in a milieu ostensibly inhospitable to them. At the other end
of the rural–urban continuum are urban men—the local-level
bureaucrats—in the village milieu. On the face of it, they represent a
set of values antithetical to those of villagers. The interesting fact is
that in many situations not only are they unable to impose these
values on villagers but also they are unable to prevent traditional
rural values from being imposed on themselves. The village council
law specifically provides that kinship and sectarian divisions be
taken into account in choosing representatives to the council. Although election to the council is provided for, selection (by consensus) is allowed. In Kufr al-Ma the subdistrict officer acceded to the
desire of the villagers to select their own representatives, thereby
assuring representation on the basis of descent groups. Many villages rejected the establishment of councils, because councils would
have rendered precise what villagers preferred to remain ambiguous
or at least unofficial—the superiority in power and status of some
men in relation to others. The governor and the subdistrict officer
spend a considerable amount of time cultivating the leading families
of the area and often they use traditional techniques in doing so, e.g.,
acting as mediators in a wide variety of situations and giving and
receiving hospitality in the traditional manner (squatting around a

tray of lamb meat and rice with numerous others—the more tightly packed the circle the better—and eating the contents with palm and fingers). Exemptions from tax collection are in fact determined by the mayors, on the basis of local notions of justice rather than by any external set of norms. Besides accepting encounter-by-mediation in many situations, local-level bureaucrats often accept and apply tribal law or some rendering of it in cases of honor. Although attempts are always made to avoid violent retaliation, governors and subdistrict officers recognize the stages of tribal reconciliation: seeking protection (*dakhal*), truce-money payment (*'atwa*), banishment of the culprits' close patrilineal relatives (*Tard*), compensation (*madda*), and formal peacemaking (*sulHa*). In many instances the subdistrict officer forces the culprit's patrilineal group to produce a patrilineal genealogy that defines the limits of culpability for the breach of honor just committed to insure that the tribal rules are followed precisely. Both the subdistrict officer and the judges of the religious and civil courts often take local custom into account, referring many cases back to village mediation, urging reconciliation and forgiveness, and when possible taking account of the practical possibilities of the situation in the local context as well as the requirements of the letter of the law.

However much local-level bureaucrats, from their own point of view, may be hampered by the necessity of having to work according to traditional norms, they remain, from the villager's point of view, a potential shortcut for tapping into the resources of the external arena. Due to the revolution of rising expectations villagers now claim as a matter of right a wide variety of services and resources that formerly, if anything, would have been a matter of supplication.[30] Appealing to government officials can be on a level-by-level basis, with some villagers, mainly the educated, holding that the government can be compelled to deliver, if not at one level of the hierarchy, then at the next. This assumption involves another truly revolutionary one, namely, that the government exists for the good of the people. On one occasion the village schoolmaster met with the two mayors and other notables and told them that they must go jointly to the subdistrict officer to petition for an additional schoolteacher. If the subdistrict officer refused to consider the matter, they could go to the governor or the minister of education. On another occasion one mayor said that he was going to present a petition in person to Prince Hasan (who was passing through the district on an official visit) asking for (1) the expansion of the school, (2) the extension of a piped water system to the village (it was so extended months later though not as a result of the petition), (3) the funds to build a new mosque, and (4) a local health officer. Another villager said he was organizing a petition to get a regular bus service established. Villagers resort to government officials when they have failed to achieve objectives through the use of local social sanctions such as gossip, avoidance, flight, refusal to provide economic aid, or cooperation. Thus men take their daughters to court to petition for judicial separation if the women's husbands continue to mistreat them after long and repeated attempts at mediation. Similarly, protracted disputes over land are sometimes taken to the land registry officer for an official disposition. Local-level government officials are also shortcuts employed in the destruction of resources. One villager addressed a letter to the governor stating that the local clerk of court, a resident villager, was guilty of accepting bribes. If the accusation had been accepted as valid—it was not—the man's reputation and, more important, his means of subsistence could have been destroyed. One mayor wheedled the subdistrict officer into tearing up an important document affecting compensation for village school lands after many other avenues to achieve the same result had failed. Men who would otherwise have been compensated for their lands were not, and others whose lands would have been sold reclaimed them and started ploughing.[31]

Factors Discouraging Competition in the External Arena

In light of the considerable payoffs available in the external arena, why don't more villagers turn to it—specifically to one or another of the local-level bureaucrats in the subdistrict center? A number of answers have already been discussed: the intercalary role of the mayor, one of whose primary duties is to ward off the consequences of government action and to reduce the contact of the ordinary villager with government officials; the fact that the village is regarded as the proper locus of social control and that villagers are reluctant to seek outside support even against members of the opposite faction; the nature of the village as a close-knit multiplex social control unit in which many incipient attempts to broadcast issues and make claims for resources in the wider arena are intercepted and cut off, and the presence of an alternative role/resource in the external arena —the Pasha.

Another factor is the poverty of most villagers. In an area where it has been estimated that the agricultural labor force works only about 150 days a year, with high seasonal unemployment and relatively low returns from most forms of wage labor in cities, villagers are not in a financial position to make the most of the opportunities provided by the government's drive for modernization.[32] For example, the government extended water pipes to the entrance of the village. The government official told the mayor that if twenty-five village households purchased water meters (at $10 per meter), they would extend the water pipes along every main village byway *gratis*. Since the village improvement tax had been collected a few months before, the required number of commitments to purchase could not be collected, and the households remained deprived of piped water, although the single outlet at the village entrance remained. Likewise villagers very rarely seek loans from banks rather than from local moneylenders, who charge high rates of interest, because banks require collateral and the loan must be paid back in cash, not in kind. Although villagers are much better off today than they were even ten years ago—the above-mentioned tax could not have been collected ten years ago—they are not well enough off to utilize many of the role/resources available to them in the external arena.

Logistical and social factors combine with worldview to discourage resort to the external arena. In a study of rural credit and thrift cooperatives in the villages of Jordan, Qutub has elucidated a number of considerations that lead villagers to avoid using governmental credit agencies and commercial banks: the process of obtaining a loan is always complicated and involves a lot of red tape; the application for a loan requires travel to towns and cities and a loss of both time and money; it is seldom, if ever, possible to postpone repayment of a loan for a long period.[33] Borrowing from traditional credit sources involves a well-understood process, often requires no interest payment (if it is a personal loan over a short period), allows repayment in crops (grain, olives, olive oil, or seeds) or services as well as cash. Furthermore, even when the loan is from a moneylender charging a high rate of interest, it is usually readily given when needed, provided some sort of security is available— olive trees, land, houses, shops (rather than officially documented collateral). Finally, it is almost always possible to postpone the repayment until the next agricultural season.[34] The substantial investment of time and energy into a poorly understood process is perhaps the most important factor of all, and the one Gubser underlines in his remarks about the difficulties peasants encounter dealing with the local bureaucracy in the Al-Kerak district. The average

Keraki must visit many offices, obtain numerous signatures, and affix stamps for each. These procedures are understood by few and actually deter many from dealing with the government.[35]

Competition may not take place in the external arena because there is greater potential for developing internal arena resources (which may later be redeployed in the external arena). This situation does not apply to Kufr al-Ma but often it does apply to instances in which the community suffers some peculiar handicap in the competition for external resources.[36]

The last factor discouraging competition in the external arena, one particularly pertinent for Kufr al-Ma, is ideological. I have already discussed briefly one of the ideologies that leads villagers to resort to the external arena (the revolution of rising expectations) and one of the ideologies (associated with local custom and the former semitribal system) that leads them to resort to a restricted part of that arena (the Pasha). These ideologies are tempered by the factors I have mentioned and by the realization, specifically with regard to the village improvement program or the village council, that the government will, willy-nilly, introduce whatever changes it wishes. Some aspects of the Muslim belief system seem to discourage resort to the external arena. In 1960 the area agricultural officer came a number of times to Kufr al-Ma seeking to form a village improvement committee to work in conjunction with the Village Improvement Program. He finally failed; one contributing factor being the refusal of two elders from the two largest clans to attend any meeting. They justified their attitude by saying that the committee intended to take out a bank or government loan involving interest and this would constitute usury (*ribā'*) according to Islamic law. Yet when I returned to the village in 1965, I found that the former clerk-usher of the local religious court, recognized in the village as a pious man, had resigned from his position and bought a tractor with a bank loan (involving the payment of interest); he was using the income gained from hiring out the tractor to give one of his sons a higher education. At that time I also noted that the village preacher, by many standards an archconservative, was leading the village in certain aspects of change: he had outfitted his guest room with chairs, he was the first to buy a water meter and to install water pipes, and he was very active in figuring the costs of purchase and installation of meter, faucet, pipes, and tank for other families. He was also the one who in 1960 had preached that the ties of clanship and patrilineal descent were divisive and had to be subordinated to the good of the community.

There is one set of beliefs, however, almost universally held by villagers, that effectively cuts off one potential role/resource in the external arena—the set of beliefs related to political parties. Branches of Jordanian, inter-Arab, socialist, communist, and Muslim parties were formed in the cities and large towns of Jordan during the 1950s but the central government curtailed their activities and in most cases suppressed them by the early 1960s.[37] However their sympathizers, mainly educated and often operating clandestinely, remained. Villagers came into contact with their views primarily through their children, whose teachers often were partial to one party or another, if not actual members. In the 1950s and early 1960s teachers often made active attempts to win their students over to their own point of view—this was particularly true in the so-called "party period" in Jordan (1954–1957), when party activity was unfettered.

The adult generation in Kufr al-Ma had an overwhelmingly negative reaction to this kind of political party activity. This reaction is part of a much wider set of attitudes and beliefs. Of all the ideas originating in the external arena, those villagers most consistently reject relate to the political process and to decision-making: village councils, elections, per capita taxation, political parties. Of these, by far the most widely and decisively rejected is political party activity.

In the first place, political parties are associated with the activity of foreigners and particularly with colonialism:

> The National Syrian Party, the Resurrection Party, the National Socialist Party, the Communist Party—they're all the same, communist.

When I asked the village preacher, who made this statement, why these parties were so popular, he replied:

> Colonialism—it was what gave birth to the parties. There is a saying, 'Divide and rule.' The English are the origin of the parties. This happened in the time of the English; the father was for a party, the son was for [another] party, and the daughter was for [another] party; and when they sat down at the table together to eat, they fought with one another.

Foreign parties and foreign knowledge (al-ʿilm al-ajnabi) are associated; and both are considered corrupting. An illiterate villager put it in the following manner:

> Nothing destroyed us except foreign knowledge; the parties call for foreign ideas.

This association is strengthened by the widely held and often justified belief, that the school teachers are mainly responsible for propagating political party opinions in rural areas. The preacher made the connection explicit:

> [During the party period] there were many political parties in Deir Abu Said [where the junior high school for the area was located]. Teachers were not on speaking terms with one another and each had their own coterie of students who were always quarreling on the playground; and education went by the boards. Teachers went around flunking students not of their party.

To the villagers one of the most serious consequences of political party activity is precisely this weakening of the social fabric. Besides the divided family quarreling at the dinner table was the situation described by a village shopkeeper:

> One reason we hate communism is that they take the small child away from its mother and father, and he does not know them and is brought up by the school and the university; he doesn't know his sister and in fact he may marry her.

I once asked a literate villager who was fairly knowledgeable about a wide variety of topics having to do with the world outside the village what the meaning of socialism (*ishtirakiyya*) was. He began talking of the Shadhiliya, a dervish order, which, he said, when it met congregationally, brought in a naked woman who danced around in the circle and was then enjoyed by all: the order, he said, was located in northern Syria.

There is no doubt that one profound source of hostility to political party activity is the Islamic belief system as interpreted for the peasants by judges of rural religious courts, and by village preachers. The term *Hizb*, today translated as political party, appears in many Quranic verses, almost invariably with an invidious connotation.[38] The term could be translated in some contexts as "splinter group," or "faction," and almost always suggests corrupting divisiveness. In a Friday sermon delivered in the village mosque, the guest preacher from the subdistrict center referred to *Hizbiyyūn*, "people associated with parties," in the context of the proliferation of differences that would arise between partisans of different groups just before the Day of Judgement. And in the same breath he referred to "the apostate parties [*al-aHzāb al mulhida*] that have come to our country"; he added that were it not for the king, "our redeemer,

Husayn," who was constantly warring against the parties, the struggle would have been lost. He continued:

> What unites people is religion. Language does not unify people: Walid ibn Mughira, 'Ubay ibn Khalaf, Abu Lahab, and Abu Jahl were all patrilineal kinsmen of the Prophet and speakers of Arabic; they did not accept his message, while Bilal an Ethopian did so. The most honorable among you with God is the most God-fearing.

The judges of the subdistrict religious court also addressed themselves to the subject of "parties," though in a somewhat different manner. One judge said that Islam didn't need *aHzāb* (parties) because in a Muslim state the ruler is just; therefore there was no need for an opposition to check injustice. He went on to say that there was no necessity for parties since Islam was "the party." On the other hand, he said that Islam was "political" (*siyāsi*): it must take on all the problems of society. The remarkable fact is that the villagers—and not just villagers associated with the religious hierarchy—condemn party activity in general, not just those of the left or left-center. The Liberation Party, a conservative Islamic party, was rejected along with the others, and many villagers viewed with considerable satisfaction the arrest of a village primary school teacher for passing out Liberation Party propaganda in the market town. Thus even during the party period villagers were by and large actively hostile to political parties. The preacher's dogmatic statement, "There are no parties in the villages," was certainly true for Kufr al-Ma. Interestingly enough, he went on to say, "We do not know their principles," which was only a half-truth, since at least a garbled version of their principles was known, if only through the children. He went on to explain this absence—both of party affiliation and knowledge of party principles—by the absence of newspapers. He had a point, for newspapers were often associated with and sometimes subsidized by particular political parties. I knew of only one villager, the clerk of the local civil court, who bought a newspaper on a regular basis. Hardly anyone else ever bought one at all. Villagers frequently used the term, "party man" (hizbi) to describe not only individuals known to be affiliated with political parties but also individuals with views that were at all similar to those enunciated by party members or party sympathizers. It was not simply a pejorative term; it indicated strong condemnation of the individual because to the peasants it connotes lack of solidarity among kinsmen, covillagers at odds, and even the split of the nuclear family. The ideology of the hizbiyyun (party people) also conflicted with fundamental values and processes characterizing village life, for that ideology called for decisions by elections. This mode of decision-making was incompatible with the traditional forms—encounter-through-mediation and consensus—and the fundamental value that underlay them—the necessity for social harmony within the community.

Becoming a "party man," then, often involved a considerable wrench away from traditional loyalties, since party loyalties were to be given precedence in many situations. However, in the party period becoming a party man could open up many new resources in the external arena if the individual party proved successful at the election box. But being a party man in a state that increasingly became a nonparty state could bring great misfortune. One villager had been a lieutenant in the Arab Legion and an adherent of a political party. He continued to announce his political opinions vociferously despite the increasing hostility of the state to such public statements. Finally he was jailed, first for a short period, but after a second attack on the government for a prolonged period. He returned to the village practically penniless, borrowed some money, and was raising chickens when I left the village. He was a social isolate in the village—he did not visit others and they did not visit him; this avoidance extended to his own brothers, one of whom was a village mayor. Conversations revealed him to be as psychologically alienated from village values and the village way of life as he was, by his own choice, socially isolated. This particular instance of personal misfortune, albeit an extreme case, requires that we examine the costs of resorting to the external arena more closely.

The Cost of Utilizing the Resources of the External Arena

Paradoxically to resort to the external arena wastes resources—time, energy, and money—especially when no results are achieved. One can go through the complicated red tape for a bank loan or bribe officials to get one's sons into the army; yet after long, strenuous efforts and considerable expenditure accomplish nothing. Another prominent example of such waste is education. During a revolution of rising expectations, education is the elixir to success. Peasants spend considerable amounts of money to forward their children's education—for room and board in schools in town and for school materials even when the schooling is local. Often the students are not able to pass their school courses at one level or another, so they terminate without the certificate that would enable them to qualify for a low-level bureaucratic post. But they have also become unfit either by training or disposition to revert to the traditional roles of cultivator or migrant laborer. One peasant, perhaps an extreme example, sold all his lands to enable his son to finish high school—the son failed to pass his examinations three times.

Resort to the external arena also leads to the idling and sometimes dissipation of internal resources. In Kufr al-Ma between 1960 and 1965 increased migrant labor to towns caused a considerable reduction in village livestock holdings, for there were not enough shepherds to care for them. Much formerly tilled land remained fallow because not enough agricultural labor was on hand during the ploughing and/or harvesting seasons. Resort to the external arena can also cost one social credit or honor. During elections to the Jordanian parliament in 1967, one mayor absented himself from the village on the day the candidates had arranged to come to the village to campaign. He said later that if he had met with the candidates, some villagers would eventually have accused him of taking bribes from one of them. The case of the former Arab Legion lieutenant presents an even more extreme example of how much social credit can be lost through association with political party activity.

From the villager's point of view there are also certain value costs, as when the police sergeant exploited the village's code of hospitality. Outsiders can violate the code in a public manner and get away with it. The migrant laborer's exposure to congestion, dirt, alcoholism, prostitution, and immodesty sometimes takes its toll; the fact that many migrants return intermittently to the village may in part be explained by the need to "recharge psychological batteries" and reassert the value of a way of life worn down under the impact of urban conditions and folkways. Prolonged absence from the village and exposure to town ways often produces departures from fundamental village values. One soldier who retired to the village after twenty years of service had a sizable piece of land in the village, but since he had gone directly from primary school into the army, he did not know how to plough it; he had to hire someone, reducing his agricultural income by half. He opened up a small grocery shop, but could not make a success of it. He was always giving away sweets and sugar to the children who played around the shop; the ethos of the successful village shopkeeper (and indeed of most villagers)—skimping, penny-pinching, driving a hard bargain, saving for shop expansion, and if spending is necessary, spending on the honored guest rather than on one's own family or friends—was alien to his own. This man often asked fellow villagers for favors in a straightforward manner at the beginning of a conversation and not, after uttering numerous politeness formulas, at the end of it. He lacked the villager's duplicity and his propensity to use circumlocution. The external arena, specifically, the new money that it offers, has also resulted in a decline of filial piety; the judge of the local religious court stated that an unprecedented kind of case had begun to appear on the court dockets: fathers were appearing as plaintiffs against their sons, charging them with lack of maintenance. Almost invariably the sons had employment in towns (as petty bureaucrats or soldiers), earned monthly salaries, and were the main economic support of the extended family—or at least so the father expected and claimed.

Valuable external resources bring external values in their tow. The village improvement program macadamized the roads, introduced piped water, and hired an extra primary school teacher, but only because each head of a household in the village paid taxes. Recalcitrant taxpayers were finally jailed, for this was an obligation that could not be canceled through mediation or the politics of hospitality or by any appeal to the necessities of a system of multiplex social relations. Once the village improvement program was utilized, the universalistic legal obligations it entailed came into effect.[39] Moreover the conception of "village improvement" is formulated in Amman and, although villagers feed in their own proposals, the projects are chosen in and directed from the governate or subdistrict capital. The temporal and procedural framework of implementation is alien to the village way of life: if village leaders do not specify to the governor the location of construction, the materials needed, the necessary preparations, the project's starting date, the number of persons available to work, and the kinds of services needed by a certain date, the governor may implement projects in his own way according to his own schedule. Bureaucratic constraints are clearly demonstrated in the local Islamic court. For a villager to gain a court order demanding wifely obedience (ta'a zawjiyya) (the return of a wife who has run away to her father's house), the husband must prove not only that he has inflicted no unduly severe punishment on her but also that he has provided her with a "legal (proper) house" (bayt shar'i). This house must be provided with certain items and maintain a certain standard of modesty—for instance there must be a courtyard with a high wall around it to insure privacy. Often such demands conflict with village custom, but if the husband wants his wife back, he must behave according to the expectations of the court.

A further stage in this process by which the internal arena is integrated into an overarching external arena occurs when villagers are not simply constrained by the actions, procedures, and norms governing the external arena but actually embrace them. One example was when the Dumi mayor embraced majority rule by asserting three times before various public officials that his coalition represented more than half the village and was therefore entitled to more than half the seats in the village council. And some villagers were not upset by the arrest of others for nonpayment of taxes, but actually called for such action. Embracing majority rule is particularly significant, for it assumes acceptance of the principle of political equality on a per capita basis and implies that the poor and the illiterate play an important role in local-level politics—an assumption that certainly did not underlie traditional politicking.

Actually, of course, the values and social processes of the external arena do not stand out dramatically against the values and social processes of the internal arena. Within the external arena significant options exist between kinds of roles/resources—the Pasha on the one hand and the bureaucracy on the other. But even within the government contradictions between ethical norms and processes exist, whether such contradictions exist in the same person at different times or in different situations or in different persons with respect to the same situation. Sometimes such contradictions even exist concerning the same principle. Government officials often attack patrilineal descent groups (clans and lineages), decry the influence of their elders, and urge the subordination of family interests to those of the community and the nation: they often blame such groups for any opposition to government plans and programs. At the same time they have reinforced the strength of patrilineal descent ties by making them pertinent to all cases of honor. Even when the parties do not know their genealogies fully or when they cannot produce them, the subdistrict officer insists that they be produced. Until they are, the process of mediation is often held up. The action of government officials does not always or perhaps even usually produce new customs and procedures (heterogenetic change); it often results in the reaffirmation or extension of old customs and procedures (orthogenetic change).[40] The necessity to produce genealogies is an instance of orthogenetic change both with respect to ideology and action, for not only must the patrilineal genealogy be collected, but relatives defined by it as being within a certain degree of kinship are banished from the area pending a final and formal reconciliation (*sulHa*).[41]

Sometimes bureaucrats hold two incompatible principles, for example the principles of decentralization and local participation. Attempts to strengthen the rights and obligations of regional and local-level bureaucrats also imply their enhanced capability of overriding local initiative when it conflicts with governmental policy or procedures. As Grassmuck pointed out, the principles of decentralization and state security are also opposed in many situations. The regular rotation of all district and subdistrict officers and, until recently, the independence of the local police detachments from regional control, although it realized the principle of local participation to a great extent also seriously undermined that of decentralization.

Occasionally options reflecting the values of both arenas are built into bureaucratic procedures, as when villagers are given a choice of either electing or selecting the members of the village council. Or bureaucratic procedure may reflect different and contrasting values at different stages of the process. For instance the Islamic court operates within the rather narrow limits stipulated by Islamic law with respect to evidence, court procedure, and verdicts; sometimes these verdicts are quite opposed to village or tribal custom. On the other hand, the Islamic court often takes local custom into account: parties to a dispute are enjoined to settle or reconcile out of court according to traditional procedures of mediation and the realities of the social context; when a village girl complained that her husband had not provided a fine pair of shoes as part of her bridal outfit, the judge retorted, "Since when have peasant girls worn shoes"; and a village shepherd was counseled by the judge to divorce his wife, since his wife, over a period of two years, had run away from her husband's home four times, taken suck from the teat of her mother-in-law—to invoke the incest taboo—and finally tried to poison him.

The values and social processes of the internal arena are not uniform either. A considerable range exists: from those acting mainly in terms of tribal and/or Islamic norms, who boycotted all meetings related to the Village Improvement Program (because of its alleged intention of engaging in usury), to the individual who engaged in blatant political party activity and violated fundamental norms of community behavior by refusing to marry, give or receive hospitality, or operate by duplicity or circumlocution. Some variation is occupation-related. Agricultural households tend to have larger families, more sons working and living at home under the father's authority, and higher rates of cousin and sister-exchange marriage. In nonagricultural households (e.g. army, migrant labor, low-level bureaucracy), sons tend to be economically independent and to live separate from the father; these households tend to be smaller and some of their women have developed a disdain of physical labor. In terms of consumption patterns, the former tend to buy sheep, marry a second wife, extend hospitality to their kinsmen and neighbors, marry off a son, or buy a horse with any surplus earnings; the latter tend to spend any savings on the education of sons, the purchase of town-style house furnishings (chairs, tables, beds), bribery for army and government positions, and the building of a new house.

In addition village men display different attitudes regarding the utilization of the external arena, which do not necessarily correlate with the above-mentioned differences. Some denounce the appeal to and reliance on government officials while others regard such utilization as the just and proper exercise of their rights as citizens. Not infrequently the same person oscillates between these two attitudes depending on the situation. The former clerk-usher of the religious court who purchased a tractor with a bank loan vociferously condemned a village shopkeeper (who was accused of selling putrid meat) for calling village women to testify in his defense in the civil court; by taking the case to court he was accused of violating the modesty of the women and scandalizing the village. Even with regard to such a fundamental value as honor, the villagers cannot be said to take a perfectly uniform stance, since some men are too poor to effectively compete for or assert it (men living in a one-room house cannot protect the modesty of their women from strange guests because there is no place to which the women can retire). Finally with respect to political norms and political behavior within the internal arena, it has already been pointed out that both machine and movement modes of political competition exist. Although the two mayors have built their followings primarily in terms of one mode or the other, it is clear from table 5 that elements of both modes are reflected in the backing of each, for the Yasin mayor has received some ad hoc payments and the Dumi mayor has received some annual payments. As with the external arena the same individual at different times espouses and acts in accord with contradictory norms: the villagers of Shujur, who justified their secession from the Yasin clan on the basis of specified failures and insults by the Yasin mayor (implying a machine context of politics), later de-

nied the reality of the secession on the basis of indissoluble movement solidarity.

Bailey has suggested in a number of places (for instance on page
291 of "Parapolitical Systems" and page 23 of "Political Activity in
Village India") that a major cost of resorting to the external arena is
escalation of the competition. It must be noted that this does not
always occur. Resort to external roles/resources may even settle an
issue and deescalate the competition. For instance in Jordan a sur-
veyor can decide disputes over land boundaries; if asked, the land
registry officer can divide lands definitively between quarreling
cousins or brothers by registering separate plots in their names. The
police and the subdistrict officer, if called upon early enough, can
control and shorten periods of violence that occur in conjunction
with cases of honor. One reason resort to the external arena often
leads to deescalation is that the external roles/resources are not in
and of themselves indicators of status. In Bailey's terms, they are
ordinarily used as "technical rules" to gain certain objectives, such
as money, jobs, or licenses. On the other hand, internal roles/
resources (see table 4), such as guest houses, agricultural land, visiting relations, patrilineal genealogies, or the deferential services of
specialists are in and of themselves indicators of social status. Thus
resort to them directly involves competition for social status, while
resort to the former does not.

Of course on many occasions resort to the external arena does
exacerbate internal dissension and escalate competition. This sometimes occurs simply because the conflict has been pushed up to a
higher structural level, as when the Dumi mayor goes on behalf of
his coalition to seek aid from the head of the municipality and the
Yasin mayor goes on behalf of his coalition to seek aid from the
Pasha. In the case of the bogus magician escalation occurred in the
same way: once the news of his activities in Kufr al-Ma had been
published in the town newspaper, it was no longer the honor of particular households vis-à-vis one another that was at stake but the
honor of the village vis-à-vis other villages. Resort to the external
arena often publicizes and makes scandalous what would otherwise
be private intravillage or intraclan or intralineage disputes and
events; the cases of the putrid meat and of Abu Fayid's letter are
cases in point. Because the competition now involves a higher social
structural level and/or because publication and scandal has occurred,
settlement becomes much more difficult. When both factors are involved simultaneously and consecutively—as when the Dumi

mayor and the Yasin mayor made contradictory claims about the size of their followings in public, first before the village elders, then before the subdistrict officer, and then before the governor—the scandal, internal dissension, and, as a result, the escalation of the competition is likely to be greatest.

A number of other reasons, some obvious and others not so obvious, can be suggested for the fact that competition often escalates following resort to the external arena. Since the external arena represents a much wider arc of roles and resources on which to draw, the prizes are greater and/or new.[42] In the examples discussed the prizes include money, electricity, and prestige (from the village council), compensation for lands sold, new teaching or janitorial posts, trees and water-tank guards (from the village improvement program), and bureaucratic posts (from the winning political party). Escalation also occurs for the opposite reason—the penalties risked in resorting to the external arena are much greater: fining, jailing, public dishonor in the courts or government offices, and scandal through newspaper publication; in the village, insult, ostracism, and economic boycott are the maximum penalties. Resort to the external arena also escalates competition because it breaks the in-built checks on factionalism or renders them irrelevant. Chapter two briefly discussed these checks—the cross-cutting ties of descent, affinity, and factionalism, the existence of the village as a unit of social control, and the importance of clan paternalism and multiplex relations; since those who play external roles are usually not susceptible to such checks, they tend to impose their own demands regarding prizes, personnel, and rules of competition. Escalation also tends to occur for certain social psychologial reasons, which Bailey has phrased in the following way:

> [external arena] rules bring in resources which are by definition unfamiliar: no one quite knows where things are going to stop. One's expectations of where the limits will be are important in setting those limits. Without this knowledge the conflict has an escalating tendency, for, since the rules and expectations remain to be discovered experimentally, each side tends to over-insure by committing more resources to be on the safe side.[43]

Finally, resort to the external arena results in escalation of competition because of certain symbolic effects. I have already indicated that the use of internal roles and resources have certain symbolic effects—namely, the denotations and connotations associated with the gain or loss of social status. If one accepts Bailey's view that "confrontations" are both potentially signals of resources martialed to one's own side and challenges hurled at the opponent to respond or lose (power, money, office, honor, land, etc.),[44] then it follows that certain situations dramatize one signal more than the other. Resort to the external arena tends to be interpreted as a challenge precisely because, in terms of traditional movement politics, such resort violates community norms regarding the proper locus of political competition. That locus is still the village whether with respect to the personnel qualified to compete or the rules of the competition.[45]

Much of what has been said about resort to the external arena does not differ substantially from Bailey's analysis of this process in the villages of Bisipara and Baderi in India. In one respect, however, the situation in Kufr al-Ma differs: resort to the external arena does not necessarily lead to either escalation, deescalation, or no change of competition. It can also produce a feedback loop—an appeal for a confrontation or an encounter in the external arena can lead back to an encounter-by-mediation and/or the politics of hospitality in the internal arena. A woman whose father had sought to obtain for her a judicial separation lost his case in the religious court; the judge recommended that the couple be reconciled. She, however, continued to live separately in her father's house, until finally the couple was reconciled in the traditional manner in the guest house after the payment of compensation (the son-in-law had cursed the father and his daughter), mutual bussing, and the eating of a common meal. After the case of the putrid meat was tried in the civil court, causing considerable hard feelings and increasing animosity between the grocer's relatives, the relatives of the mayor (who reported the grocer to the authorities), and the relatives of the women who were called on to testify, the case was finally settled in a village guest house in the traditional manner. In some instances the villagers themselves decide for various reasons, including the waste of time and money in the external arena without the desired result, that the most appropriate solution is encounter-by-mediation in the village guest houses. Other times government agents themselves suggest and encourage solution of the problems brought to them by traditional processes. Thus the feedback solution finds support in both arenas. The prominence of this solution in Kufr al-Ma and its relative unimportance in Baderi and Bisipara suggests that the value gap separating villagers and bureaucrats in India is greater than that which separates villagers and bureaucrats in Jordan. There is evidence that this is indeed the case. Many Jordanian bureaucrats who are in some respects extremely westernized, whether in terms of dress, political views, house furnishings, or attitudes toward modernization, often wear the Bedouin shawl and headband along with their western-style suit, drink coffee village style, enforce the modesty code on their women quite strictly, and enforce tribal law. In spite of their immediate urban backgrounds and their western ways, they too are "the sons of tribes and clans." It is this fact that establishes the feedback loop as an important option, one that allows the adjustment and partial integration of the institutions of both arenas with one another. The Kond-Oriya contrast in Baderi and the clean caste-outcaste cleavage in Bisipara do not allow for the articulation of the two arenas in this manner. As Bailey points out, the adjustments and integrations that do occur come either through the economic frontier or through the administrative frontier and not through the mores and folkways of a still partially tribal and increasingly Islamic way of life.

The Articulation of the Two Arenas

In his first book on India, *Caste and the Economic Frontier* (1957), Bailey attributed the failure of the untouchables to win the main prize available in the internal (village) arena—honor-purity—to two factors, "localization" and untouchability.[46] The first factor prevented a man from sloughing off his social origins anywhere in the vicinity of his home district in order to maximize economic gain and social mobility and the second constituted a barrier which it was impossible to overcome through the usual processes of "subversion," "confrontation," and "encounter." In other words Bailey argued that the internal and external arenas were articulated administratively and economically rather than in terms of ethical norms and the values inferred from them. In the initial stages of the Pan (untouchable)-clean caste conflict, it was a "competition" and not a "fight," since both sides agreed on the main prize (honor-purity) and on tactics (barring resort to external resources). They only seriously disagreed on the rules defining which personnel were to be eligible to compete—the untouchables insisted that they were eligible and the clean castes denied such a possibility. Basically, then, the value gap was still between the bureaucrats of the external arena and the villagers—clean caste or untouchables—of the internal arena.

However the untouchables' bold attempt to enter the temple (to gain the prize of honor-purity) and their repulsion by the clean castes, who employed economic and political sanctions (through the village council) and the threat of force, led to a significant change. The untouchables contacted the police and eventually the courts and the politicians of the Congress Party in order to make good their attempt to enter the temple; they had now violated the rules regarding tactics, since they had drawn upon resources in the external arena in order to win the competition in the internal arena. And we are led to believe that in the future some untouchables would abandon the quest for the main prize in the internal arena (honor-purity) and embrace the main prize in the external arena (political office and influence).[47] At this point the conflict between the Pans and the clean castes had become more like a "fight," since the two sides within the village were in disagreement about the rules governing tactics as well as personnel and some villagers were beginning to question the value of the prize. The untouchables were becoming integrated into the external arena much more rapidly than the clean castes, who, willy-nilly, had to take up the untouchables newfound tactics (drawing on external roles/resources) to hold their own in the "fight" cum "competition."[48] In the second stage, then, the untouchables were integrated into the external arena with respect to the rules governing personnel and tactics, while in the third stage the clean castes were becoming integrated with respect to tactics and the untouchables in an incipient fashion with respect to prizes.

In more general terms Bailey has outlined four types of articulation between what he has termed "Structure A" and "Structure B" or what I have termed, respectively, the internal and the external arena. In the first the integration of A into B or, as Bailey puts it, the "encapsulation" of A by B is nominal; that is, local communities, although formally part of an overarching political structure, are in fact unadministered, as, for instance, large areas of the Ottoman Empire in the nineteenth century. The second type of articulation is "predatory"; in return for the payment of taxes, local communities are left alone to conduct their own affairs according to their own folkways and mores. A third type of articulation, "is founded on an agreement to leave intact the broad structure of A, providing this does not do violence to certain fundamental principles (natural justice) which are embodied in Structure B."[49] The British colonial policy of "indirect rule" in Nigeria is an example of this type—it is based on the view "that people are entitled to their own beliefs and should be allowed, as far as possible, to preserve cherished institutions."[50] Finally, national or imperial governments can decide that local communities must be integrated; that is, in the terms used above, local communities must accept the rules with respect to prizes, personnel, and tactics laid down by the bureaucrats of the central government. As Bailey notes, this type of articulation is espoused and worked for in most developing nations, and Harik describes an interesting recent case of this in an Egyptian Delta village.[51] There, in a policy he describes as "the mobilization of peasants," the government through land reform, the establishment of cooperatives, the introduction of technocrats, the establishment of political party branches at the local level (the Arab Socialist Union), and the appointment of village mayors, who may or may not be natives of the community, has substantially reshaped the rules regarding prizes, tactics, and personnel.

Many instances are not nearly as clear-cut as this Egyptian case. The Arab village in Israel that Cohen studied poses a number of problems, particularly when one considers whether to classify it as an example of type one or type two.[52] On the one hand, a considerable degree of cultural autonomy exists: villagers eat their own food, dress in their own way, follow their own marriage customs, regulate interpersonal behavior between men and women according to their own mores, and follow the rituals, beliefs, and law of their own religion. On the other hand, these villagers are completely integrated into the county's economic life—many are members of the Histadrut, the national trade union; they are integrated into political life at both national and local levels—competition for election to the village council occurs at the local level and political parties woo villagers' votes in parliamentary elections; and, willy-nilly, they are integrated into the state's legal system—aspects of Islamic or tribal law that contradict national legislation or policy are nullified; thus, for instance although Islamic law allows polygyny, Israeli national law forbids it. To some degree Cohen has suggested that there exists an inverse relationship between economic and political integration on the one hand and cultural assimilation on the other: the more thoroughly Arab villagers are enmeshed in the economic, political, and legal institutions of the state of Israel, the more strongly they affirm and in a real sense expand upon (by adding culture content) their own cultural identity. These villagers would be placed at different points on Bailey's continuum depending on which institutional complex one considered.

The situation in Kufr al-Ma is even more complex. With respect to the rules about prizes, structure A (associated with the village) values honor, modesty, and prestige as defined by traditional indicators (land, sheep, hospitality, eloquence, patience, and judicial wisdom). On the other hand, structure A increasingly accepts and values education, money, and government position. Structure B (associated mainly with the bureaucracy) to a large degree values honor and modesty and accepts the legitimacy of certain indices of traditional prestige. Even when they do not value them, they accept them, often selectively, on a pragmatic basis—as, for instance, their acceptance of tribal law as the most efficient way to facilitate conflict resolution. However structure B values more strongly prestige as defined by modern indicators (education, government position, and money). With respect to prizes, then, structures A and B include the same values with a difference in the weighting of the values and a tendency for structure B to interpret the norms associated with some values as pragmatic bases of action rather than as ethical imperatives.

With respect to the rules about personnel eligible to compete, the situation is fairly straightforward for structure B. This structure assumes that all citizens of the village are eligible to compete for prizes at the local level; all citizens, therefore, are eligible to run for positions on the village council or for the mayorship.[53] However structure B also assumes that a local power elite exists (the Pasha and the head of the municipality of Deir Abu Said would be the most prominent members) which must be dealt with in matters of importance. Structure A is divided over who is eligible to compete in the local-level political arena. One view (mainly but not completely) associated with the Dumi-'Amr coalition accepts the view that all residents of the village are eligible to compete for prizes made available at the local level. But another view (mainly but not completely) associated with Beni Yasin holds that only village notables are able to do so. However structure A is undivided in its assumption that a local power elite exists (personified by the Pasha) and that on important matters it must be consulted. Structure A and structure B are similar in this regard except that whereas structure B regards consultation with the local power elite a pragmatic norm, structure A, at least with respect to the Pasha, regards it as an ethical norm. With respect to personnel, then, part of structure A is distinctively different from structure B and part is basically similar.[54]

In Kufr al-Ma and its subdistrict, the rules about tactics, specifically, with respect to the use of external roles/resources are the most complicated of all. Structure B holds that all external roles/ resources, with the exception of political parties, can be used by all citizens unreservedly—these include the police, the subdistrict officer, the forest ranger, the land registry officer, the agricultural inspector, the judges of the civil and religious courts, the village improvement program (for grants), and banks and cooperatives (for loans). It also proclaims the right of bureaucrats to intervene in village affairs when it is deemed necessary. Structure B also assumes that majority rule will prevail in the deliberations of the village council. Structure A, on the other hand, holds that certain external roles/resources not only may be but should be used unreservedly (the Pasha); it approves selective use of other external roles/resources for the purpose of achieving culturally approved limited goals, e.g., petitioning the subdistrict officer for an extra teacher. It accepts the use of still other external roles/resources for narrowly defined considerations of self-interest, such as cases raised in the civil and even the Islamic courts for the purpose of placing one's opponent on the defensive—that is, external roles/resources are manipulated in the context of a given competition. Finally, structure A accepts resort to other external roles/resources (the police) only as a last resort, when all other options have either been exhausted or are considered ineffective. Although it is in no position to negate it, structure A resents structure B's absolute right of intervention and seeks selectively to nullify it through "fixing," circumlocution, procrastination, and evasion. Apart from the village council arena, with respect to which structure A is bifurcated, structure A assumes that decision-making is through consensus rather than majority vote. With respect to tactics, then, structure A accepts structure B's tactics selectively, with mounting limitations and more pejorative evaluations, as one moves from roles/resources that confer honor to those that attach odium.

It must be said in conclusion that the terms used in this analysis of the articulation of arenas are value-laden. One section of this chapter has been labeled, "The Cost of Utilizing the Resources of the External Arena"; it might just as well have been labeled, "The Process of Modernization." The first phrase clearly reflects the values of most actors in the internal arena and the second clearly reflects the values of most actors in the external arena. Even when a more third-party or societal point of view is adopted, the terms continue to reflect value judgments, e.g., "encapsulation" as opposed to "integration." I recognize my bias toward the internal arena point of view and justify it on the basis of two considerations: first, because of the vicissitudes of field work I am more acquainted with that point of view, have documented it more fully, and can speak about it more convincingly; second, the great majority of publications by social scientists deal at length with the external arena (e.g., the vast literature on "elites") and either completely neglect the internal arena or deal with it superficially and with scant interest.

Subversion, Confrontation, Encounter:
The Case For and Against
Cyclical Change

If one fact has become apparent from the recent writing by anthropologists on local-level politics, it has been the necessity of
focusing on political process rather than on political structure.
Whether one takes M. G. Smith's landmark article, "Segmentary
Lineage Systems" (1956), Barth's "Segmentary Opposition and the
Theory of Games" (1959), or J. Bujra's "The Dynamics of Political
Action" (1973), to name a selected few, the same message appears:
students of politics must not only gather more longitudinal data
that will make possible the study of process, but they must also
develop concepts capable of organizing such data in a way that for-
wards analysis.[1] It is not so much that studies of political structures
have little value; it is rather that without a temporal dimension they
can only provide limited insight into political behavior.

No anthropologist has done more to rectify this deficiency than F.
G. Bailey. His interest in process extends not only to processes re-
storing equilibrium but also to processes producing cumulative
change. He has developed three key concepts for the purpose of
analyzing the political process: "subversion," "confrontation," and
"encounter." Like core and support, these concepts require considerable refinement, but they constitute a thoughtful beginning in the
quest for conceptual clarity. This chapter begins by outlining these
concepts and suggesting both problems involved in their use and
possible refinements, it continues by demonstrating their relevance
in Kufr al-Ma, and it ends by pointing out the implications of the
analysis for the study of factionalism.

Bailey has defined confrontations and encounters and their relationship to one another in the following manner:

> A confrontation is a message about one's own strength to an
> opponent or to potential opponents: it can also be a challenge.
> An encounter takes place when the challenge is accepted and
> the competitors may set upon one another and continue until
> one has won and the other is defeated. . . . The difference be-
> tween confrontation and encounter is, . . . analogous to the
> difference between a debate and a decision. Confrontations are
> messages and claims . . . about command over political re-
> sources, about political credit: an encounter occurs when both
> sides agree on a version of what their relative strength is. This
> may occur through an actual battle, either literally or in the
> form of a vote or in whatever other mode is characteristic of the
> culture concerned; or it may be brought about by the
> withdrawal of one side, conceding victory to the other; or
> finally, it may be the result of a mediated settlement.[2]

In another context Bailey defines confrontation and encounter and
their relationship to one another as follows:

> A competitor confronts his opponent by making statements
> (either in words or actions) about his own command over re-
> sources (both human and material) in order to intimidate an op-
> ponent. . . . A confrontation may result in an encounter through
> which both contestants publically agree about their relative
> strength. Sometimes this arrangement is only reached after a
> combat, men being killed and property destroyed, in cultures
> which go in for violent political games. In other cultures the
> contest is played out through law courts when fortunes and
> reputations are destroyed. But a "showdown" (encounter) may
> also take place without too much expenditure of material re-
> sources, as when the votes were counted. . . . The importance of
> confrontation and encounter should now be clear: they may en-
> able competitions to be settled without the destruction of re-
> sources on which the whole society, not merely the political
> structure, depends.[3]

Bailey has defined subversion and its relationship to confrontation
and encounter in the following way:

> Subversion is the activity of altering the balance of support
> . . . [dependents] in your own favor by recruiting previously neu-

tral people to your own side, by persuading the rival . . . [depen-
dents] to retire from the contest or otherwise incapacitating
them, or by winning the rival . . . [dependents] to your own side.
The same process may also be worked with . . . [external
political] resources. Subversion is the substantive activity of
changing the pattern of political resources by increasing your
own and diminishing those of a rival. But confrontation is an act
of communication; a signal (whether accurate or a bluff) of one's
command over resources; and, in the situation of conflict, a
threat. . . . As in the case of subversion, in encounter there is a
substantive shifting of political resources from one side to the
other. But there is also, as in the case of confrontation, a simultaneous act of public communication about relative strength.
. . . If subversion is the substantive change in the relative
resource pattern of two contestants, and confrontation is an
assertion about control over resources, and encounter is merely both of these, why do we need a separate term for "encounter"? . . . (a) We need to distinguish an "episode" from a
"sequence". . . : to sound a bell to end rounds, so to speak. . . .
(b) There is a sense in which all the acts of subversion and confrontation lead up to encounter: like the series of short moves
which bring you to the head of the snake or the foot of the lad-
der; a kind of climactic intensity of conflict activity. . . . The
three kinds of activity—subversion, confrontation, encounter—make up an episode. A number of these episodes are
related to one another in sequence (and usually in other ways
too) to form a sequence. The form is that of rounds in boxing or
battles in war.[4]

If one departs from Bailey's definition of subversion as the process
of altering the balance of support in one's own favor, then at least
five separate options should be considered: (1) winning the supporter
of the opposition to one's own side; (2) getting the supporter of the
opposition to retire to a neutral position; (3) winning a previous neutral to one's own side; (4) getting a previous neutral (but potential
supporter) to withdraw from the contest; and (5) destroying the
effectiveness of the opponent's supporter either by violence or the
discard ploy. As the analysis at the end of chapter two indicated,
only the third option is utilized in Kufr al-Ma with any regularity—
the division of the independent families and members of 'Amr between the two mayors. Even in this instance the subversion is indirect, gradual, and incomplete. Muted subversion on the leader's side

and muted renegadism on the supporter's side are, then, the rule. An outright switch of support from one side to the other is rare, but if it occurs at all, it results from a dispute between a supporter (the future renegade) and his leader, not from open or even covert attempts at subversion by the opposition leader. That this is, in fact, the state of affairs is indicated by the existence of the gentlemen's agreement and also by the analysis of core and support elements in table 5 and chart 1 in chapter three. The degrees of backing reflected in this chart and table can only be understood in the light of the presence of the principle of partible allegiance, which not only makes muted subversion and muted renegadism possible, but also fosters their incidence. As the end of chapters four and five indicated, one of the mayors has made the gentleman's agreement (and its implications for restriction of subversion) the foundation of his strategy, while the other, although seemingly departing from it in a radical fashion, emerged from one sequence upholding it; indeed, it became one cornerstone of his strategy too. Although Bailey's analysis of the Indian situation in "Parapolitical Systems" (1968) indicates that in certain kinds of competition (caste-caste) subversion is absent and in others (faction-faction) it is infrequent, the thrust of the examples used and analyzed in *Strategems and Spoils* indicates that the essence of subversion is to be found in option one and to a lesser extent in option five. The surprising result of analyzing subversion in Kufr al-Ma is not simply the focus on option three, but also the fact that the most rarely used options are precisely options one and five. Instances of low-key politics such as those in Kufr al-Ma may be more numerous than Bailey's analysis suggests and may possibly be more representative of local-level politics than the abrasive competition described for the Swat Pathans and Gaullist France. In any case an interesting problem for comparative analysis emerges: what factors lead to the development of abrasive processes of political competition on the one hand and to low-key politics on the other?

What happens to genealogical neutrals and/or politically minor segments after they have been subverted, and at what point does subversion become confrontation? A comparison of Atareb, Kufr al-Ma, and Bisipara is instructive. In Atareb, the Syrian village analyzed in chapter three, subversion by one alliance against the other is usually followed by a long period of political support, the exchange of brides, mutual consultation, and, finally, if a long enough period has elapsed, the assumption of genealogical unity. This process is relatively long and gradual, and if the substantive act of switching sides has not been publicized by the subverter or reacted to by the opponents, it is difficult to determine any one point in time that could be identified as confrontation or encounter. In Kufr al-Ma certain independent families, such as Ikhtaba (with Dumi) and Majadbi (with Yasin), have become closely linked to and partially identified with the major clans. As chapter two pointed out, however, this phenomenon in Kufr al-Ma is the process by which a movement increases its membership rather than one by which a machine wins support elements to its side. Although the concept of subversion is applicable to the analysis of the political arenas defined by the mayorship and the village council, provided refinements are introduced (e.g., muted subversion and muted renegadism), it is not applicable to the analysis of the long-term process by which descent groups grow or contract. A wider theoretical implication of the Kufr al-Ma case is that Bailey's concepts of subversion, confrontation, and encounter may not be appropriate for analyzing large fields of social relations, at least without considerable refinement, in societies where the basic building blocks and the main competitors are descent groups and the idiom of competition is kinship.

Bailey's analysis of subversion within the framework of caste-climbing in Bisipara[5] raises another difficult problem which Bailey himself has recognized but not satisfactorily resolved: if subversion, confrontation, and encounter are sequential and processual, how does the observer recognize the end of one process and the beginning of another?

Bailey identified four steps in the process of subversion of a low-caste specialist (e.g., barber or washerman) by an aspiring upwardly mobile entrepreneur of a low caste; the entrepreneur first makes the specialist materially beholden, e.g., by debt; then he extracts specialist services from him for cash; then he turns the relationship into a regular long-term (*jajmani*) patron-client tie; and finally he establishes with the specialist the same commensal relation that the specialist has with the Brahmin. Bailey considers the first two steps as subversion proper, but he regards the last two as implying confrontation, since they are open claims to purity (superiority). If these claims are not disputed by the opponent (a bye), an encounter occurs, for the shift in resources has taken place (the first leader has gained in political credit).[6] The conceptual confusion arises from the fact that the shift in resources which marks subversion is not actually complete (in the sense of confirmed) until the opponent reacts, e.g., by committing greater resources (issuing a counterchallenge), or fails to react (a bye), and this reaction or lack of it marks the occurrence of an encounter.

Moreover although subversion, confrontation, and encounter are assumed to be sequential, subversion does not necessarily lead to encounter or, for that matter, confrontation, unless control of resources is publicized and/or the opponent recognizes the change of resources either by committing more resources himself or by employing the discard ploy. Otherwise a bye occurs. Bailey construes a bye as an encounter, but to do so denies two fundamental attributes of encounter, both symbolic: the signal that the challenge is taken up and the signal that ends the round and begins a new one. The key problem here is that a shift of resources may occur without being publicized by the subverter or recognized by the opponent.

One way of beginning to deal with these problems is to identify more precisely the elements of each process. One type of confrontation is a signal-confrontation, in which the element of challenge is missing and a reply is not necessary. Many of Bailey's "general" confrontations fall into this category; in Kufr al-Ma filling one's guest house with guests every night, conspicuous hospitality at weddings and funerals, or building a big house constitute signal-confrontations. Challenge-confrontations, on the other hand, must be responded to or else political credit is lost. This type of confrontation does not coincide with Bailey's "specific" confrontations, since certain acts not aimed at specific persons, e.g., potlatches, sometimes require reaction or credit is lost. In Kufr al-Ma violating a woman or breaking the gentlemen's agreement constitute challenge-confrontations; another example is the Yasin mayor's denouncing a member of Beni ʿAmr who had failed to pay the mathbata for services after the lapse of some time and after promising to do so. Since the mayor of Yasin was attempting to operate a full-blown mayorship and the mayor of Dumi was not, and since the former required the collection of more revenue than the latter, one might posit that the relative number of challenge-confrontations between the Yasin mayor and his followers would be much higher than the number of challenge-confrontations between the Dumi mayor and his followers. My personal observations over sixteen months of field work tend to confirm this assumption. This challenge-confrontation was also significant in that it indicated a change in the mayor-follower relationship—it proclaimed that the mayor would no longer render services to followers, particularly nonclansmen, *gratis*. Confrontations, then, can signal important changes in relationships, more specifically in the rules of the political game, as well as claims over resources.

In a community characterized by low-key politics signal-confrontations of a generalized kind preponderate. The fact that these confrontations are general does not mean, however, that they cannot be assessed as to significance. It is certainly true that many such confrontations relate to such prizes as status, honor, and purity, which seem themselves ambiguous. However indices are available, in some cases rather precise indices. They include the gifts and payments made at weddings and funerals, the number of people attending guest houses, the number of sheep slaughtered in offering hospitality, and the number of days such activities take up. Furthermore in a community characterized by low-key politics, precisely because the scope for encounters and challenge-confrontations is normatively restricted, e.g., by a gentlemen's agreement or by clan paternalism or by a norm disapproving resort to external resources, innocent acts construed as nonconfrontations in other societies are regarded as signal-confrontations: verbal jests become insults and acts of omission (such as not visiting or not extending an invitation) become indications of nonsupport. The analysis of core and support elements in chapter three provides evidence for such a view.

Of all the actions related to confrontation in Kufr al-Ma the most conspicuous is "deconfrontation."[7] Deconfrontation is the process by which confrontations are wound down and possible encounters avoided. Again one might posit that in a community characterized by low-key politics deconfrontations would be particularly important. The gentleman's agreement is an example of institutionalized deconfrontation in Kufr al-Ma. Another example is when Abu Fayid, a leader of the Yasin clan, informed Shaykh Basim, the head of the incipient village council and a leader of the Dumi-'Amr coalition, that he was about to visit the subdistrict officer to advise him to postpone the implementation of the village council. Tipping off one's opponent of one's next move in the hopes that he will agree with you, or at least not object, is certainly not behavior characteristic of a "contest," but it is quite appropriate to the overall process of low-key politics.

At the end of the last chapter I discussed a number of factors which tended to escalate competition. The argument can be pursued here in a broader fashion and with respect to confrontation. What factors determine the degree of confrontation or, more precisely, which factors tend to produce challenge-confrontations rather than signal-confrontations? It appears that the amount of publicity accompanying the confrontation is important, whether that publicity stems from either of the competitors or from the new role/resources enlisted. The hierarchical level of personnel involved in the confrontation is also important. Both of these factors suggest that confrontations involving external personnel and/or resources will tend to produce challenge-confrontations rather than signal-confrontations. A third factor is the range of social structural involvement at the local level. Confrontations involving clans will tend to be of a higher degree than confrontations involving their component lineages, and confrontations involving the whole community will tend to be of a higher degree than those involving its component clans. A fourth factor is whether the values of the competitors on each side and as a whole are similar or dissimilar to those of the personnel of the external arena, particularly the values regarding prizes, personnel eligible to compete, and tactics. Great similarity reduces challenge-confrontations, reduces encounters, and accentuates signal-confrontations; there is also a tendency to construe innocent behavior as a signal-confrontation. Where low-key politics are practiced, deconfrontations are institutionalized. Great dissimilarity of values produces a direct leap from subversion to encounter. The possibilities suggested so far may be represented in the following manner:

Just as it is sometimes difficult to distinguish the last phase of subversion from the first phase of confrontation, it is also difficult to distinguish the end of confrontation from the beginning of encounter. Again the problem can be illuminated by stipulating the elements of encounter in a clearer fashion than has heretofore been the case. Analytically encounter can be broken into four separate parts with two paired segments, each of which has a substantive and symbolic element as follows:

{ (1) The challenge is taken up (symbolic).
  (2) Commitment of greater resources (substantive).
{ (3) Shift of political resources (substantive).
  (4) The bell that ends the round and begins a new one (symbolic).

The initial element of encounter is symbolic; it is the response which indicates that the contest has begun. It may or may not coincide with a substantive act committing greater resources to the contest: when the mayor of Dumi denied the Yasin mayor's statement that Yasin represented more than half the village and insisted that they were only 35 percent of it, that act represented the first element of encounter but not the second. However when the Dumi mayor accepted the support of the renegade Yasin lineage (Shujur), he not only signaled the end of the gentleman's agreement but also increased his own support considerably; that single act comprehended elements two, three, and four of encounter. Thus the elements of encounter may be sequential, but there is no necessity that they be so. Indeed we must investigate further different kinds of situations to determine which elements of encounters combine in which ways and which factors affect the types of combinations produced. Subversion almost always involves elements two and three of encounter but never elements one and four. Challenge-confrontations, like encounters but unlike subversion and signal-confrontations, can partake of both symbolic and substantive elements. For instance, in many parts of the Middle East violating a man's daughter not only challenges her father's honor, it also substantially reduces that honor. Other groups who previously have given women in marriage to the now dishonored family are very reluctant to do so again until that honor has been vindicated. Another example of a challenge-confrontation with both substantive and symbolic elements is the letter a villager wrote to the district officer charging Abu Fayid, a leader of the Yasin coalition, with bribery. Until the matter was cleared up, not only was Abu Fayid's honesty impugned, but also the threat of removal from office had to be considered. Every subversion, then, and every challenge-confrontation has elements of encounter. The same is true of the bye and the discard ploy. The bye (nonaction) is the negative counterpart of element two: a refusal to commit greater resources. The discard ploy comprehends both element one and element three. It is a symbolic act (often a statement) that destroys the opponent's political resources by assessing them as being of no worth. Neither the bye nor the discard ploy, however, comprise more than a few of the elements of the encounter. Analytic clarity demands that the encounter proper be distinguished from the bye and the discard ploy, although all can follow upon a confrontation, so the three have been distinguished in the preceding diagram. The problem that the four-element breakdown of encounter helps to resolve is that some elements Bailey ascribed to encounter are also found in subversion and confrontation, which fosters conceptual ambiguity. The four-way breakdown clarifies the relationship of the concepts to one another by specifying which elements of each do or do not overlap with the others.

One way of shifting political resources in encounters is to destroy them. One can destroy material resources, such as money, land, or personnel, but one can also destroy reputation and influence. Destruction of resources may even extend to existent decisions and contracts, such as when the subdistrict officer ripped up the school land sales agreement. Political principles can also be destroyed. When the Dumi mayor, in front of the subdistrict officer, rejected the possibility of selecting the village council head by lot and insisted that the process of democratic selection prevail and when the subdistrict officer accepted his view, one principle of political domination was destroyed and another took its place: the principle of political domination based on superior wealth, social status, and number of specialists gave way to majority rule.

One might ask whether encounters in Kufr al-Ma don't break down into "fights," that is, conflicts in which rules are suspended, goals and strategies are absent, and the only end is to eliminate the opponent.[8] Competitions tend to break down into fights when there is no agreement as to what constitute prizes, personnel, and tactics. But in Kufr al-Ma, except for the issue of majority rule (as opposed to the principle of elite consensus) and that only with respect to the field of social relations defined by the village council, the two competitors within the village arena agree substantially. A second critial factor bringing about the breakdown of encounters and the development of fights is the lack of a neutral umpire. Of course members of the local bureaucracy occupy a neutral position social structurally, but they are not neutral with respect to values held. The umpire should be neutral social structurally, but he should be sympathetic to the contestants' values or at least empathetic to them. In the Pasha the people of Kufr al-Ma have an umpire who is sympathetic, constantly available, highly proficient, and possessed of great influence. For these two reasons, Kufr al-Ma stands at the end of the continuum where encounters are held to a minimum (although some evidence of incipient development away from this position is discussed in the remainder of this chapter) and not at the end where encounters threaten to become fights, the situation at least partially applicable to Bisipara after the untouchables attempted to enter the temple.

To describe encounters in Kufr al-Ma in this fashion, however, is to put the case too mildly and formulate it too narrowly, because almost all encounters and confrontations eventually wind up as encounters-by-mediation not simply those resolved by the Pasha's mediation (a very small minority of cases, although some of the most important). This widespread tendency to resolve competition through go-betweens (*wasTa*), delegations (*jaha*), and peacemaking (*SulHa*) is what the last chapter called "the feedback loop." These encounters-by-mediation are not in fact encounters; they are institutionalized deconfrontations: issues are resolved in the guest house by manipulating the idiom of blame and honor, weighing it against the nature of the breach and the social status and structural position of the parties involved, and balancing it against goods which are given to the aggrieved party. At the end of the process a fiction of amity is established; it is unclear who has "won" and who has "lost," since intangible rewards (honor, respect, prestige) are balanced against tangible rewards in a skillful manner, and the parties resume social relations. A process that began as a political process, a competition between clearly delineated opponents for scarce resources and prizes, has ended as a process of social control in which men are led to subordinate their interests for the sake of the wider social unit. An initial focus on the competition and the dynamics of winning and losing transmutes into a theoretical question of a different nature, why do men obey? That this happens leads to the conclusion that Bailey's gamelike conceptual framework may not be completely adequate for describing the local-level political process in many societies and cultures. As indicated in chapter one, Bailey's framework may have to be combined with one that focuses on social control as well. To do otherwise would be to utilize concepts such as encounter to describe events whose attributes are more easily and usefully comprehended in another way. Although one can talk of politics and encounters when discussing peacemaking and mediation, these latter processes can be analyzed more appropriately within the framework of social control There are two empirical considerations that give added credence to this view. One has already been mentioned: in Kufr al-Ma most confrontations and encounters become deconfrontations. But second, and equally important, certain personnel and fields of social relations have been quite clearly exempted from the consequences of political competition, i.e., they have been defined as inappropriate for confrontations and encounters. Using women in the political game is ruled out; utilizing the external arena to prosecute one's own lineagemates is greatly frowned upon; and most important, the field of dispute settlement, tribal law, and peacemaking are exempted from political competition—all villagers consult the Pasha regardless of coalition membership and all villagers contribute compensation in outstanding cases of honor regardless of what coalition the family involved adheres to. To phrase it in another way, the field of high-level social control is exempted from the game of village politics.

The Village Council and School
Lands Dispute Sequences

The development of the Dumi-'Amr coalition to wrest control of village affairs from Yasin and the government attempts to modernize the village came to a head in the disputes over the formation of the village council and the sale of village lands for the new village school. The chronology of key events connected with attempts to establish a committee for village improvement and subsequently a village council appear in chart 4.

The Dumi-'Amr coalition that finally formed in 1965 was foreshadowed by earlier events and social structures. The village had long been physically divided between an upper eastern side, inhabited almost completely by Yasin members, and a lower western side, occupied preponderantly by Dumi and 'Amr members. This division was particularly striking in the part of the village built up before 1940, when some households had to move out of the central part of the village because of congestion.[9] This division may have occurred because Yasin settled the village first and occupied the top of the hill, while Dumi and 'Amr came later and settled below them, at least this is the view held by a number of knowledgeable village informants. This would also help explain the peripheral spatial location of the independent families. The articulation of Dumi and 'Amr members with one another and with the independents rather than with Yasin is also confirmed by the location of village grocery shops. No Dumi or 'Amr shops are located in the Yasin quarter and vice-versa. One Yasin shopkeeper had a shop on the edge of the 'Amr quarter, but when I returned to the village in 1965, it had gone out of business. Dumi and 'Amr grocery shops, however, frequently stand next door to one another. Moreover, and much to the point, several families from Dumi and 'Amr are tied through marriage and in a few cases through partnership in grocery shops. Judging from the customers that patronize these shops, I would hazard that the members of Dumi, 'Amr, and the independents are tied in a credit ring. As the events in the lands case and the village council sequence amply demonstrate, the independents have played an

Chart 4
Chronology of Events Connected with Attempts
to Establish a Village Council

April 1960   Village reform officer attempts to establish a "committee for village reform" (*lajna qarawiya*) in order to negotiate a loan for the building of a new village school; he fails.

July 1960   Village reform officer again attempts to establish a committee for village reform. He meets with a number of old-timers, mainly from the independent families and Beni ʿAmr (but with a few from Yasin) who voice their opposition to the committee saying they are being bypassed in village decision-making and that they fear the committee's taxing power. The reform officer succeeds for the moment; then a Dumi-ʿAmr coalition asks for the dissolution of the committee after they find themselves in a *de facto* minority.

August 1960   A member of Shuqayrat and a dissident Yasin member go to the subdistrict officer and complain that they are not represented on the committee. He tells them that the committee didn't really represent anybody; it was only a means of having a certain number of villagers go to the district capital to sign documents allowing the village to get further grants of money.

1964   [Government introduces a new regulation stipulating a new basis for compensation of mayors on the basis of specific services rendered rather than annual contributions from clansmen.] *

February 1965   The Ministry of Municipal and Rural Affairs, with Qasim Rimawi as its head, is created in Amman.

August 1965   A letter is sent from Rimawi to the district officer (muhafith) of Irbid ordering the establishment of a village council (*majlis qarawi*) in every village in the district.

Early November 1965   [The subdistrict officer (qaimaqam) of Al-Kura rips up the contract between the government and the Sibbaʿi brothers stipulating compensation at a certain rate for lands taken by eminent domain for the purpose of building a village school.]

Late November 1965   Villagers meet with the qaimaqam in the village school to explore the means of choosing the village council, with Yasin and Dumi choosing four representatives, ʿAmr choosing three, and one additional member representing the independents.

Next Day   (Morning) Village notables meet and select Shaykh Basim of Beni Dumi as head of the village council, after a notable of Beni Yasin, Abu Kamil, declines the honor. Abu Yasin, the mukhtar of Beni Yasin is not present at the time of selection.

(Afternoon) An "encounter" occurs in the office of the qaimaqam. Abu Yasin rejects the possibility of selecting the head of the village council by lot and Abu Tahir the Dumi mukhtar rejects the view of the elders of Beni Yasin that they (Yasin) compose half the village.

	A vote is taken and Shaykh Basim is again chosen as council head by an eight-to-four vote.
December 1965	A petition is sent to the qaimaqam by Beni Yasin asking for the cancellation of the village council.
December 1965	[Sulayman Hasan's telegram is intercepted by a village shopkeeper.]
December 1965	Abu Fayid talks to Shaykh Basim regarding the purpose of his impending visit to the qaimaqam: to dissuade the latter from implementing the establishment of the village council.
December 1965	Abu Fayid visits the qaimaqam and convinces him to shelve the implementation of the village council, citing Sulayman Hasan's telegram as evidence of village dissension caused by the village council vote.
January 1966	[Abu Fayid defeats Mahmoud al-Khatib's land claim.]
January 1966	The government begins to collect the village improvement tax.
February 1966	Confrontations take place at the village school on the occasion of the district officer's visit. Abu Yasin requests the attachment of Kufr al-Ma to the municipality of Deir Abu Said (in order to avoid implementation of the village council) and Abu Tahir requests a reevaluation of the compensation rates to be paid out to villagers whose lands had been taken by eminent domain for the purpose of building the village school.
March 1966	A letter is received by the minister of interior signed by an individual who designates himself a resident of Kufr al-Ma describing Abu Fayid as a big landowner in the village and charging him with obstructing the establishment of a village council and accepting bribes during his past service with the customs department. The letter is referred to the mukhtars by the subdistrict officer. The mukhtars testify that the signature does not correspond to any individual living in the village and that they have no idea of who could have written the letter.
April 1966	A letter is sent from the minister of rural affairs to the district officer of Irbid asking why only seven of sixty-one villages in the district had established village councils.
June 1966	Beni Yasin draws up an official petition asking for attachment to the municipality of Deir Abu Said (discard ploy).
March 1967	Abu Tahir says that the government still wishes to implement the village council. He said, "In ten days we will have a new qaimaqam, and I will take the matter up with him then."

* Brackets indicate important events not directly related to the sequence being described.

Chart 5
The Village Council: First Round 1960

The Committee for Village Reform (*Lajna Qarawiya*)

April 1960

YASIN	DUMI	'AMR	DUMI
Mustafa Abd al-Qadir	Muhammad al-Hilu	Salih al-'Asali	Abu Tahir

PIOUS ELDERS	POOR PEASANT	POLITICAL MODERNIZER: CONTRACT THEORY
They refuse to sign any document or attend any meeting with the village reform officer because of the usury (*ribā*) involved in negotiating a loan for the building of a school.	Opposes the building of a school. "The government only eats up the money."	"The village can certainly pick up 100 dinars for a new school; any responsible townsman—not just landowners—can sign a petition obligating the village to support a school or establish a village council."

July 1960

	DUMI		'AMR	
Abu Tahir	Ahmed al-Hamad	Ali al-Husayn	Muhammad al-Yusuf	

COMMITTEE MEMBERS
They ask for the dissolution of the committee for village reform and the formation of a village council (*majlis qarawi*). This request is made in the presence of the village reform officer, after a Dumani was replaced by a Yasini on the committee, giving Yasin a de facto majority. (Yasin now possessed five members and Dumi and 'Amr possessed six; but Sulayman Hasan (a committee member) was pro-Yasin and Raji al-Wazir (another member) was an affine of Yasin. Thus Dumi-'Amr stood in a seven-to-five minority.)

important role in the Dumi-'Amr coalition: many of them signed a petition against the Yasin mayor (after the wheat distribution); they composed the majority of the old-timers who opposed the formation of the committee for village improvement that Yasin would have dominated; and their members were victimized in both the lands case and the robbery case along with members of Dumi and 'Amr.

The division between Yasin and Dumi and 'Amr seems to have been symbolized by the soccer teams that formed in an *ad hoc* fashion on the threshing grounds: informants declared that Yasin members always formed one team and Dumi and 'Amr members the other; moreover each team was given a distinctive nickname. It

Chart 6
The Village Council: Second Round 1965

Important Yasin Leaders and "Supporters"

YASIN
Abu Yasin

The mukhtar of Yasin who supports traditional mayorship on a non-contractual basis. He opposes the establishment of a village council and the recognition of Shaykh Basim as its head. He supports the gentlemen's agreement and seeks the adhesion of Kufr al-Ma to the municipality of Deir Abu Said.

YASIN
Abu Fayid

A local government official, large landowner and Yasin notable. Together with the mukhtar he leads the opposition to the Dumi-ʿAmr alliance. Abu Fayid was instrumental in convincing the qaimaqam to postpone implementation of the village council, claiming Sulayman Hasan's telegram proved the dissension that resulted from attempts to establish the council. He was the object of the slanderous letter sent to the district officer.

ʿAMR
Sulayman Hasan

The former mukhtar of Beni ʿAmr who supports Abu Yasin against his own ʿAmr clansmen. Author of the telegram to the district officer accusing the village schoolmaster (of Dumi) of disobeying administrative policy

YASIN
The Sibbaʿi Brothers

Benefactors of the second school lands evaluation, first patrilateral cousins of Abu Yasin, and his staunch backers.

should be quickly added that the situation in Kufr al-Ma is not at all like that in Atareb, where spatial opponents were also enemies. On the contrary, the practice of low-key politics in Kufr al-Ma assumes the muffling of competition and the existence of underlying solidarity.

It came as no surprise, then, that Dumi and ʿAmr leaders rejected attempts of the village improvement officer to establish a committee. The reaction of the Dumi and ʿAmr committee members in July 1960 (depicted at the bottom of chart 5) also indicates that both competing "teams" were coalitions. Yasin counted on the support of one prominent ʿAmr member and one independent, although most ʿAmr and independents supported the Dumi-ʿAmr coalition. Conversely one prominent Yasin elder refused to support the committee (see the top of chart 5). As these examples and the following charts illustrate, for the purposes of political competition the three clans are far from being solidary corporate groups; to a lesser extent, the

Chart 7
The Village Council: Second Round 1965

Important Dumi Leaders and "Supporters" of the Dumi-'Amr Coalition

DUMI Abu Tahir	DUMI Shaykh Basim	IKHTABA (Independent Family) Mahmoud al-Khatib
The mukhtar of Beni Dumi, who led the coalition against Yasin. He supported the village council and the principle of majority rule in two separate encounters and one confrontation: (1) The initial "consensus" that selected Shaykh Basim in a guest house of the village; (2) The vote electing Basim in the qaimaqam's office; (3) The request for a re-evaluation of school lands compensation made before the district officer.	Magician, tractor owner, and shopkeeper, who was selected and later elected as head of the village council. He was jailed temporarily in the case of the accused robbers and consulted by Abu Fayid before Abu Fayid went on his mission of dissuasion to the qaimaqam. The letter accusing Abu Fayid was brought to him for examination.	Shaykh Basim's neighbor who lost out in a land dispute with Abu Fayid. He was detained in the case of the accused robbers.

same holds true of their component lineages. Friendship (as in the case of Sulayman Hasan on chart 6), ties through marriage (as in the case of Saeed al-Salim on chart 8), religious conviction (as in the case of Mustafa Abd al-Qadir on chart 5), as well as economic interests and social grudges lead men to line up against the majority of their patrilineal kinsmen on specific issues. It is the absence of solidary corporate patrilineal descent groups within the context of political competition that makes the concepts of core/support analyzed in chapter three particularly appropriate for analyzing local-level politics in Kufr al-Ma.

Two facts about the first round of the struggle to establish the village council are noteworthy. The Dumi-'Amr coalition first crystalized in a successful encounter that used obstruction and withdrawal (from the committee) to destroy the principle of majority

DUMI	SHUQAYRAT	DUMI	INDEPENDENT FAMILY
Sulayman Esa	Muhammad Mahmoud Abu Shuqayr	Al-Hilu	Abu 'Asri
A poor peasant who began ploughing the school lands in protest against their unfair evaluation.	Another "victim" of the school lands evaluation.	The shopkeeper who intercepted Sulayman Hasan's telegram, notified the accused's family of its contents, and alerted the qaimaqam.	The Palestinian refugee who became involved with a Yasin member in an assault and battery case in a civil court. Members of the Dumi-'Amr coalition claimed Abu Fayid used his influence with the judge to influence the verdict.

DUMI	SHUQAYRAT
Mahmoud Abd al-Qadir	"Muhammad Bashir Abu Shuqayr"
The schoolmaster of the boy's school in Kufr al-Ma accused in Sulayman Hasan's telegram. Mahmoud is a good friend of Abu Yasin, while his father is a respected elder of Beni Dumi.	Purported author of the letter accusing Abu Fayid of corruption and obstruction of the village council.

rule (at this point the Dumi-'Amr coalition opposed such a principle because representation was not based on numbers but rather on elite [mainly Yasin] representation). Later Yasin leaders employed the same tactics, withdrawal and obstruction, to oppose majority rule with partial success (implementation of the village council with Shaykh Basim at its head was still pending in the spring of 1967, although the vote electing him had been held in the autumn of 1965). Second, the mayor of Dumi publically espoused the contractual basis of politics as well as the aim of modernization as early as 1960: he rejected the view that only the elite (landowners, sheepowners, and grand old men) could make critical decisions for the village (see top of chart 5).

The second round was climaxed by the double encounter (before the villagers and then the subdistrict officer) in which the Dumi

Chart 8
The Village Council: Second Round 1965

Important ʿAmr Leaders and "Supporters" of the Dumi-ʿAmr Coalition

ʿAMR Ahmed al-Yasin	YASIN Saeed al-Salim	ʿAMR Sons of Rashid al-Samad	ʿAMR Hasan Salih ʿIbadi
He complained to Shaykh Luqman regarding the penetration of Abu Fayid's chickens into the mosque courtyard. Abu Fayid regarded him as the author of the letter to the district officer charging Abu Fayid with accepting bribes and obstructing the village council.	A poor peasant tied to Beni ʿAmr by the marriages of his father and sister. He attributed the failure of his friend to win a court case to Abu Fayid's intervention in favor of his relatives.	"Victims" of the school lands evaluation.	A "victim" of the school lands evaluation.

mayor asserted the relevance of the rule of numbers and openly rejected the principle of political domination based on superiority of wealth, social status, and number of specialists and the political finesse of the grand old men (mediators). The most important fact to note is that of the five critical encounters in the combined village council-school lands dispute sequence (the dissolution of the committee for village improvement, the destruction of the school lands contract, the first village council encounter within the village, the second village council encounter before the subdistrict officer, and Abu Fayid's conversation with the subdistrict officer that resulted in the indefinite postponement of the implementation of the council), only one occurred with the leaders of both coalitions present. That is, most critical encounters in Kufr al-Ma take place with key competitors *in absentia*. This phenomenon reinforces and rounds out the characterization of the low-key political process that has already been identified by the attributes of muted subversion, muted renegadism, and institutionalized deconfrontations: the gentleman's agreement, encounters-by-mediation, and the tip-off ploy (letting your opponent know your next move).

The village council sequence contains two other notable matters with respect to encounters. Government collection of the village improvement tax in Kufr al-Ma in January 1966 provides an excellent example of the fourth (symbolic) element of encounter. It was the bell that ended one round and began another, for initiation of the tax collection was an open government admission that plans to implement the village council were being shelved. Had the village council been implemented, it would immediately have had the power to collect its own taxes, which would probably have exceeded the village improvement tax. Thus the government action gave notice of temporary surrender or perhaps, more accurately, a truce in the drive to modernize the village through a council.

Second, the words of the Dumi mayor at the end of the sequence are important—he intended to renew the drive for implementation when a new subdistrict officer arrived on the scene. Subdistrict officers are regularly circulated for reasons of state security; they can also be shifted because they are too honest and impartial or because they are too corrupt and play favorites. In either case many complaints are taken to higher authorities and the transfer is accelerated. Regular replacements of key local-level officials establish cutoff and beginning points for competition sequences. Both the winners and the losers in the foregoing sequence, particularly the latter, realized that a shift in personnel would create new opportunities and a new competitive situation. Thus although national policymakers do not usually sound the bell that ends the rounds, (though they can do so in competitions that threaten public order), willy-nilly they mark off the longer sequences from one another through the power of appointment and dismissal.[10]

The key issue in the school lands dispute sequence outlined in chart 9 is the differential evaluation of land to be sold to the village for the purpose of building the school. Originally (early 1963) the land of the Sibba'i brothers (members of Yasin and the Yasin mayor's close patrilateral cousins) was evaluated at fifteen pounds a dunum. Later that same year government engineers selected the exact site for building, moving the building back from the main road by at least one hundred feet more than had been previously indicated. Unlike the other villagers who sold land for the school, the Sibba'i brothers had houses near their land. Locating the school so close to their domiciles threatened their privacy and, particularly, the modesty of their women, since the houses had no courtyard. They refused to sell at the previously agreed-upon price and raised a court case against the government. In order to satisfy them and facilitate

Chart 9
Chronology of the School Lands Dispute

1960	Disagreement between Beni Yasin on the one hand and Beni Dumi and Beni ʿAmr on the other as to the appropriate location of the new village school. The former wants it placed in the Pasha's vacant house in the upper quarter. The latter wants it built on the main road close to the lower quarter.
1960	Subdistrict officer rejects the Yasin mayor's view that the location of the village school has to take account of clan sensibilities and rivalries saying, "I don't want to hear about clans and tribes. I only want to work with those who are working for the good of the village."
Early 1963	First evaluation of school lands with compensation of the land of the Sibbaʿi brothers estimated at 15 dinars per dunum.
Late 1963	Engineers select exact site for the school building.
Spring 1964	The building of the school begins.
Early Summer 1964	Following the advice of Abu Fayid, the Sibbaʿi brothers raise a suit in the civil court against the government, charging that a change in the location of the school had been determined after the signing of the agreement stipulating the rate of compensation for lands taken by eminent domain.
Late Summer 1964	After consultation with the subdistrict officer and both mukhtars, the Sibbaʿi brothers agree to a new and higher rate of compensation for their lands at 35 dinars per dunum to cover the damages done to the Sibbaʿi household (including the modesty of its women) by the building of the school.
October 1964	The building of the school is commenced a second time.
July 1965	The building of the school is completed.
November 1965	The subdistrict officer rips up the school lands contract at Abu Tahir's instigation.
December 27, 1965	Abu Yasin says that he is going to complain to the district officer about the subdistrict officer's "losing" the document stipulating the rate of compensation for school lands; later, he is dissuaded from the course of action by Abu Fayid.
January 1, 1966	Sulayman Esa and the sons of Rashid al-Samad begin ploughing the school lands.
February 7, 1966	There is a "confrontation" at the school on the occasion of the annual visit of the district officer. Abu Tahir requests a reassessment of the value of school lands. Abu Yasin requests attachment of Kufr al-Ma to Deir Abu Said. A heated argument takes place between the two mukhtars and the district officer departs abruptly, rebuking the peasants for their selfish quarrels.

CHART 10
SCHOOL LANDS CASE

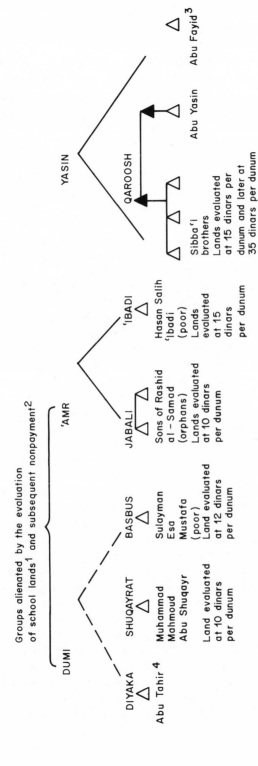

Groups alienated by the evaluation
of school lands[1] and subsequent nonpayment[2]

DUMI

'AMR

DIYAKA

Abu Tahir [4]

SHUQAYRAT

Muhammad
Mahmoud
Abu Shuqayr

Land evaluated
at 10 dinars
per dunum

BASBUS

Sulayman
Esa
Mustafa
(poor)

Land evaluated
at 12 dinars
per dunum

JABALI

Sons of Rashid
al - Samad
(orphans)

Lands evaluated
at 10 dinars
per dunum

'IBADI

Hasan Salih
'Ibadi
(poor)

Lands
evaluated
at 15
dinars
per dunum

YASIN

QAROOSH

Abu Yasin   Abu Fayid [3]

Sibba'i
brothers

Lands evaluated
at 15 dinars per
dunum and later at
35 dinars per dunum

1. The five estimates made evaluating the worth of the school lands were those of the
subdistrict officer, the agricultural inspector, the civil law court clerk, and the mukhtars;
thus two of the five evaluations were made by Yasin members.

2. Eighteen months elapsed between the final evaluation of school lands and the definitive alienation (evidenced by ploughing of school lands) of the Dumi and 'Amr members
listed above. Thus the hardening of the Dumi-'Amr alliance against Yasin was not the
result of the initial evaluation of lands but of subsequent events.

3. Abu Fayid advises the Sibba'i brothers not to sell their lands until they have received
"their price." He later writes a petition for them to the subdistrict officer requesting
payment of the agreed-upon sum.

4. Abu Tahir incites the subdistrict officer to rip up the contract stipulating the rates of
compensation for school lands. He publically requests the district officer to make a reevaluation of the rates of compensation established for school lands.

the building of the school, the school lands evaluation committee evaluated their land at more than twice the value of the next highest land and more than three times the value of the least highly evaluated land (see chart 10). Although all parties had agreed upon the evaluations, as time passed and the government did not pay the stipulated compensation, the owners of the least valued lands, and their friends and lineagemates began to grumble. Since all of these owners were members of either Dumi, 'Amr, or the independent families supporting them (and none were of Yasin), and since two of the land evaluation committee were members of Yasin (although one was also the mayor of Dumi), the impression grew that a "fast one" had been pulled over the eyes of the Dumi mayor at the expense of his coalition. He began to suffer ridicule and increasing pressure to do something about the situation.

By January of 1966 some members of the Dumi-'Amr coalition phrased the issue not simply in terms of favoritism by the Yasin committee members to their own clansmen but also in class terms. One 'Amr shopkeeper said that those who got very little money for their land were poor weak peasants who didn't know how to protect their own interests. Others shared this view, particularly since Abu Fayid, one of the evaluators and a Yasin member, had a government position as clerk of the civil court in the subdistrict center, where he was thought to have considerable influence, which he was believed to have used in the civil court in two cases against members of independent families (see chart 7). His critical role in the second round of the village council sequence has already been commented upon. In the school lands sequence he played a critical role in helping the Sibba'i brothers get an upward reevaluation of their lands. This was not the first time that certain acts by villagers had class connotations. In 1960 a number of villagers had signed a petition against the Yasin mayor charging that the wheat distribution had discriminated against the poor; the meeting of old-timers to oppose the village improvement committee had somewhat the same protest quality, although its class connotation was weaker, since the group was also identified in terms of generation and conservatism.

As the next chapter makes clear, the Dumi mayor was little interested in the ideological ramifications of the issue. However he must have been concerned with his own coalition members' view that he had been duped, for it was fundamental to his watered-down contractual mayorship, that he be able to deliver the goods, whether they were jobs, invitations to official functions, or, as in the present case, relief from the encumbrance of lands that occurred after land

sale. One day in early November the Dumi mayor met privately with
the sub-district officer in the latter's office and told him, "The peasants are laughing at you." When the subdistrict officer, somewhat
upset, asked why, the mayor replied, "They are saying that Abu
Yasin has bought you with a pile of food." This referred to the fact
that the mayor of Yasin and other Yasin notables had lavishly entertained the subdistrict officer (slaughtering sheep and inviting him for
a meal) on a number of occasions. Of course the politics of hospitality underlay Yasin strategy, along with the gentleman's agreement.
The mayor's remarks implied directly that the subdistrict officer had
unwittingly become a dupe and political captive of the Yasin leaders. When the mayor cited the wide discrepancy between the evaluation of the Sibbaʻi brothers' lands and that of all the other villagers
as proof of his naïveté, the subdistrict officer asked his clerk to bring
him the contract in question. He perused it in private, then ripped it
up. When the Yasin mayor came to inquire the next day about when
the government was going to pay the long-due compensation for
school lands, the subdistrict officer denied that a signed contract
existed, even asking his clerk to consult the files. The clerk, of
course, could find no contract.

Besides representing a definitive shift in political resources, which
was not officially recognized until Sulayman Esa and the sons of
Rashid al-Samad began ploughing their own lands (the bell that
ended one round and began another), this incident demonstrates
that in local-level politics encounters between villagers and external
authorities can be as or more significant for the outcome of an
episode as the encounters between the competitors themselves. In
this particular instance the victory went to the local-level competitor, but probably more often the external authority wins. In the
early stages of the school dispute, when the school's location was
the issue, the subdistrict officer rejected the Yasin mayor's view that
clan sensibilities and rivalries had to be taken into account. The
school was finally built on precisely the location that the government engineers recommended, despite the unhappiness of the Yasin
clan in general and the Sibbaʻi brothers in particular.

Two other observations about this sequence should be made. Deconfrontation was again apparent when Abu Fayid dissuaded the
Yasin mayor from carrying the case to higher authorities. Such an
appeal would have had considerable costs—loss of the mayor's time
and energy, perhaps even his incarceration for obstruction—without
much chance of success, for it would have been the mayor's word
against the subdistrict officer's, unless the other members of the

lands evaluation committee backed him up. Such a broad and high-level encounter, involving bureaucrats against one another, bureaucrats against villagers, and villagers against one another, had to be avoided. It was, moreover, the village council dispute and the school lands dispute and their interaction (the critical encounters in each sequence occurred in November 1965) that alienated members of six separate lineages and more than any other events galvanized the Dumi-ʿAmr coalition to a position of open opposition to the Yasin coalition's dominance of village politics.

The Politics of Intragroup Relations: The Secession of Shujur

The previous chapters have indicated that local-level politics in Kufr al-Ma involves a wide variety of issues which cut across a number of institutional complexes. But my analysis has focused on the competition between clan coalitions for control over the village's public institutions, e.g., the village council, the village school, the mayorship. When nonpublic matters have been analyzed it has always been with a view of how these matters affected that competition. However this picture has been too simple. Private issues completely unrelated in any direct fashion to the competition for public prizes also affected the competition, since their development, resolution, or nonresolution affected the relative strength of the competing coalitions. More generally stated, the dynamics of intragroup relations dramatically affects the dynamics of intergroup, or more precisely intercoalition, relations. In what follows, marriage, divorce, the disposition of inheritance, the modesty of women, theft, the control of olive trees, and magic all played a role in the events that led to the secession of an important lineage from one clan, thereby weakening it vis-à-vis the opposing coalition.

Informants recounted five separate incidents (referred to as "cases") to explain the climactic event—the secession of Shujur.[11] Each informant favored one incident as an explanation and either discounted the others completely or considered them much less important. Each incident will be described in rough chronological order as I transcribed them in my notebook, usually paraphrasing the informant's words, sometimes quoting him, and occasionally interpolating my own observations. The informant usually assessed the significance of the incident. However the chart that follows each incident summarizes each case by delineating the personnel involved, the issue at stake, the norms violated, and the identity of the interpreter(s). At the end of the descriptive rendition, I will analyze briefly the significance of the cases for the themes pursued in this book.

Case One: The Case of The Disobedient Wife

The prayer leader of the village told me that Shujur's[12] separation from Beni Yasin was all the work of Khalil Marwan (C6 on chart 11). Abdullah Jagayni (C4 on chart 11) went to the civil court to file a claim for wifely obedience (tā'a zawjiyya) against his wife (C3), who had run off to her father's house. The wife, in turn, had filed a countercharge against her husband in court, charging contention and dispute (shiqāq wa nizā').[13] Each side was called on to bring forward witnesses to affirm or deny that a state of contention and dispute existed. The testimony of the witnesses conflicted on this point. The prayer leader (who was interpreting the history of the case for me) said that the charge of contention and dispute was hard to prove, since a witness had to see the blows of the husband fall on the wife with his own eyes. When the witnesses were not able to support the charge with firsthand observation, the judge selected a number of arbitrators and charged them to attempt to reconcile the couple. The prayer leader said that the fourth chapter of the Quran stipulates that the first job of the arbitrators is to reconcile the couple but if that proves impossible, they determine who is at fault and arrange for a division or return of the marriage payment (mahr); if the fault is the husband's, the arbitrators recommend judicial separation with no return of any part of the marriage payment to the husband; if the fault is the wife's, she must return all or some portion of the marriage payment to the husband. The arbitrators decided that the fault was the wife's, since she refused to return to her husband's house or to be party to a reconciliation; she was ordered to pay back £115 (sterling) of the marriage payment. The father of the girl (B3 on chart 11) refused to guarantee repayment. The judge then announced a verdict of wifely obedience. The wife still refused and the court was not able to carry out its verdict. Then the prayer leader and two other villagers attempted to reconcile the couple, but failed. Then the prayer leader and the village mediators divided the furnishings between the couple and the formula of conditional divorce (talaq mu'allaq) was agreed upon. By this formula divorce would take place contingent on the payment of £115 to the husband

CHART II

CASE ONE: THE CASE OF THE DISOBEDIENT WIFE

DATE: 1963 – 1965

INTERPRETATION: SHAYKH LUQMAN

VIOLATION: CONJUGAL OBEDIENCE

ISSUE: DIVORCE

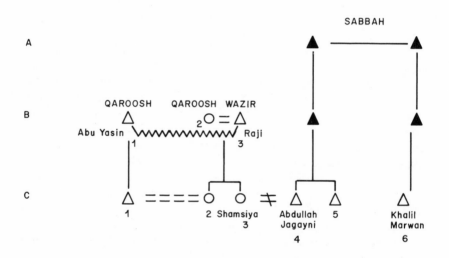

△ MALE

▲ DECEASED MALE

○ FEMALE

⚌ MARRIAGE

⚵ DIVORCE

〰 FRIENDSHIP

— DESCENT

⚌⚌ BETROTHAL

NON – SHUJUR ALIENATED:
KHALIL MARWAN
ABDULLAH JAGAYNI

within a year. The father of the girl made repayment within the time period stipulated and the couple were divorced. The Jagayni brothers (C4 and C5) accused the mayor of Yasin (B1) of supporting Raji Wazir (B3), the father of the girl, in his successful attempt to prevent her from returning to her husband. It was well known that the mayor was related to the girl's father—the mother of the girl was a member of the mayor's (Qaroosh) lineage—and it was well known that the mayor's son (C1) was about to be betrothed to one of Raji's daughters (C2). Besides, the mayor was Raji's friend. During much of the two-year period in which these events took place the husband, who was a soldier, was residing in the army camp; he had appointed his close patrilineal cousin Khalil (C6) as his agent in the case both in and out of court. The prayer leader ended by noting what he believed to be the case's significance: "It was Khalil," he said, "who wrote the official document submitted to the subdistrict officer that severed the Shujur lineage from Beni Yasin."

Case Two: The Case of the Contested Betrothal

The prayer leader said that the case of Shamsiyya Raji was the background for the case of the contested betrothal.He said that the secession of Shujur from Yasin occurred long after the case of the bogus magician (case 3) and that the latter case was not its cause. He said that many men had come to ask for the hand of his ward Zuhriyya (C4 on chart 12) in marriage, and he named a number of men from both the Massadi and Qaroosh lineages (of which the prayer leader was a member). The girl's father, who was of the Shujur lineage of Yasin, was deceased and the prayer leader had married her mother. The prayer leader told all of these men (the fathers of the men who wished to marry her) that she was still too young. Later the son of Abd al-Aziz Ali came with his father (C5 and B7 on chart 12 respectively) to ask her hand in marriage. Both the girl (C4) and the prayer leader (B6) approved of the match, since the suitor was a carpenter who earned a good living in the nearest market town; she would lead a good life in town in comfortable circumstances. The father of the suitor was a son of the village, a member of the Qaroosh lineage, who had settled in town and opened a small restaurant; he was pious and was well regarded by the prayer leader. Although the girl's mother was legally charged with her upbringing as fosterer, and the prayer leader had been legally charged by the court as the trustee of her property, her legal marriage guardians were her closest patrilineal kinsmen, the members of the Shujur lineage (C2, C3, D1,

CHART 12

CASE TWO: THE CASE OF THE CONTESTED BETROTHAL

DATE: MAY 1964 – JULY 1965

INTERPRETATION: SHAYKH LUQMAN

VIOLATION: ISLAMIC LAW OF GUARDIANSHIP

ISSUE: CONTROL OF PROPERTY

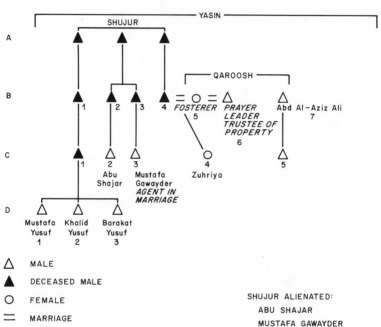

△	MALE
▲	DECEASED MALE
○	FEMALE
=	MARRIAGE
≠	DIVORCE
∿∿	FRIENDSHIP
—	DESCENT

SHUJUR ALIENATED:
ABU SHAJAR
MUSTAFA GAWAYDER
KHALID YUSUF
BARAKAT YUSUF
MUSTAFA YUSUF

D2, and D3 on chart 12). Acting according to local custom, the prayer leader sent several go-betweens to the legal guardians of the girl to get their official consent for the marriage. The men sent were more closely related to the girl's lineage than either the prayer leader or the father of the suitor, that is, they were the appropriate social structural "intermediaries." At first the men of Shujur appeared to agree to the request of the go-betweens, with three stipulations: that the slaughtering of the betrothal be held in their house (as befitted the legal guardians' status); that the official delegation of elders that came to ask for the hand of the girl in marriage (the jaha) come to their house and make the request (and not the prayer leader's house); and that Mustafa Gawayder (C3) act as the girl's legal marriage guardian and receive the marriage payment. They further said that they wished to postpone their official approval until the next day, since one prominent elder (C2) whom they wished to consult was not present. The father of the suitor and the prayer leader went to C2's house the next morning to make arrangements for the sending of the formal delegation (*jaha*) that would ask the girl's hand in marriage (since the go-betweens operated only as unofficial preliminary intermediaries). Upon arrival they found that the men of Shujur had changed their minds. Mustafa Yusuf (D1 on chart 12) wanted one of his own sons to take the girl in marriage. The prayer leader said that would be all right with him if the girl gave her consent. A member of the Shujur lineage was sent to the prayer leader's house to inquire whether she would consent.[14] She said she would never take any of the sons of Mustafa al-Yusuf as a husband. "They never paid any attention to me before," she said. "Why all this interest now?" This last retort obliquely referred to the fact that she believed they were only interested in getting control over her property—she owned several acres of the best agricultural land in the village. With this turn of events the prayer leader and the suitor's father decided to send a second go-between to the Shujur elders. The second go-between seemed to have succeeded in his mission, but when the prayer leader and the father of the suitor came the next morning to make the formal arrangements, they found that Mustafa Yusuf again had changed his mind, now saying that he would never agree to the marriage. The next day the prayer leader wrote a petition to the religious court in Zuhriyya's name, asking for an investigation of the opposition of her relatives to her marriage. Mustafa Gawaydar and the Yusuf brothers were called to appear in court. The judge asked for her closest patrilineal kinsman (who would be her legal guardian) to step forward. Mustafa Gawaydar did so, since he was her second cousin, while the Yusuf brothers were her third cousins. The judge asked him whether he opposed the marriage and if so, on what grounds. Mustafa replied that he was not opposed to the marriage and on the spot he signed the marriage contract and accepted the £50 down payment from the suitor in the name of the girl. The prayer leader told me that a year earlier Khalid Yusuf (D2) had tried to take the position of trustee of Zuhriyya's property away from him. He had hired a lawyer who went to the Islamic court and claimed that as a close patrilineal kinsman of the girl Khalid was the proper trustee for her property rather than the prayer leader, who was not related to her consanguineally. The judge solicited the patrilineal genealogy of the Shujur lineage, which showed that Khalid was a genuine third patrilateral cousin. However the judge had to reject Khalid's claim of wardship, since Islamic law did not allow a girl beyond the age of puberty to be given in custody to relatives other than those that fell within the prohibited categories of kinship, that is, those covered by the incest taboo. Since Khalid was her third cousin he was an eligible marriage partner and not covered by the incest taboo; therefore, he could not act as her property guardian. The prayer leader, on the other hand, through his marriage with her mother did fall within the prohibited categories of kinship, could live with her in the same house and act as the trustee of her property. Subsequently Khalid raised another claim in the religious court, seeking to make Zuhriyya a ward of her father's sister. The judge again had to reject the claim, for her father's sister was married to a man who was not related to Zuhriyya and, not, therefore, covered by the incest taboo. The prayer leader said that he had learned a month before that Khalil Marwan had agreed to give Khalid Yusuf £50 if the latter would raise a case in court for the guardianship of Zuhriyya; Khalil wanted the girl for his own nephew. He said that a formal delegation was finally sent to Mustafa Gawaydar's house, the slaughtering of the betrothal took place, and Zuhriyya was betrothed to the carpenter from the market town. The prayer leader went on to say that the document severing Shujur from Beni Yasin was written on the same night that the second go-between had been sent to Shujur asking their consent for the marriage. He said that the Shujur had not come to pay him the festival visit (after the end of Ramadan), a gross violation of the norms of behavior among patrilineal kinsmen. There was no question in his mind that the secession of Shujur from Yasin resulted from the bitter feelings that the case of the contested betrothal aroused.

Case Three: The Case of the Bogus Magician

I recorded four separate accounts of this case. The first three informants, members of the independents, Dumi, and ʿAmr respectively, clearly regarded the incident as the key to the secession of Shujur; the last informant (the Yasin mayor) was at first reluctant to speak about the case; when he finally did, he denied it was relevant to their secession.

(From a member of the Rifaʿiya lineage): He said that the magician (*hajjāb*)[15] (B2 on chart 13) was writing amulets in the house of his (the informant's) kinsman, Haris al-Milhem (B1 on chart 13). Village women were coming to him without the knowledge of their husbands and he was preparing amulets to treat barrenness and induce fertility. Finally the sons of the Yasin mayor (C8 and C9), the sons of another Yasin elder of the Qaroosh lineage (who was also the father of the prayer leader) (C6 and C7), and the son of Abu Fayid (C10), ganged up on Haris and the magician and pummeled them. Both the magician and Haris were taken off to jail.

(From the Dumi mayor): He said that Shujur left the Yasin clan over a year ago over a misrepresented case of honor. The Yasin mayor apprehended a magician from Palestine who was staying at the house of Haris al-Milhem al-Rifaʿi on the outskirts of town. He had been there for three days. The Yasin mayor "belted him" and accused him publicly of rending the honor of a Shujur girl. All of the Shujur members denied any such happening. "It was a case of one lie on top of another," he said. The Shujur were boiling mad at Abu Yasin (a teknonym and the term by which the village referred to the Yasin mayor) for making this accusation. The police came and an investigation took place. The magician and Haris were taken off to jail. That was a year ago. He said that Shujur have been with him ever since that time. He also said that Abu Fayid and others had berated Abu Yasin for his precipitate action. The latter had even broken in on him in the middle of the night to denounce the magician's violation of modesty.

(From the ʿAmr watchman): He said that the magician used to sit with women alone. They menstruated into the dish mounted on a pile of dirt in front of him, while the magician wrote amulets to do away with their inability to bear children. Those who had gone to be treated by the magician included the daughter of a Yasin member, the daughter of a Shuqayrat member, the daughter of Haris al-

Milhem (C1 on chart 13) and his mother (A1), as well as the daughter of Khalil (C11 on chart 13). The police came at night to Haris al-Milhem's house and he hosted them by killing four chickens. The police took the magician off to jail and kept him there fifteen days. Abu Yasin beat up both Haris and the magician. He said that the magician shouldn't have been allowed to remain alone with women. He said that apart from the women mentioned above, fifteen others had gone to the magician for treatment. Some had male children but wanted more. Later a piece appeared in the local paper (of Deir Abu Said) describing the whole incident. One of the Shujur women was alone with the magician when Abu Yasin entered the house. The Shujur denied this. The Shujur seceded from Beni Yasin on account of this incident and signed officially with Abu Tahir (the Dumi mayor). He said that the Shuqayrat are for Abu Tahir, the Ikhtaba are for Abu Tahir, the Rifaʿiya for for Abu Tahir—all because of the anger over the beating up of Haris. "Why did you blacken our face," they asked, "Why inform the government? Why beat us up? Why not just kick the magician out of town?"

(From Abu Yasin, the Yasin mayor): He said the following had come to the magician to be treated for barrenness: two women from Beni Dumi, the daughter of Abu Shajar (C5 on chart 13), the daughter of Mustafa Gawaydar (C2), and the wife of Muslih Mustafa Gawaydar (C4). She was the woman whom he found alone with the magician when he walked in. The mayor said that the formal charge made against the magician was imposture (*dajjāla*). He said that he saw the women going to Haris's house and he went there but found no one. When he went to Haris's shop and asked him the identity of the magician, Haris refused to give it. Then he ran across the magician in the street and asked him his identity; the magician refused to give it. He asked him where he was staying. The magician replied that he was at the house of Muslih Mustafa Gawaydar along with a number of other guests. The mayor went to the house of Muslih, but found only Muslih's wife there. The magician had been alone with her. The mayor berated the magician and Haris as well as Mustafa Gawaydar and Mustafa Yusuf and swore at them for not protecting their women. Then he tied the magician up until the police came to get him. He said that the magician admitted his imposture later: he worked with phosphorus and put it on the forehead of the women; he touched their legs; he lay down along side them. He mixed the phosphorus with oil and water and said, "If you see light, your barrenness will depart." Haris had told him that he (Haris) was keeping

CHART 13

CASE THREE: THE CASE OF THE BOGUS MAGICIAN

DATE: APRIL 1965

INTERPRETATION: ABU TAHIR, DUMI MUKHTAR; ABU WASFI (RIFA'I); WATCHMAN OF 'AMR

VIOLATION: MODESTY, SECRECY, CIRCUMLOCUTION

ISSUE: FRAUDULENT MAGIC

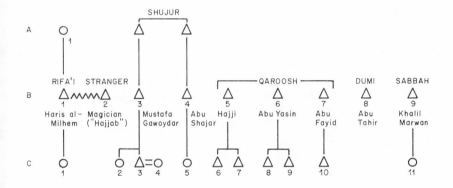

△   MALE

▲   DECEASED MALE

○   FEMALE

═   MARRIAGE

≠   DIVORCE

ʌʌʌ FRIENDSHIP

─   DESCENT

INDEPENDENTS ALIENATED:
    ALL THE RIFA'IYA (DUE TO
    THE BEATING OF HARIS);
    SEVERAL SHUQAYRAT MEMBERS

OTHER YASIN MEMBERS ALIENATED:
    KHALIL MARWAN
    HUSAYN ABD AL-QADIR

SHUJUR ALIENATED:
    MUSTAFA GAWAYDAR
    MUSLIH MUSTAFA
    ABU SHAJAR

the money. If the women did give birth, he would pass it on to the magician. The mayor said that Shaykh Basim (the hometown magician) was not like that: he did not stay alone with women or touch them or lie along side them. The mayor said that Haris had collected about £70 from the village; part he had been forced to give back and part was still with the government. The mayor said that he had hit Haris as well as the imposter. He said that Abu Tahir had acted in a cowardly manner during the whole affair and had failed to come with him to confront the magician. The Dumi mayor had seen the bogus magician operating in the village but had failed to do anything about it. Abu Yasin said he would never stand for imposture. Yusuf Sibba'i, the mayor's first cousin, interrupted the mayor's monologue to say that he would not visit the members of the Shujur lineage, Ramadan or no Ramadan (to indicate forgiveness and reconciliation), because the fault was theirs. The mayor said, "He who believes in magicians has no religion whatsoever; there are doctors [now]." Yusuf replied by saying that some amulets were all right— those that utilized Quranic verses. [That same afternoon Mustafa Gawaydar told me, "Women have been consulting magicians all their lives."]. The mayor told me that the magician had been imprisoned for three months and that Haris had been bailed out by his brother and was later declared innocent. A few months later Haris left the village to seek permanent employment in Palestine, because, it was said, he was hit so hard by Abu Yasin and his son.

Case Four: The Case of the Disputed Olive Trees

For many years a certain olive tree belonged to the family of Abd al-Aziz Ali (B8 on chart 14, the father of the suitor involved in case two). The tree was located in Tibne, the mother village, in the middle of a grove of trees owned by members of the Shujur lineage (D1, D2, D3, D4 on chart 14). At the time of the registration of lands of the village in 1939, the grove was registered in the name of the Shujur with the understanding that the members of the Qaroosh lineage who owned the tree would have access rights to it and the right to pick its fruit. However no written document was drawn up to that effect at that time. In 1965 the Shujur concerned sold the grove of trees and received ten dinars for each tree. They would not give Abd al-Aziz the ten dinars for his olive tree. The mayor of Beni Yasin attempted to arbitrate the matter and they seemed to have come to an agreement of five dinars compensation, but finally the above-mentioned Shujur members refused to pay. Abd al-Aziz took

CHART 14

CASE FOUR: THE CASE OF THE DISPUTED OLIVE TREES

DATE: SEPTEMBER 1965

INTERPRETATION: ABU YASIN, YASIN MUKHTAR

VIOLATION: RIGHTS OF USUFRUCT TO ORCHARD

ISSUE: LAND DISPUTE

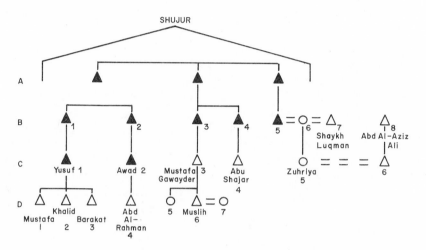

MALE

DECEASED MALE

FEMALE

MARRIAGE

DIVORCE

FRIENDSHIP

DESCENT

SHUJUR ALIENATED:

MUSTAFA YUSUF
KHALID YUSUF
BARAKAT YUSUF
ABD AL-RAHMAN AWAD

(Their fathers owned the olive grove)

the case to court and a number of old-timers called as witnesses swore that the tree belonged to Qaroosh under the terms of the oral agreement. The Shujur were found guilty and fined four pounds for court costs and ten pounds which was to be handed over as the value of the tree. The Yasin mayor ended his description of the incident by saying that the Shujur involved were so mad at him as a result of the verdict that they went off to Abu Tahir and told him that they would now support him and not Abu Yasin.

Case Five: The Case of the Accused Robbers

Khalid al-Yusuf, Mustafa Gawaydar, Khalil Marwan, Hasan al-Milhem and Shaykh Basim (C1, B3, B4, B7, and B6 respectively on chart 15) looked out one night in response to cries of alarm raised by Daoud al-Khatib (B5) who said that he had just been robbed of 167 pounds. All the above-mentioned except Khalil Marwan came out. Later the same four men were jailed for a week on the charge of giving false testimony in court with regard to the circumstances of the robbery. They blamed the Yasin mayor, saying, "Why did he sign a paper affirming the suspicions of Daoud al-Khatib against us?" They told Khalil Marwan that it was the Yasin mayor who had given his name to the police. The mayor replied that he did not charge them in court with stealing; he had merely said that the plaintiff, Daoud al-Khatib, has suspicions, and that he, the mayor, affirmed such suspicions. Mustafa Gawaydar (B3) said that the Yasin mayor had let them all stay in jail seven days without once going to see them or attempting to bail them out. Finally Abu Tahir bailed them out. Mustafa said that he and Khalid al-Yusuf were jailed for saying that they hadn't touched the pilfered trunk (which was found lying outside Mahmoud's house) and hadn't returned it to the house, that is, for disassociating themselves from the acts of Shaykh Basim and Hasan al-Milhem. Mustafa said that after the Dumi mayor bailed them out, the Shujur signed up with him. He said that previously he had always paid the *makhtara* to Abu Yasin, even when times were hard, because he knew that the mayor was weak (i.e., poor) and needed help. But this year he had not paid. He ended by saying, "Anyway, there is no *makhtara* anymore; the mayorship was now the government's responsibility."

The five cases demonstrate that in a community characterized by multiplex relationships it is not possible to understand any particular event except by reviewing a very wide arc of social relations involving the personnel concerned. Indeed the arc of social relations is

CHART 15

CASE FIVE: THE CASE OF THE ACCUSED ROBBERS

DATE: OCTOBER 1965

INTERPRETATION: MUSTAFA GAWAYDAR AND MUSTAFA YUSUF OF SHUJUR

VIOLATION: NORMS OF CLANSHIP, CONCERN OF MUKHTAR FOR HIS CLANSMEN'S WELFARE

ISSUE: ROBBERY

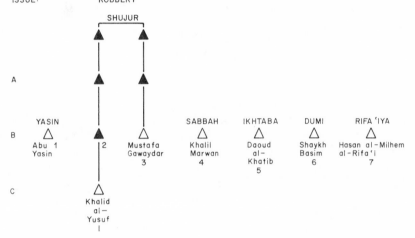

△	MALE	
▲	DECEASED MALE	
○	FEMALE	
=	MARRIAGE	
⚏	DIVORCE	
⋀⋀	FRIENDSHIP	
—	DESCENT	

SHUJUR ALIENATED:
    KHALID aL-YUSUF
    MUSTAFA GAWAYDAR

NON-SHUJUR ALIENATED:
    KHALIL MARWAN
    SHAYKH BASIM
    HASAN aL-MILHEM
    DAOUD aL-KHATIB

so wide and the interrelationships of the people involved are so intertwined that I cannot claim that these five cases were the only ones relevant to Shujur's secession. In fact I have fragmentary information to suggest that Khalil Marwan (whom the prayer leader regarded as the mastermind of the secession, because he forged the chain of evil by tying together four separate grudges to bring schism) was involved in still another incident through a complaint his wife raised against her brother, who was also the first patrilateral cousin of the Yasin mayor.

In addition to demonstrating dramatically the tangled history of grudge relationships in such a community, these cases also show how frequently these relationships cause people to resort to the external arena (the civil court, the religious court, the police). The norms that guide behavior in the external arena then become as important as the grudge relationships themselves. Good examples are the first two cases both of which involved the application of Islamic law. In the second case the law recognized the girl's mother as the fosterer (*Hādin*) until she reached the age of eleven, when her legal guardian (*wali*) had the right to exert his jurisdiction over her. The legal guardian is the father, but in his absence that responsibility and right passes on to her nearest patrilineal kinsman. However because the girl was an orphan, the law required that a trustee of her property (*waSi*) be appointed, and this trustee was the prayer leader. Thus the Shujur had the right to assert their legal guardianship over Zuhriyya, but this right had to be accommodated to the rights of fosterage, the obligations of the trustee, and the preservation of the girl's modesty. In this case, the court decided that modesty had to be given preeminence. What from the Shujur's point of view was a legitimate economic struggle to prevent a daughter of the lineage from alienating land became overshadowed by Islamic norms regarding modesty, fosterage, and guardianship.

The issue in the third case was not magic as such but its fraudulent practice. Most villagers regarded the practice of magic as an acceptable folk tradition and would have agreed with Mustafa Gawaydar's pronouncement, although some would have given conditional approval (like Yusuf Sibba'i) and a tiny minority would have agreed with the Yasin mayor in his outright condemnation. The norms violated were those of modesty and secrecy. The magician had abused the women's modesty in a flagrant manner, treating them in private without the knowledge of their husbands and in such a way as to jeopardize the honor of their families. But in trying to put things right the mayor compounded the offense by making public accusations which finally became common knowledge in the whole sub-district through the newspaper. Violations of modesty are private matters which bring disgrace once publicized. Shaykh Basim, the hometown magician, was contrasted with the bogus magician on precisely this point. Even the Yasin mayor, who disapproved of magic itself, declared that Basim would never resort to such im-modest behavior. Basim always practiced his magic within an Is-lamic framework, beginning and ending his divination with Quranic verses, and the people of all the surrounding villages regarded him as a genuine magician. He had, it seemed, as a very young man suffered from epileptic fits which after some time stopped; this event was interpreted as indicating that he had achieved mastery over certain semisupernatural creatures, the *jinn*.

The villagers' indulgent attitude toward Basim sharply contrasts with the treatment given to the bogus magician: he was questioned in the street, beaten, run out of town, and imprisoned. To some de-gree this relates to his being a stranger; he was not the first stranger to elicit suspicion, questioning in the street, threats after refusal to give satisfactory answers, and banishment.

Although many informants considered the case of the bogus magician the emotionally crucial case (the 'Amr watchman named four separate lineages alienated by it), many others thought the rob-bery to be the immediate precipitating incident: some stressed Abu Yasin's giving the names of suspected villagers to the police, while others cited his failure to bail out his clansmen as the final critical act.

In all the cases informants tended to interpret all events in terms of preceding grudge relationships and to extend the significance of these relationships to all kinsmen within the patrilineage, i.e., they assumed a unity within the lineage or close consultation group. In some instances such an assumption was correct, but in others it was not. For instance in case two the prayer leader assumed that the hard feelings between himself and the members of Shujur over the be-trothal extended to Abu Yasin, who was his close kinsman and Qaroosh lineage mate. This was probably so, for the mayor and the prayer leader were good friends, neighbors, and frequent visitors of one another's guest houses; besides they shared an ideology that was traditional with respect to religious matters while modernizing with respect to initiating village development projects. On the other hand my informants from Dumi and 'Amr frequently implied that the case of the bogus magician caused all Shujur members to shift sup-port from the Yasin mayor to the Dumi mayor. This was not strictly

true, since not all Shujur household heads signed the official document of secession that was presented to the subdistrict officer. Some
Shujur household heads were not directly involved in the case, for
their women had not consulted the magician, and Khalil Marwan's
close patrilineal kinsman simply ignored his exhortation to boycott
Abu Yasin. The view that the patrilineal descent groups referred to
in these cases acted and reacted in a unified corporate manner is,
therefore, of dubious validity, but my informants' ideological view
is not completely false for two reasons. Although all Shujur household heads were not directly involved in all the cases, nearly all were
involved in at least one case and most were involved in more than
one. Given the multiplex nature of social relations within the group,
such involvements tend to become more intense and extend to
cover interests not first concerned. Second, although it is not a corporate group in a strict economic or political sense, the patrilineage
is a corporate prestige unit: to impugn the honor of any component
family diminishes the honor of the whole lineage. Therefore there is
a sense in which the totality of the Shujur lineage as well as the
totality of the Rifaʿiya lineage were victimized: they lost a substantial amount of an important resource—honor.

The five cases also demonstrate the pertinence of the different
analytical approaches to core and support discussed in chapter three.
Abu Yasin never repudiated Khalil Marwan as a clansman, even
though he shared the prayer leader's pronounced negative ethical
evaluation of him, even though Khalil had helped engineer the
Shujur secession, and even though Khalil had never contributed
money to Abu Yasin's mayorship, for Abu Yasin adhered very
strictly to an ideological view of core/support. From an economic
point of view, Khalil Marwan was neither core nor support for the
Yasin coalition, and Mustafa Gawaydar, after announcing that he
would no longer pay the *makhtara*, switched from a core to a support element in the Yasin coalition. His statement that the mayorship was now the government's financial responsibility marked the
disappearance of the distinction between primary and secondary
core that had been the economic basis of the Yasin mayorship for
more than fifty years.

Examined from a processual point of view, Mustafa Gawaydar's
statement, together with the substantive shift away from the
makhatara and towards the mathbata seems to indicate a movement
from a status-based to a contract-based political process. This view
is reinforced by Shujur's secession and their adherence to the Dumi

mayorship and the subsequent offer of a Dumi lineage (Khalaf) to adhere to Abu Yasin's mayorship. Mustafa Gawaydar's statement seems to indicate that villagers were aware that new rules of the game now prevailed. The following section will examine whether and to what extent that was true.

One final point about the five cases needs to be made. If one took only the village council sequence and the school lands sequence, one might conclude that local-level politics comprehends merely competition for control of the village's public institutions, e.g., the village council, the village school, the mayorship. But the third sequence demonstrates that to understand such "public" politics involves all kinds of nonpublic matters—e.g., divorce, marriage, inheritance, land claims, and matters that take place in a variety of situations and institutional frameworks that bear no direct relation to the public competition—e.g., divination sessions, Islamic courts, festivals, and funerals.[16] It is only by following the ramifications of the interfamilial, intralineage, and intraclan grudge patterns that one can determine why a family or a lineage begins or terminates its political support for a coalition at a particular time. And it is the assessment of any particular coalition's strength and an understanding of how that strength is gained or lost that is essential to an understanding of how the political process works.

Cyclical Change and Cumulative Change

The five cases illustrate how a core element for one coalition was converted into a support element for the other. What seems to have occurred is a linear change from movement-like politics to more machine-like politics (see chapter two). As was observed in chapter one, whether change is to be considered cumulative and linear or cyclical is usually very difficult to judge, since the number of episodes examined is limited. This temporal limitation is particularly telling in social anthropological analysis, where the span of time considered is usually the year or two of field work. The present study has the advantage of an eight-year span between the first observation and the last, although I must hasten to add that I did not make systematic observations at regular intervals during this time. Still the evidence from the last section seems to indicate that some kind of distinct change in the political process had taken place, a change that could be interpreted as linear in direction; after all, offi-

Chart 16
The Case for the Cyclical Movement of
Politics in Kufr al-Ma

1
On the Way Back: Shujur-Abu Yasin

December 1965	Abu Tahir says that Shujur will never go back (to supporting Abu Yasin).
Early January 1966	(Morning) Mustafa Yusuf shakes hands with Abu Yasin immediately after the festival prayer ending the fast of Ramadan, but his brother Khalid does not.
Early January 1966	(Afternoon) Mustafa Gawaydar visits Abu Yasin after the festival prayer, but leaves soon after coming.
13 January 1966	Abu Tahir says that all members of Shujur are with him.
February 1966	Mustafa Yusuf has lunch with Abu Yasin. (The mukhtar needed him to build his son a house; multiplexity breaks the grudge relationship).
Early March 1966	Khalid Yusuf refuses to sign a letter accusing Abu Fayid of bribery. (The presentation of the letter to Khalid by members of Beni Dumi indicates that they regarded him on their side).
29 August 1966	Abu Tahir says he doesn't take Shujur's support seriously; he doesn't need them; he has Dumi and 'Amr and Shuqayrat and Rifa'i, and that is enough. Besides, he says, he doesn't charge Shujur when they come to him for his signature on a document. He says he doesn't feel as if he has the right to charge them. He doesn't care if they go back (to Yasin).
31 August 1966	Mustafa Yusuf says there is no necessity for a reconciliation meeting between himself and Abu Yasin—that it was a case of vexation (za'al) among kinsmen. "Will anyone desert his brother for his cousin?" he asked. "At any rate," he continued, "the petition for the official attachment of Shujur to Beni Dumi was never signed."
29 March 1967	Abu Yasin says all the Shujur have come back (support him).
31 March 1967	Abu Tahir says Shujur still brings him documents for signature, but they also go to Abu Yasin for the same purpose.

cial secession by a component lineage from its clan had been unheard of in the village's history.

However for analytical purposes I have been guilty of holding back part of the evidence. That evidence, set out in chart 16, presents the case for a cyclical movement of politics. The chart marks the sig-

2
On the Way Back: Abu Yasin-Abu Tahir

31 December 1965	The mayors speak to one another but without approval (*raDā*).
2 January 1966	Abu Yasin says that he regards Abu Tahir's taking on Shujur as an act of personal treachery. He says that he kept the "gentleman's agreement" (by collecting the makhtara from discontented Dumi and handing it over to Abu Tahir and by refusing to accept the support of the Khalaf and Abu Hadabi lineages). Abu Tahir did not. He says that the Dumi mayor's lineage are noted for their dishonesty.
Early August 1966	The end of nonofficial avoidance between the mayors occurs: Abu Tahir enters the same grocery shop in which Abu Yasin sits and proceeds to joke and make light conversation.
4 September 1966	The end of official avoidance between mayors occurs: the mayors consult one another regarding village business (mathbata). They move back to a day-to-day cooperating and speaking relationship —but still "aren't sincere with one another" (*mush mukhlisīn ma a ba'aD*).
Early March 1967	Abu Tahir comes to Abu Yasin's house to give him a shot against the grippe.
30 March 1967	Abu Yasin praises Abu Tahir. When Abu Tahir leaves a gathering and a visitor becomes apprehensive lest he not return, Abu Yasin reassures him: "No, he (Abu Tahir) is a good man and will return."
31 March 1967	Abu Tahir says of the estrangement (*za'al*) existing between himself and Abu Yasin: "Abu Yasin and I are all right now. (*ana wa Abu Yasin malah halla'*). There was no meeting to reconcile us. (After all) we are the symbol of the town. Anger to the last degree—no! We can't allow it. We fell out over public matters, not private."

nificant events regarding Shujur's return to the Yasin mayorship as well as the events that marked the reconciliation of the two mayors with respect to both public and private affairs.

Again the cycle of events is significant in terms of identifying core and support elements. With respect to Shujur, Abu Yasin kept strictly to an ideological point of view—he never admitted that they had seceded, and by the end of the sequence the Shujur themselves adhered to that point of view, denying that they had ever left. Although Abu Tahir clearly broke the gentleman's agreement, he, too, revealed that he had not entirely emancipated himself from an ideological view of core/support. Although he took on Shujur members as support, he denied that he needed them and never solicited either the makhtara or the mathbata from them. Although at an early point in the sequence he stated flatly that Shujur would never return to Yasin, he told me soon after in another context that sometimes it did happen that one mayor took on the adherents of another—but this was only until they were reconciled with their own mayor. In this statement Abu Tahir recognized switching only as a temporary pragmatic circumstance not as a new policy reflecting new rules of competition.

From an ethical point of view, Abu Yasin condemned Abu Tahir for breaking the gentleman's agreement as unequivocally as Mustafa Gawaydar had condemned Abu Yasin for not bailing a fellow clansman out of jail. Abu Tahir, on the other hand, construed breaking the gentleman's agreement as a pragmatic act for which ethical evaluation was inappropriate. But he described Abu Yasin as motivated by overweening greed during the school lands sequence. Significantly neither mayor made once-and-for-all ethical evaluations, for by spring 1967 both mayors in word and in deed wished one another well. A number of factors made the cycle of return to good feelings after back-biting and estrangement inevitable: it was not, as Abu Tahir had suggested, that the moral authority of the mayorship was so great. Rather multiplexity made estrangements that derived from one set of interests incompatible with another set of interests that tied the same two persons together. Abu Tahir served not only as the Dumi mayor, but also as the village medic. At one time or another every family in the village had to use his services—estrangement over political matters did not prevent Abu Yasin's requesting treatment for the grippe, and such visits could not but influence their political relationship. Similarly Mustafa Yusuf and Abu Yasin were not simply bound by patrilineal clanship; Abu Yasin wanted Mustafa, an accomplished builder, to build a house for his son. Multiplex social relations operate not merely in the present, but have historical roots. When I asked the Yasin mayor in the spring of 1967 how it was that he and Abu Tahir were now friendly after all that had gone before, he said, "His father and my father were friends."

However there is another good reason for the cyclical movement of politics in Kufr al-Ma—the requirements of the office and the demands of the government do not permit estrangement to run its natural course. The two mayors are often required to appear together in the subdistrict center's various government offices and they sometimes must consult together in the village. Such continuous interaction is incompatible with the central characteristic of estrangement—avoidance.

From a processual point of view it is difficult to determine whether Shujur on the Yasin side or Khalaf on the Dumi side have now in fact become support elements rather than core elements for their respective coalitions. Until another round occurs, i.e., until another case of estrangement occurs involving these lineages with their respective mayors, it is not possible to tell whether they view their attachment to their clan and their clan's mayor in a different way than before.

Finally the cycle of events recorded on chart 16 provides further insight into the different strategies the opposing coalition leaders pursued. The end of the cycle indicated a return of both sides to the gentleman's agreement. As chapter four pointed out, the Dumi-ʿAmr coalition based their strategy on that agreement, on the rule of numbers in the village council, and on increasing confrontation and encounter with the opposing coalition. This strategy combines old (the gentleman's agreement and the static view of politics) and new (voting, majority rule) elements; if utilized consistently and applied skillfully, it would seem to guarantee victory for that coalition. It is a conservative strategy that aims at cutting down the risk of attrition from one's own coalition (rather than attracting supporters from the opposing coalition), thereby guaranteeing victory through the superiority of numbers. For Yasin the return to the gentleman's agreement confirms its own ideology and value system but also portends its defeat: if the village council becomes operative and majority rule prevails (admittedly, two big ifs), they will lose.

There are two catches to the Dumi-ʿAmr strategy. The first is that ʿAmr, as documented in chapter two, is the least solidary of the clans. The Yasin leaders may hope to maintain the static view of politics and play the new game successfully by winning over enough supporters from ʿAmr and the independents. This possibility is enhanced by the greater services the Yasin mayorship renders compared to the Dumi mayorship. Second, an inherent contradiction exists between the elements of the Dumi strategy itself. On the one hand it depends on increased use of confrontations and encounters, but it is equally founded on adherence to the gentleman's agreement (in order to guarantee its majority). It is quite possible, indeed probable, that the increasing use of confrontations and encounters in intercoalition competition will lead to an increasing use of it in intracoalition affairs. In that event dissension would grow within the coalition, creating obvious possibilities for violations of the gentleman's agreement.

There is an alternative strategy that Yasin could, but under the present leadership will not, follow: repudiation of the gentleman's agreement in order to play a more free-wheeling political game. With its superior resources, Yasin could provide more payoffs to supporters than Dumi, while continuing to offer enough rewards to its own core members to keep them in line. Yasin so far has opted for the minimum-risk strategy—reducing the chances of losing its own followers by sacrificing the possibility of attracting broader support. The present Dumi strategy would be jeopardized by such a shift in the Yasin strategy, but as things stand, Dumi seems fated to win.

The strategy the Dumi-ʿAmr coalition follows is particularly apropos, for it seems to have anticipated socioeconomic trends that have weakened the politics of hospitality. Between 1959 and 1967 the offering of hospitality has declined in Kufr al-Ma and with it the political influence and prestige generated by its extension. Yasin, by relying on the politics of hospitality and the gentleman's agreement, is ignoring the trend and acting against its own interest.

There is one more factor that gives credence to the view that cumulative as well as cyclical change has occurred in Kufr al-Ma. Bailey argues that contests about change are those at the end of the continuum where uncertainty prevails. Where uncertainty exists about which rules of the game apply, the competitors are likely to miscalculate. Evidence of this exists in Kufr al-Ma. The leaders of Yasin misread Dumi's commitment to the rule of numbers, as evidenced by three successive encounters and confrontations, each progressively more public than the previous one, over the issue of selecting the village council head and adjusting the school lands claims. Yasin lost the two encounters and came out badly before the district officer in the exchange of confrontations. The Dumi coalition, on the other hand, miscalculated how attached Yasin was to the old rules of the game—encounter-by-mediation and the politics of hospitality. The miscalculations on both sides resulted from a different interpretation as to how committed the central government was to a policy of establishing village councils. To substantiate its view Dumi had the promulgated laws of the country (since 1954) and the new drive by Rimawi to execute those laws, as well as the efforts of the subdistrict officer to implement the new minister's demands. To substantiate its view Yasin had the fact that by late 1965 only 14 of 235 villages in the Ajlun district had established village councils and that Abu Fayid had been successful in convincing the subdistrict officer to shelve implementation of the council for the time being. In other words both sides miscalculated because both were truly uncertain as to whether the regional and local-level officials would execute national-level policy.

The cyclical movement back to the gentleman's agreement may have affirmed the value system and the sociopolitical structure the great majority of Yasin members and many other villagers uphold, but that victory, both substantive and psychological, may defeat Yasin in the local-level political arena. Thus although the cyclical movement of politics in Kufr al-Ma reflects the strong stabilizing forces at work in the political process, it tends to obscure the fact that cumulative change has occurred which has placed the competitors in quite a different posture at the end of the sequence of competition than they held at its beginning.

Factionalism

Since the late 1950s a number of anthropologists have become interested in a phenomenon they have labeled "factionalism." One of the first analyses, "Pervasive Factionalism," by Alan Beals and Bernard Siegel, distinguished "pervasive" factionalism from "schismatic" factionalism (competition between cohesive groups within the larger group often leading to its dissolution) and from competition between parties and interest groups. Beals and Siegel argued that pervasive factionalism is characterized by overt "conflict" between nonideological transient groups affecting all levels of the social structure including the basic social structural units (e.g., the family, the subcaste), a conflict that leads to the increasing abandonment of cooperative activities.[17] Besides the fact that it is pervasive, the most important characteristic of pervasive factionalism is that it signifies a kind of social *malaise* ("A hated brother was often in one group and a hated neighbor in the other"),[18] or, as Beals and Siegel put it, "strain." The fact that they describe the relationship between opposing factions in terms of "conflict" rather than "competition" (my usage) reflects this view point. Ralph Nicholas agreed with

Beals and Seigel in many respects: factions are "conflict groups"; they are not corporate groups; faction members are recruited by a leader. But he goes on to add that factions are "political" groups vying for "public power" and that faction members are recruited on diverse principles.[19] B. D. Graham, in analyzing how a "dominant" factional system became "bifactional" in the Indian state of Uttar Pradesh, described factions as being informal, impermanent, and recruited on simple and specialized terms "so that the line of cleavage between factions usually cuts across the line separating established political groups. . . ."[20] He went on to add the important qualification that factions are not regarded as "legitimate" by many in the community and that their members can be divided into two categories, core and support. In "Factionalism and Politics in Village Burma" Melford Spiro also defines factionalism as the competition of nonideological noncorporate groups recruited by a leader on the basis of diverse principles. He adds, however at least for his Burmese case, that factionalism covers a narrow range of behavior; alignments are fluid, competition is covert, and the factions seldom realize their goals.[21] Spiro posited four important variables to consider in studying factionalism: factional scope, factional visibility, factional efficiency, and factional solidarity.

Janet Bujra has made the most incisive comprehensive analysis of the general characteristics of factionalism by an anthropologist in "The Dynamics of Political Action: A New Look at Factionalism."[22] She agrees that the leader is the key to the faction, that the ties between leaders and followers are contractual rather than ideological, that factions cannot usually sustain themselves over time (the exceptions are "ritualized" factions), and that factions are governed by informal pragmatic rules. As an implication of these attributes she adds that factions are small. But her essay breaks new ground with three propositions. First, factions are dynamic phenomena; they are going somewhere—either toward schism, resolution of conflict and withering away, or institutionalization (as pressure groups or associations). For example she identified Bailey's Bisipara as a community in an advanced institutionalized stage of factionalism when Bailey arrived for his first-field study—a stage she characterizes as "ritualized factionalism"—in which the competition is no longer violent (but usually merely verbal), because the prizes are no longer substantial and the rules governing the competition are not only recognized but adhered to on all sides. But by the time Bailey left the field, the competition had become largely nonfactional; that is, more and more the significant groups in opposition were the subcastes rather than cores of factions and their diversified support elements. The pervasive factionalism Beals and Siegel describe in their Indian and New Mexican communities was, she claims, already in the process of becoming something else.

Second, Bujra assumes that the competing groups must be structurally and functionally equivalent; she does not differ in this respect with similar assumptions Bailey and Nicholas made. Her insight is that the similarity is only essential in the long run; drawing on Bossevain's well-documented study of Maltese factionalism, she noted that it was quite possible for village factions to compete with pressure groups or pressure groups to compete with political parties in the short run and that only in the long run did pressures to institutionalize political activity along party lines become overwhelming.

Third, and by far the least developed of her arguments, Bujra maintains that the direction of the lines of political division within a particular community, the composition of the political support for any particular coalition (whether vertical, horizontal, or diagonal), and whether factional "quasi-groups"[23] dissolve, ritualize, or develop into pressure groups or political parties depends as much or more on the external political situation as it does on the internal balance of power.[24]

To what degree can the local-level political competition in Kufr al-Ma be described as factionalism and what new insights does it yield into the process of factional development and the various phenomena associated with it? If one takes Graham's attributes of factional groupings—informality, impermanence, recruitment on simple and specialized terms, such that the resulting groups cut across established political groups—and applies them to the clan coalitions in Kufr al-Ma, they are clearly inappropriate. The clans are permanent groups; they have a formal existence and a historical identity associated with a genealogy and a place of origin. From an ideological point of view (patrilineality) the clans coalitions do not crosscut one another at all, but from an economic point of view (see table 5) they do to some degree. This is so, however, only if one excludes the two main competitors, Yasin and Dumi, whose members do not comprise one another's followings; even in the case of Shujur's secession economic contributions were neither solicited nor given after the switchover. On the other hand, Graham's observation that corporate groups from whom factions recruit regard the factions as nonlegitimate is quite apropos in Kufr al-Ma, as the gentleman's agreement which prohibits contractual politics (and incipient factionalism) attests. Precisely as Graham argued, such factionalism threatens the corporate (or in this case corporate-like) group by dividing it and draining its resources.

In his essay on schismatic factionalism in Burma, Spiro specified a number of additional attributes of factionalism and asked the question, To what degree are these attributes generic characteristics of factionalism? Since, as pointed out above, Kufr al-Ma lacks many of the defining attributes of factionalism, the existence of a number of attributes specified by Spiro there would provide evidence against their inclusion as generic attributes of factionalism; contrarily, their absence in Kufr al-Ma would provide some evidence for the existence of such generic attributes. Regarding the scope of factionalism, Spiro noted that in Burma factionalism covered a very narrow range of behavior, that confrontations when they occurred were exclusively verbal, and that there were no encounters. Undoubtedly there actually were encounters in the Burmese village, but they were not face-to-face. However Kufr al-Ma does not possess any of these attributes of factionalism: competition for public power involves a very wide range of behavior, and one coalition has increasingly utilized encounters and confrontations. Nor have confrontations been exclusively verbal (witness the letter accusing Abu Fayid and the petitions submitted to government offices). It is questionable whether verbal confrontation is very useful as an index of factional scope anyway, since surely the great majority of confrontations in most societies are verbal. Much more important are the particular arenas in which such verbal confrontations take place—the courtroom as opposed to the village guest house as opposed to the domicile—and the number and kind of interests that are involved in the confrontation—economic, political, religious, kinship, etc. Regarding factional visibility, however, Kufr al-Ma bears some resemblance to the Burmese case. Spiro noted that opposing parties never faced one another, charges were often anonymous, and one assumed a mask of friendliness in the other's presence. In Kufr al-Ma many encounters occur *in absentia* and it is quite common for villagers known to be estranged to deny the fact repeatedly both to third parties and in one another's presence; yet bitter feelings and mistrust do characterize the relations between opposing sides, as is apparent in the school lands, village council, and bogus magician sequences. These attributes are not, then, generic to factionalism but probably specific to the culture. Kufr al-Ma differs in one important respect, however, from the Burmese situation Spiro described. In Kufr al-Ma a state of nonconfrontation is not allowed to continue indefinitely; sooner or later attempts are made to reconcile estranged parties, and eventually these attempts succeed. As a result of the commitment to encounter-through-mediation, bitterness and ill-feeling are cyclical in their incidence rather than permanent. Regarding factional efficiency, Spiro noted that factions seldom realized goals; however clan leaders in Kufr al-Ma were not all that good with respect to goal realization. It is true that the Dumi mayor got jobs and that the Yasin mayor in conjunction with prominent clan elders was adept at the politics of hospitality, but the number of clear-cut payoffs was small. Moreover I can remember numerous occasions when petitions drawn up were never submitted and plans for action were never acted upon. Rather than being a generic attribute of factionalism, such behavior may reflect a cultural reluctance to formalize plans and goals or to publicize division. The evidence from Kufr al-Ma, then, supports Spiro's views regarding factional scope (if one accepts his definition of encounters), but does not support his views regarding factional visibility; the evidence regarding factional efficiency is inconclusive.

To what degree does the evidence from Kufr al-Ma substantiate Bujra's analysis and to what degree can it advance the general argument? Bujra stated that external political factors are critical in determining how factions develop. The evidence from Kufr al-Ma suggests not only that external fators are critical in how factions develop but also in *whether* they develop. It would be difficult to conceive how the inchoate factionalism of the Dumi-'Amr coalition and the breaking of the gentleman's agreement could have started without the impetus provided by the government's village council policy and its establishment of a legal basis for a contractual mayorship; and if these policies are not carried out, it is difficult to imagine how the challengers (Dumi-'Amr) can effectively compete. Bujra argued that local opposition always arises against the institutionalization of factionalism, for such institutionalization divides the community and violates the norm of community harmony. Analysis of the Shujur secession cycle indicates that opposition arises not only against the institutionalization of factionalism but also against its very inception. The fact that factionalism in Kufr al-Ma is inchoate and probably abortive also procedes from the fact that offices (mayorship, subdistrict officership) and roles (grand old mediator—the Pasha) already exist within and outside of formal structures that can bring economic or political advantages.

Institutionalization of factionalism can take the form of ritualized factionalism, where limits to the competition are clearly developed and recognized: the commitment of resources must not be great, external powers may not be utilized, leadership tends to be hereditary, and encounters must be nonviolent. Although Kufr al-Ma is far from having institutionalized ritualized factionalism, it does seem to have many of its attributes. Processes such as muted subversion and muted renegadism result in muffled competition, and encounters between village opponents are nonviolent (though this does not hold with strangers, as the case of the bogus magician illustrates); although resort to external resources are frequent, they are viewed with various degrees of disapproval; and the mayorship, though not hereditary, is a permanent appointment. That what is basically a nonfactional process of local-level political competition should approximate so closely Bujra's characterization of a type of institutionalized factionalism seems to negate the generality of her argument. The contradiction is resolved, however, by Bujra's basic assumption that factionalism embraces disparate phenomena arranged in a continuum, all of which are in a state of flux; there is no reason for believing that at one end of the continuum the attributes of institutionalized factionalism cannot be similar to those characterizing the competition of corporate-like but not fully corporate groups (the clans of Kufr al-Ma)—indeed, that is just what is to be expected.

Although local-level competition in Kufr al-Ma does fit with certain lesser attributes which Bujra and others use to characterize factionalism, it does not accord with the basic attributes they identify: lineal leader-follower relations are not critical (leadership is substitutable in both coalitions), the leader is not the focus of all actions and does not initiate recruitment, the basis of his following is not short-term individual interests, switching is of minor importance. However there is another, more important problem that the data from Kufr al-Ma raises. Bujra assumes that though competing groups are not structural-functional equivalents in the short run, they will become so in the long run. Indeed this is the rationale for the continuum of factional types she posits. According to this assumption, the Yasin coalition should begin to develop along the lines of the more free-wheeling contractual mayorship that the Dumi coalition has already embraced, yet there is very little evidence of such an incipient development. As a corollary of the above assumption, Bujra asserts that the leaders of competing groups arise within a dominant category of some description (e.g., seniority, wealth, ritual status) and appeal to the same value system for support. It is certainly true that both Abu Yasin and Abu Tahir were leading members of their respective clans and as such had a similar field of recruitment for both men and money. But the next chapter demonstrates in detail that the two mayors differed strikingly in a number of respects, e.g., one was young, the other was in late middle age; one worked for harmony, the other for justice; one subjected government officials to only slightly veiled sarcasm, the other related to them through exaggerated politeness formulas. One could argue that since Kufr al-Ma lacks the critical attributes of factionalism, there is no reason to expect the political process there to develop in the direction Bujra indicates. However Kufr al-Ma can be located on the continuum she describes with respect to many attributes. There is, moreover, the broader question of whether Bujra's assumption regarding the likeness of competitors relates to factional politics or whether it is intended to apply to local-level politics generally; in the latter case, to explain the dissimilarity of political competitors in Kufr al-Ma would be generally significant for the study of local-level politics.

According to Bujra, those who hold power force an opponent to organize similarly in order to compete successfully. This conclusion is indicated both by the examples she gives[25] and her statement that "where the adversary is strongly entrenched and has institutionalized his position, then his opponent must organize similarly, or be repressed."[26] The evidence from Kufr al-Ma suggests that the challengers, not the historically dominant coalition, both initiate and pioneer in changing the oppositional context; they have done this by seizing upon certain principles the external authorities have introduced—local participation, majority rule—and turning them into political resources.

In a recent paper prepared for a symposium, The Anthropological Study of Politics, Jeremy Boissevain has taken issue with the assumption of Bujra, Bailey, and Nicholas that factional competitors are structurally and functionally alike.[27] He argues that challengers must always be unlike their entrenched competitors with respect to efficiency, ideology, and composition of support elements. The challengers must make up for the fact that they lack in power, and therefore rewards, by developing a broader ideological appeal to attract marginal support elements; and they must develop efficient administrative procedures to cut down the waste of time, energy, and resources. Although the arguments of Boissevain and Bujra are convincing in their own terms, they exclude a critical intervening variable—namely, the possibility of success. If the challengers are continually unsuccessful playing according to their own strategy but cannot match the resources of the entrenched competitor in order to play by his strategy, they have no choice but to continue playing according to their own; thus the competition continues to be between unlikes. The example of Sandombu, the Ndembu leader Turner describes, is pertinent here;[28] because he did not have close matrilineal kinsmen from whom to draw support, he had to play a game of strictly contractual politics and to depend on marginal groups and individuals for backing—while his competitors operated in a much more movement-like fashion. However if Sandombu had succeeded in attaining the headmanship through a combination of economic and political entrepreneurship—the saving of money and its parcelling out as rewards to unrelated followers—others who lacked kinsmen would have been tempted to do likewise. Even aspirants who had large followings of close kinsmen might begin to think in terms of a mixed strategy which combined a kin core with pecuniary rewards to support elements, and thus the competitors would become more similar both in strategies followed and resources utilized. In Kufr al-Ma success is also a key intervening variable. Yasin has rejected contractual politics up till now because it is still unclear that this mode of politics will prevail; after all, attempts to block implementation of the village council have so far succeeded and it is by no means certain that the politics of hospitality is still not the best strategy. If the village council is implemented and a few key votes go against the Yasin coalition, it is quite possible that they will reappraise their strategy; failing that, it is quite likely that competition for the mayorship will continue to take place between coalitions that are unlike in important respects.

Time is an important dimension that must be considered in analyzing the process by which initially unlike competitors become like one another. Friedl has pointed out that there often exists a process of "lagging emulation" connecting different social strata in the same population.[29] She notes that the lower strata of certain peasant populations tend to imitate elements of the elite's life style long after the elite has discarded those elements for others considered more modern. It is possible that such stylistic lag also applies to political competition. By the time the challengers have developed the resources to play the game the way their opponents have traditionally done, the dominant groups have developed new resources that demand a new strategy. Here cultural factors work for the development of like competitors, but economic factors work against that result.

What, then, is the significance of Kufr al-Ma for the study of factional politics? Four points stand out. First, the study of what Bujra has termed the "oppositional context" has been oversimple. To analyze factionalism in terms of the presence or absence of "dominant castes" as Nicholas does or in terms of "dominant" or "bifactional systems" as Graham does assumes that the groups identified as "dominant" or "minority" are unified. Such was clearly not the case with the ʿAmr clan in Kufr al-Ma; far from being a faction, it was a corporate-like group; even Yasin, the most unified clan, had its staunch renegades. Such was not the case with the Boad outcastes or the Warriors in Bisipara. In short there is no substantial evidence that either corporate groups, corporate-like groups (the clans of Kufr al-Ma), or factions operate as unified groups in political competition. Moreover as the whole analysis of muted subversion, muted renegadism, and partible allegiance in chapters two and three indicated, "support" of given individuals and groups for particular coalitions at any moment in time is by no means crystal clear. Indeed in communities where partible allegiance is permitted, most individuals must hedge their bets.

Second, Kufr al-Ma is significant precisely because it focuses on political processes moving in quite the opposite direction from those Boissevain and Bujra discuss. Whereas they concentrate on the process by which factions institutionalize, to become ritualized or to become political parties or corporate-like groups, the present study traces the process by which corporate-like groups might be construed as breaking down into smaller units that participate more flexibly in political competition. Such events as the split of Yasin in the 1955 election for mayor, the 1960 petition against the mayor (with its class complexion), the 1964 legislation stipulating the contractual mayorship, and the secession of Shujur in 1965 can be seen as the milestones of such a process. In this respect the present study fills a gap in the literature, for it starts at the end of the continuum which Bujra and others regard as an end point and examines a process moving in the opposite direction.

Third, this study demonstrates the existence of certain built-in limits to the trend toward what Bailey might call "machine" and Bujra "factional" politics. The previous chapters have examined a large number of such limiting factors: the existence of all-embracing movements such as the village and the peoples of Tibne, crosscutting ties (whether of marriage, social control, or descent), multiplex relationships, clan paternalism, partible allegiance, encounter-through-mediation, the existence of the mayorship as a permanent office terminated only by resignation or government displeasure (and, therefore, not the focus for repeated competitions in which contractual politics can be practiced), and the pressure exerted by the villagers' image of the good man and the model leader (to be discussed at length in the next chapter).

Finally, this study demonstrates that although the continuum may suggest it, factional or machine politics is not a linear and evolutionary development out of movement politics. It is more useful and also more realistic to view machine and movement politics as simultaneous yet opposite processes and trends: the trend for ideological neutrals (strangers, members of independent lineages and unrepresented clans, i.e., 'Amr) to be incorporated into movements (the clans and their component lineages) and the trend for all followers of movements (clan members) to be incorporated as "supporters" in machines. Thus there is the constant pressure to join a movement—by taking a woman in marriage, giving a woman in marriage, registering land together, living in a particular quarter, giving and receiving hospitality, etc.—and at the same time the constant temptation to leave it—to transact business with a leader (mayor) on the basis of calculations of mutual advantage and profit. The leader feels constant pressure to restrict the search for political support to his own movement (i.e., clan) and to focus his efforts on curbing (clan) renegadism, yet he is constantly tempted to extend the scope of his political support to the whole village and in so doing work in terms of political contracts rather than kinship obligations. This simultaneous yet opposite process or pressure or temptation or opportunity—depending on the point of view—underlies this volume's analysis of the strategy, tactics, and intercalary leadership of the two coalitions.

Individual Differences, Influence, and Leadership

Almost every chapter of this book has referred in some way to the importance of the individual in politics. The analysis of movements and machines in chapter two led to a discussion of individual motivation. The analysis of core-support elements in chapter three discussed the ethical evaluations of individuals. The focus on intercalary leadership in chapter four stressed decision-making and the options open to mayors. Chapter five analyzed a number of "roles" available as resources in the external arena. And the last chapter demonstrated that the local-level political process cannot be understood without considering the vagaries of many social situations and the outcomes of numerous individual decisions ostensibly unrelated to public affairs or the political process.

There is no doubt that villagers themselves are acutely aware of individual differences. As one informant put it, "Peasants know their men like they know their plants, down to the number of seeds in any given type." This intimate knowledge of individual differences appears in the naming system.[1] Names, particularly nicknames, reflect physical differences, deformities, personality quirks, items in personal histories dating from childhood, and any extraordinary characteristic worthy (or unworthy) of comment. Such individual differences are taken into account during the process of reconciling disputants in the guest house and are manipulated to achieve the desired end. But though this is true, villagers deliberately play down idiosyncratic differences when it comes to explaining any particular set of events; instead they magnify social structural differences and the prevailing pattern of grudges. A particular dispute between, say, a shepherd and a cultivator, is seldom explained in terms of one's heedlessness and the other's propensity to take offense, although these attributes are recognized in the nicknames they bear, but is traced to past incidents involving members of the patrilineages to which the individuals belong.[2]

Analytically there is also good reason not to exaggerate the importance of individual differences. The analysis of the politics in Kufr al-Ma indicates that although the movement basis of polities has weakened, it remains an ongoing reality. An important attribute of movement polities is the substitutability of leadership: no leader (here, mayor) is indispensable; others can and do take his place in his absence and in his presence upstage him, though they may not often choose to do so. We are not justified in overly emphasizing personality attributes or the presence of charismatic qualities, but individual differences do exist and do have a significant impact on politics, even movement politics. This chapter will be devoted to describing that impact and analyzing it in relation to the concepts of influence and leadership.

When he discusses political middlemen in the context of local-level politics Friedrich argues for recognizing and taking into account "minimal personality variables."[3] He asserts that "through the analysis of the cultural ideals and models of a particular leader" and the "topical life history," "politically decisive personality traits" can be identified.[4] In his Ph.D. thesis Friedrich made an interesting attempt to accomplish this considerable task. The present chapter makes no attempt to reconstruct a topical life history for either mayor or their "substitutes" in a systematic fashion, nor does it address itself to the psychoanalytical implications of leadership.[5] Neither my professional training nor my data base allow such an endeavor, and in that sense this chapter falls short of Friedrich's goal both in intent and substance. However, this chapter does reflect his assumption that individual differences are important and that the nonprofessional can examine them for the purpose of analyzing politics. I will focus on the individual's knowledge and effective use of custom, the degree to which his behavior approximates the cultural ideal, i.e., is "model" behavior, and conversely the degree to which his behavior is idiosyncratic. I will analyze all such differences within the framework of the concept of influence, viewed sociologically and with special reference to leadership attributes.[6]

As Barnard has pointed out, the concept of influence can best be understood with reference to the more embracing concept of authority. Authority, he argues, involves two aspects: the personal—acceptance of the order; and the objective aspect—the character of the communication by virtue of which it is accepted.[7] He notes that most persons are disposed to grant authority because they dislike personal responsibility and that the practical difficulties of operating organizations relate to this dislike rather than to the excessive desire of individuals to assume responsibility for their own or others' acts within the organization.[8] He argues further that the "authority of position" must be distinguished from "the authority of leadership." The former emanates from the objective aspect—the office, hence the importance ascribed to time, place, dress, and other circumstances of the communication; the authority of leadership, on the other hand, emanates from knowledge and understanding of the individual rather than any position he may or may not occupy. Barnard argues that a person has "influence" when people obey him apart from any authority he has as a result of his position.[9]

Bierstadt has phrased the same argument in somewhat different terms. Authority, he says, is power attached to statuses. However within any formal social organization, informal interaction takes place in which the prestige of statuses gives way to the esteem for persons. Influence relates to this "intrinsic" and "personal" interaction rather than to the "extrinsic" and "categorical" relations governing members of associations.[10] Influence, Bierstadt argues, is persuasive, while "power" is coercive. Power is located in groups and expresses itself in intergroup relations; influence is located in interpersonal relations, where differences of temperament become important. For Bierstadt, power has three "sources": numbers of people, social organization, and resources (e.g., money, land).[11]

Taking another tack, Warner argues that the basis of leadership is not wealth or occupation but the range and intensity of interaction. He developed his "reputational technique" in order to delimit the "in-group" that leads. For him, leadership is based first on recognition of such leadership (only the "ins" can tell you about the "ins") and second on interaction with leaders.[12] These three authors, then, provide three useful points of departure for the analysis of the man of influence: influence operates through persuasion rather than coercion; it flows out of a man's personal qualities rather than out of his position; and the influential is identified primarily by his peers and by his interaction with them.

If one defines power as the capacity to control men and resources, and one specializes the term authority to refer to obeisance elicited as a result of holding a position, then the relationship of power, authority, and influence become clearer. A leader's power derives from his command over numbers and wealth and to the social organizational cohesion of the core and support elements that back him. A leader's authority comes from the right to make decisions and represent groups which his position confers upon him. A leader's influence emerges from the effectiveness of his personal interactions, which in turn have their source in his knowledge, the degree to which he approximates the cultural ideals of the group (or its model personality), the idiosyncratic aspects of his personality, and the social structural appropriateness of the roles he plays (e.g., in a society attributing great importance to age differences an elder exerts more influence than a young man).[13] In what follows I will make a few preliminary remarks about the sources of power and authority in Middle Eastern peasant communities, but principally I will analyze influence and leaders as men of influence, first generally in the Middle Eastern context, then in detail regarding Kufr al-Ma.

Although the diversity of the Middle East with respect to ethnicity, social stratification, tribalization, technological modernization, and proximity to urban centers makes generalization difficult even within the peasant sector, pertinent ethnographic literature provides some material about the sources of power for local-level village leaders. The number of sons a man has is important not only for their economic contribution to the household and the prestige they confer upon their father but also for their politico-military support. The height of the father's power in this sense occurs at the maturity of his sons, but the birth of grandsons signals the beginning of his decline and the split of the family into separate units. In villages where most employed men are engaged in agriculture and related occupations, land ownership is a key political resource. In many parts of the Middle East the terms for leaders or "men" are etymologically related to the terms for particular types of land plots. In Jordan *zalameh* used to refer to a fully mature man (capable of performing a full work load and bearing arms) as well as a traditional land unit; in many parts of the Middle East *za'īm* refers to a prominent political boss with a certain localized political base, while the term *zi'āmet* used to refer to a certain kind of land grant given to loyal subjects by the Ottoman state. The literature also suggests, however, that wealth, landed or otherwise, is hard to acquire and difficult to retain. The Islamic rule of equal inheritance among siblings of the same sex may contribute to this problem, but uneven agricultural production due to a changeable, unreliable climate and sudden declines in wealth related to the vagaries of political fortunes and cases of honor may be more important. The fact that many of the really rich and successful men move to town also probably reduces the importance of wealth within the village community.

Although wealth is an important source of power, it does not necessarily elevate men to leadership or even influence; much depends on how the wealth is expended. Many wealthy men who lack other traditional attributes of influence are controlled by those who possess these attributes, probably because wealth, particularly wealth gained as a result of new opportunities and occupations, must be legitimized by traditional mechanisms: e.g., the proper marriages, the adoption of the proper attitudes and demeanor, the acquisition of traditional skills (e.g., the capacity for mediation), and the extension of hospitality in appropriate settings. In Jordan and many other parts of the Middle East, a wealthy villager is expected to open and maintain a guest room where coffee is served on a regular basis. The village notables attend the leading guest houses on a nightly basis to discuss local and national affairs and the latest gossip. The formalities of preparing coffee in the guest house, of pronouncing the appropriate politeness formulas (after drinking coffee, prayer, sneezing, the entrance of a newcomer, etc.), of seating arrangement and rearrangement to take account of differences of social status, and the absence of women lend an aura of importance to these sessions. The values of the culture are played out on a nightly basis in a semiformal context. Men celebrate the most important events of the life cycle and the annual events of the religious cycle by an effusive display of hospitality which often includes the slaughter of a sheep or goat. At the same time the atmosphere of these nightly sessions is one of close kinship and camaraderie, with all the men sitting close together on the floor round the four walls of the guest house. A man who maintains a regular guest house becomes the center of intense social interaction, an esteemed personage, and a man of influence. Indeed, the number of men of influence can be calculated by the number of on-going guest houses. A wealthy man who refuses to maintain a guest house (i.e., who refuses to extend hospitality) is not visited and is seldom consulted. He is not a man of influence, although he may possess other attributes of power and authority, and his low rate of social interaction with other influentials matches their failure to include him as one of their company, as Warner would have predicted. Not only does power not automatically translate into influence but in order to achieve influence, some power (here economic resources) must be surrendered. Indeed for initially wealthy Middle Eastern peasants there may be an inverse relationship between power and influence. One more point emerges from a review of the literature. In the village context a leader rarely decides by himself; he invariably consults others, and the guest house is the arena par excellence for developing consensus and martialling public opinion. Moreover making decisions is not the traditional leader's most important attribute. That is, the authority of position seems less important than acts performed by the influential, e.g., offering hospitality, mediating disputes, performing rituals, and contracting marriages (acting as go-between). Indeed there is evidence that the politically ambitious, i.e., those that seek to occupy formal positions, are precisely those who do not have influence.

Zecher's study of men of influence in a medium-sized town in Lebanon illustrates a number of these points and isolates a key attribute of the influential man—his capacity to please.[14] The man of influence can do things ordinary men cannot do because he has ties with government officials, he has eloquence, and he has popular support. Men of influence can get things done for the people who come to them for favors, but rarely are they able to resolve problems alone. By acting as a go-between, the man of influence personalizes the ties of the townman and peasant with the impersonal bureaucracies of the cities and the capital. Although he contacts others to satisfy a request, a man of influence sacrifices his own time and money in the process. He keeps an "open house," and all of the surrounding villagers who have identified themselves as his supporters have eaten at his table. This hospitality assumes, of course, that the man of influence has extensive land and/or stock holdings. Although men of influence are often called upon to settle disputes, they are reluctant to do so for fear of alienating supporters. Moreover although they may act to conciliate and suggest, they do not make decisions.

Although Zecher's man of influence can cause trouble and is known to have "waved the stick" (i.e., he has power), he operates principally by *musāyara*, "the art of pleasing." "He talks about things people like to hear and he talks in a way that is pleasing to the ear."[15] He never refuses to take up a request and never admits his inability to deal with a problem. The practice of musayara involves trying to please everyone, appearing to agree with claims and opinions, not confronting others with unpleasant news directly, not telling people what you think, not always acting according to the merits of the case, and not shaming others. Musayara also involves the fulfillment of all formal social obligations: attendance at funerals, weddings, and religious celebrations. Finally musayara involves the ability to solve people's problems, which in turn requires great patience and the ability to listen.[16]

In many respects Zecher's men of influence do not resemble those in Kufr al-Ma: the men of influence in Kufr al-Ma do not have numerous or important ties with bureaucrats in towns or in the capital; they do not have the ability "to wave the stick," at least in the same sense (i.e., they lack power); and they seldom give advice about education and politics (few villagers have educational options and voting campaigns and elections are infrequent). On the other hand, men of influence in Kufr al-Ma, like those of Zecher, do give advice about religious matters, about investment of money, and about traditional problems, e.g., marriage, divorce, inheritance, and agriculture; they do maintain open houses; and they also act as go-betweens both within and outside the village. Unlike Zecher's men of influence, those in Kufr al-Ma are consulted about intimate family problems and they are consulted at an early stage of the problem (Zecher's men of influence are consulted at a very late stage), probably because they are relatives, friends, and neighbors of those who come for consultation and because social status differences are minimal compared with Zecher's town. Men of influence in Kufr al-Ma not only settle disputes; they regard mediation as a duty, a primary attribute of a both "good man" and a "wise man," and undertake the task without hesitation. Most important the influentials of both locales recognize the importance of musayara and departure from its main tenets has important consequences for the prestige of the influential and the outcome of the political competition.

The main conclusion of this brief sketch, then, is that among Middle Eastern peasants the sources of power and the authority of position are far less important for the study of leadership than one might assume and, conversely, the role of influentials is much more important.

Influentials in Kufr al-Ma: Substitute Leaders

In the discussion of influentials I make frequent reference to old-style model behavior, a source of influence I contrast with new-style model behavior on table 7. Chapter two described briefly the important functions of the Shaykh of Tibne in arbitrating disputes, offering protection, and acting as a point of redistribution for surplus. Chapter four sketched the stages in the transformation from shaykhdom to mukhtarate. Chapter five analyzed the role the present-day descendant of the Shaykh plays in local-level politics, and the present chapter has commented on the importance of the guest house as an arena for the affirmation of traditional values and for the gaining of influence. It remains here to elaborate on the substance and style of old-time political leadership. The traditional leader excelled in qualities that all men aspired to and practiced to a lesser degree. Foremost among these qualities was hospitality. The head of a household stored all animal products (clarified butter, cheese) in the loft of his house and hardly ever expended them except for guests. Indeed the contents of the loft, including the flour that was stored there (flour was in short supply and considered a luxury), was referred to as "guest-work" (*shughl Tārish*). Meat was the most prized item of hospitality; at harvest time any man who could afford to do so invited his kinsmen and neighbors to help him harvest, after which he slaughtered a goat that he had staked to the threshing ground and made a feast for all who participated. A measure of wheat known as "the blessed measure" (*sā' al-baraka*) was distributed to every harvester at this time. In addition any prominent guest who happened to be in the village at harvest time was given some wheat and a bale of straw. The old-time Shaykh could indulge in hospitality on a grand scale, for he possessed much land and many sheep and goats, which were always being augmented by his supporters in the form of gifts. Even today villagers say, commenting on the fact that less than a tenth of all households have proper guest houses, "The guest house requires porridge. It's not a masquerade." Wealth in land and livestock was critical for political leadership. Apart from the Shaykh of Tibne, the politics of hospitality involved all other generous men in debt which they carried from one year to the next. The debt, however, was handled by long-term reciprocity, with the expected return hospitality put off until the next marriage, funeral, or religious festival. The extension of more modest hospitality as well as charity was also appropriate during and immediately after the fast month of Ramadan.[17]

Various social and cultural sanctions were available against those who disregarded the norms of hospitality and generosity; people scorned the miser in the course of ordinary gossip and the preacher did so formally during the Friday congregational sermon. If generosity was not possible, then the concealment of wealth was regarded as essential in order to avoid envy. Large supplies were stored out of sight in the loft; small items were placed on built-in shelves along the walls that were shielded from view by embroidered pieces of cloth. When grocery shops opened in the 1920s, goods bought there were taken away covered with paper or in an opaque vessel. Certain customs existed to preserve the norm of hospitality even when its practice was impossible; one such was the second invitation. Since the ethical norm required everyone to offer hospitality whether he could afford to or not, the host was supposed to send a second invitation by word of mouth early on the day the guest was to come; if the guest did not receive the second invitation, he assumed that the first invitation was merely an act of politeness and let it go at that.

Besides possession of wealth and extension of it in appropriate forms and on appropriate occasions, three other qualities were essential for the old-style leader. He had to be eloquent and patient, for these were the qualities that made a man effective in the long and tiring give-and-take of debate in the guest house and established his reputation as a skilled mediator and a wise man. He also had to have a reputation for valor that he earned by knowing how to handle a rifle in skirmishes with Bedouin or hostile villagers or government forces; this reputation could also be earned by daring and successful thievery from the same. Finally the Shaykh of Tibne and to a lesser extent clan leaders had to be able to raise a certain number of armed men in case of a threatened or actual skirmish with another group.

Today, as outlined in chapters two and five, economic differentiation, occupational mobility, the establishment of central government, and the abolition of the musha' system of land tenure has changed the sources of power and influence and altered the form and substance of local-level political leadership. Shaykhs no longer rule the countryside, giving protection and hospitality in return for economic contributions and armed support; rather mukhtars operate as functionaries and intercalary leaders, each for his own village. Since the registration of land ownership in individual hands and the establishment of centralized government, it is not nearly so important to be a clan member in good standing, for neither protection nor land rights are the prerogative of the clan. Moreover the numerous government offices in the subdistrict center provide alternatives to clan elders for many problems of concern to villagers. Thus although the mukhtar is not without sources of power and influence, he has no way of enforcing his will on recalcitrant clansmen: they can cut off visiting relations, refuse to pay dues, and (although few have chosen to do this) move out of the clan quarter. According to the new style of political leadership, the mayor can be a poor man (as long as others in the clan have economic resources they are willing to expend) or a young man. He does not have to have a reputation for generosity or valor, although such a reputation would contribute to his influence, but he must have some education and he must be town-wise, i.e., he must appreciate the townsman's way of life and he must be adroit enough to deal with government officials in government offices both to ward off the consequences of unwanted government action and to solicit government aid.

The following discussion of substitute leaders does not refer at all to a number of other individuals who make prominent contributions to their respective political teams. For instance several men in all three clans, but particularly in the Yasin clan, act as elders and maintain guest houses that are the locus of political activity. Other clan members provide economic support for the mayorship (see chapter three); still others act as messengers and as unofficial police for the mayor (besides the two watchmen who are unofficially charged to the mayors). Each clan, but again particularly Yasin, has men who serve in lower echelon bureaucratic posts or as officers in the army—such men provide useful contacts for their clansmen. Finally some individuals provide logistical support for their clansmen: the market-town beanery is where Yasin members gather when they go to town; a grocery shop owned by a Yasin member in Deir Abu Said provides a similar hangout for clan members. Of course a number of clan members, far from supporting their mayor, have openly opposed him.

Some individuals who apparently deserve to be considered as substitute leaders because of their official positions have been excluded. For instance, twelve members of various clans were selected as members of the incipient village council, including Shaykh Basim, who was later chosen as its head. At least four were picked as "dummies," persons who could be easily controlled and instructed by others; some of them were barely literate retired elders, others were shopkeepers, others were young unemployeds. What they all had in common was a considerable amount of leisure, which released them for such activity. Even Shaykh Basim can in some respects be considered a dummy rather than a genuine substitute leader—when I asked the Dumi mayor why Basim was chosen as council head, he replied that Basim was inexperienced and he, the mayor, would be behind him and would "train him," would "teach him." However Basim had other attributes, which qualified him as a substitute leader and man of influence.

What follows is a brief sketch of each substitute leader in terms of his principal attributes of power and influence:

Shaykh Basim

In 1960 Shaykh Basim was thirty-five years old. He was a magician and folk doctor. According to his own claims and those of all villagers with whom I spoke, he practiced only white magic. That is, he did not pronounce spells or conduct divinations for the purpose of doing harm. It was said about him that he had been sick for a year and a half; the symptoms described were those of epilepsy; villagers said that during this period he had been attacked by the *jinn*[18] and that by the end of that period, after consulting numerous other doctors, folk doctors, and magicians—all without avail—and after a long period of estrangement from his wife, he finally prevailed over the jinn. Thenceforth he was able to call upon them for aid during divinations. Basim had a reputation outside the village and clients from as far away as Amman came to consult him about their physical and mental ailments. In 1960 he lived in an ordinary adobe house with typically sparse furnishings. By 1965 his guest room conspicuously displayed modern furnishings (chairs and tables, a huge wardrobe closet, a glass crockery closet, a stove, spoons displayed in a special cloth holder along the wall) that were absent from almost all peasant households in the village, though they were common in town. Basim now shaved with a safety razor; I was the only other person who did so. Basim had opened a grocery shop in the village by 1965; he claimed to be the first shopkeeper to sell fresh vegetables in it. By 1965 he was also the owner-renter of a tractor (one of three in the village). He had five years of formal education in the primary school in Deir Abu Said. Both his mother and his wife were from an important lineage of Beni 'Amr; his mother was also a midwife. Basim was solidly built, but his outstanding features were his high-pitched childlike laugh and his wide jet-black eyes; he had the visage as well as the cleverness of a magician. As table 7 indicates, Basim's addition of shopkeeping and tractor-renting to his magical skills increased his economic resources. His high rating on knowledge of custom was not due to his mastery of tribal or Islamic law or local history or agricultural lore but to his monopoly of magical knowledge; many other villagers could write amulets, but only he could summon the jinn. Basim ranked fairly high in terms of model behavior, new style. That is, he was a pioneer in material modern-

Table 7
Rating of Leaders According to Sources of Power and Influence

SOURCES OF POWER (RESOURCES)

	Economic	Demographic	Social Organiza-tional
ABU FAYID	*1++	1	1
ABU KAMIL	2 −3	1	1
SHAYKH LUQMAN	3→2	1	1
YUSUF AL-TULUQ	1+	1 −2	1
ABU YASIN	4→2	1	1
ABU TAHIR	2 −/3+	3+	3
MAHMOUD ABD AL-QADIR &	2 −	1	1
ABD AL-QADIR AL-ALI	4	1	1
SHAYKH BASIM	3→2	3	3
MUHAMMAD AL-HILU	4	3	2
FAYID AL-HAMAD	1 −	1	1
SULAYMAN HASAN	1	2+	4
MUHAMMAD AL-YUSUF	2 −/3+	2	4
IKHLEYF AL-MUFLIH	2	1 −2	1

* Numbers are ratings on a scale of 1–4 with the former indicating a high rating (e.g., many economic resources) and the latter indicating a low rating. See the explanation of the basis of rating for each category given on the next page. Arrows indicate a shift in rating from 1959 to 1966.

Explanation of the Basis of Rating for Categories Listed on Table 7

1. Economic Resources were rated on the basis of two scales, one for annual income and one for land ownership in dunums. An annual income of 400 or more Jordanian dinars received a rating of 1; 300–400, a rating of 2; 200–300, a rating of 3; less than 200 a rating of 4. Land ownership of more than 300 dunums received a rating of 1; 200–300 dunums a rating of 2; 50–200 dunums a rating of 3; and less than 50 dunums a rating of 4. The final rating was an average of the two ratings.

2. Demographic Resources were rated on the basis of the relative size of the influential patrilineage and patriclan. See table three for the relative numbers involved.

3. Social Organizational Resources were rated on the basis of my own estimation of the relative social cohesion of the influential's patrilineages and patriclans after sixteen months of participant observation.

4. Idiosyncratic Behavior refers to personality attributes peculiar to each of the influentials. The rating was based on my own observation of such attributes and my own impressions of whether they strongly abetted, abetted, detracted, or greatly detracted from the individual's influence.

SOURCES OF INFLUENCE

Idiosyncratic Behavior	Knowledge of Custom	Model Behavior		Structural Appropriateness	
		Old	New	Old	New
4	1	2+	1 −	2	1
3	1	1	2+/1 −	2	1
2	1	2	2	3	1
1	1	1	2 − /3+	1	3
1	1	1 −2	3→3+	1+	3+
4 −	2 −	3	2 −3	3 −4	1 − /2+
2	3	4	1	3	1
4	2	2+	3	1	3 −
1	1	3	2	3	2
4	2	2+	2 −	1	3+
4	2 −3	3	2 −	2	1
1	1	2	3	2	3+
4	2 −	3	3 −	3 −4	4
4	2 −	3+	3 −	2 −	4

5. Knowledge of Custom refers to five categories of knowledge and my own evaluation of the influential's expertness in them: local history, tribal law, Islamic law, agricultural custom, and magic.

6. Old-Style Model Behavior was rated on the basis of my own evaluation of the degree to which the influential lived up to the ideal norms of the village concerning the following: the offering of hospitality, the visiting of relatives and neighbors, skill in mediation, piety, the practice of modesty, the giving of advice, the taking of an antipolitical stance (see chapter five), and the practice of musayara. The final rating was based on balancing off the ratings for the specific items.

7. New-Style Model Behavior was rated on the basis of the presence or absence of the following attributes for each influential: literacy, government position, contacts with local-level government officials, education of sons beyond the junior high school level, investment and entrepreneurship, and material modernization.

8. Old-Style Social Structural Appropriateness was rated on the basis of the presence or absence of the following attributes for each influential: advanced age (to be considered an elder), parental status (father of grown sons), possession of important patrilineal ties, possession of important matrilateral ties, and possession of important affinal ties.

9. New-Style Social Structural Appropriateness was rated on the basis of the presence or absence of two attributes: relative youth and important links outside the village.

ization and he was a successful entrepreneur. But in terms of model old-style behavior, he was ranked low: he did not offer regular hospitality; he had little skill as a mediator; and he was lax in his enforcement of the modesty code—often his wife remained in the room in my presence and in that of other strangers.

Abd al-Qadir al-Ali and Mahmoud Abd al-Qadir

Abd al-Qadir al-Ali, age fifty-one in 1960, was a prominent elder of Dumi. For many years he had been a livestock merchant, buying sheep and goats in Transjordan and selling them in Palestine. Later he was a butcher in Irbid, the nearest market town; finally he settled down as a shopkeeper in Kufr al-Ma in partnership with another clansman, Muhammad al-Hilu (see below). Abd al-Qadir was illiterate and, as table 7 indicates his annual income was less than 200 pounds a year. Mahmoud Abd al-Qadir, age twenty in 1960, was his son. In 1960 he had just graduated from the teacher's college in Ramallah and was teaching in Palestine; by 1965 he had become the schoolmaster of the primary school in his home village, Kufr al-Ma. Mahmoud and his father's main resources were demographic and social organizational; they came from one of the largest and most cohesive lineages of Dumi. I have dealt with them together because they complement one another both in terms of resources and influence attributes and because although considered separately they are not substitute leaders, together they combine their attributes. Mahmoud's regular salary as a schoolteacher provided the wherewithal to maintain his father's guest house and his age, advanced education, government position, belief in progress and outspokenness in claiming the village's rights made him a model for new-style village leadership.[19] But, as table 7 indicates, Mahmoud rates low in terms of old-style model ladership and old-style social structural appropriateness. His father rates high on precisely these attributes: he is an accepted mediator for his clan, he is pious, and he maintains one of the few guest houses in the clan; his age, his parental status (father of three grown sons), his membership in a large and prominent lineage of the clan, and the marriages of his brother and daughter into a lineage of 'Amr and his son into an important lineage of Yasin make his leadership structurally appropriate according to the old style. Abd al-Qadir al-Ali has a lackluster personality, but his son is sharp, agile, and effective in debate, although a trifle forward considering his age in a culture that respects seniority.

Muhammad al-Hilu

Muhammad al-Hilu, age fifty in 1960, is a prominent elder of Dumi and the partner of Abd al-Qadir al-Ali in the grocery shop. He had been a fisherman in Haifa for four years as a young man, later a builder in his home village, and finally a shopkeeper. His resources are much more meager than Abd al-Qadir's, for he comes from a smaller lineage and his income is not yet supplemented by a son with a white-collar job. Like Abd al-Qadir, he is a highly respected pious elder who maintains a guest house and is a recognized mediator. Although he does not rate high according to the norms of new-style village leadership, he rates higher than Abd al-Qadir, since he is literate and not only has a son who has finished teacher's college but, exceptionally in the village, also a daughter who has finished primary school. Muhammad rates high in terms of old-style structural appropriateness—in terms of his age, parental status, and marriage into the largest lineage of Yasin. Both he and Abd al-Qadir used the profits from their shop to finance their sons' high school educations. Muhammad was the only shopkeeper I ever witnessed reading the Quran in his shop during a slack period.

Fayid al-Hamad

Fayid al-Hamad, age thirty-two in 1960, is of the same Dumi lineage as Mahmoud Abd al-Qadir; consequently, he has the same social organizational and demographic resources; in addition, he has the economic resources provided by a regular army salary and a large bloc of land in the village held jointly by his father and brothers. He served in the Arab Legion from 1947–50, quit the service, opened a shop in the village for five years, then reenlisted. Ten years earlier, at age twenty-two, he served as mayor for two years. He had five years of primary education in Deir Abu Said and being young and town-wise (he had been a livestock merchant between Transjordan and Palestine in addition to his army service there) rated high in terms of new-style social structural appropriateness and new-style model behavior. In addition he had links into a prominent family of the area through his mother's marriage and into an important landed 'Amr lineage through his own marriage, which combined with his own lineage affiliation, gave him a high rating in old-style structural appropriateness as well (see table 7). The fact that he was on duty away from the village most of the year limited his political effectiveness, but his two brothers, one a shopkeeper, the other who acted informally as a messenger and policeman for the Dumi mayor, represented the interests of the family in his absence.

Yusuf al-Tuluq

Yusuf al-Tuluq, age fifty-two in 1960, was the largest landowner in Kufr al-Ma and also one of its most colorful figures: he was a persuasive speaker, an accomplished raconteur, a charming host, and a happy spirit. He had served as mayor of the village for several years during and after World War II and undoubtedly would have served again had not a fall from a horse rendered him paraplegic. Apart from six months in the secular school of Deir Abu Said, his education was strictly traditional—two years of instruction in the Islamic kuttab; however, he was able to read the Quran and the newspaper and his intelligence made up considerably for his meager education. Yusuf was also the largest livestock holder in the village, possessing a hundred head of sheep; in addition he possessed one of the few pure-bred horses. Yusuf was as high-ranking in his model traditional behavior as he was in his material resources (see table 7): he maintained an on-going guest house of first rank, he was a prominent mediator and giver of advice, and his knowledge of local history, tribal law, and village custom was considerable. Although his age, meager education, lack of entrepreneurship, and failure to lead in material modernization does not give him too high a rating in new-style model behavior, his intelligence and the contacts and prestige he has as a result of his son's position as clerk of court in the market town does not give him too low a rating either. Although his demographic resources are somewhat lower than other substitute leaders of his clan e.g., Shaykh Luqman, Abu Kamil, Abu Fayid (since he comes from a smaller lineage), his age, parental status (father of grown sons), patrilineal clan ties and matrilateral ties to a prominent Dumi lineage give him a high rating in old-style structural appropriateness. Although Yusuf's charismatic qualities make him popular among many villagers, his wealth makes him envied, and disliked among some. Compared to other villagers, Yusuf was little traveled. His wealth made it unnecessary to supplement his income by working in Palestine. Therefore unlike most men of his generation, he has had no significant contact with westerners (Englishmen and Jews).

Shaykh Luqman

Shaykh Luqman, age thirty-two in 1960, was the village preacher and prayer leader and had been since the age of twenty-four. He had an unusual life history in that he was one of the few village men who defied his father's occupational choice (as ploughman) and pursued his own vocation (man of learning and preacher) even at the cost of being expelled from his household.[20] Luqman studied for six years in the secular primary school in Deir Abu Said and continued his Islamic education with a preacher in the subdistrict capital for another four years. By 1965 he had doubled his income as a result of a monthly stipend the government provided to preachers and he was confirmed as the drawer-up of marriage contracts, *ma'thūn*, for the district. By 1965 he had renovated his traditional small two-room house by raising the ceiling, installing chairs and tables in the guest room, and a large built-in bookcase with a sliding glass cover. He also dressed in clothes of good quality as compared with his rather shoddy dress of five years earlier. He was the first in the village to buy a water meter and pipes for the purpose of getting piped running water to his house and was active in encouraging others to do likewise. He subscribed to an Islamic weekly and occasionally bought the daily newspaper sold in Deir Abu Said. Since he came from one of the largest and most closely knit lineages of Yasin, he had demographic and social organizational resources to match his new-won economic resources. Although he had no special knowledge of tribal law, local history, or agricultural custom, and was not a noted mediator, he had a good general knowledge of local customs and, of course, he had an expert's knowledge of Islamic law and ethics—no one matched his knowledge of these matters in the village. On that account he was frequently consulted. Like Shaykh Basim, his monopoly of a special type of knowledge made him a man of influence. Shaykh Luqman's influence was, however, much more extensive and institutionalized than Basim's, for he delivered the congregational sermon in the village mosque every Friday. Since attendance at the Friday congregational prayer was a duty for all village men, Shaykh Luqman's views were heard by every family in the village. In the pulpit his personality was transformed from that of a rather quiet, earnest, knowledgeable young man to that of a powerful evangelist. Because he was straightforward about laying blame on those who had committed wrongdoing (though he never mentioned names in his sermons, everyone knew the identity of those whose acts he condemned) and therefore, did not practice musayara (the art of pleasing) and because he often preached against acts and principles villagers regarded as proper and fundamental (for instance the primacy of kinship and clanship), Luqman was not given the highest rating (though he was still high) in terms of old-style model behavior. On the other hand, although he did not have a government position and was not an entrepreneur, his pioneering in the material aspects of modernization, his contacts with government officials, particularly in the religious court, his literacy, and his forward-looking views on many matters gave him a rather high rating in terms of new-style model behavior. Interestingly enough, in the ideological questionnaire the results of which are given in table 8, Luqman was the only person in the village (out of twenty asked) who supported the unqualified right of free speech.

Abu Kamil

Abu Kamil, age forty in 1960, was a respected man of the largest lineage of Yasin. He had been a village shopkeeper for fifteen years, but by 1960 he had worked for several years as a clerk-usher in the religious court in Deir Abu Said. At that time he maintained the most active guest house in the clan and in so doing contributed critical economic backing to the Yasin mayorship, because at that time the Yasin mayor was impoverished. Abu Kamil had six years of primary education in the secular school in Deir Abu Said in addition to one year of traditional Islamic education from his father, a former village preacher and prayer leader. Abu Kamil had gone to Palestine for the purpose of working only once and had remained only forty days. Compared to other men of his generation he was not well traveled. Several years before he had served as mayor of the village for one year, and in 1965 he turned down the offer of becoming the first head of the incipient village council, claiming that his work with his tractors and his orchard in the Jordan valley took him out of the village a good part of the time and did not afford him the leisure to serve in that position. By 1965 he had resigned his position in the court, taken out a loan from the bank, bought a tractor and a stonecutter, and with one of his sons was making a living by renting them out to the area's cultivators. He was using the profits from the enterprise to finance his son's medical education in Turkey and to modernize his home: he replaced its stone and adobe walls and floors with cement, installed a cement ceiling, and added a colorful painted grille around each window. He previously bought land in the Jordan valley, where, again with a bank loan, he had planted fruit trees. His second son also seems to have developed some minor entrepreneurial skills: he was working in Lebanon selling goods and stamping farm produce. Abu Kamil had a wide knowledge of custom, including local history, Islamic law, and tribal law. Abu Kamil was also a model of old-style behavior: he was pious, hospitable, a recognized mediator, a giver of advice, a modest man (he protected his womenfolk), and a practitioner of musayara—but not if it involved dishonesty. His behavior rated high according to new-style norms too: although he had traveled little and did not have a government position, he was highly literate, was giving one of his sons a higher education, was engaged in material modernization, and, above all, was a pioneering entrepreneur—he was the first in the village to buy a tractor for entrepreneurial purposes and one of the first to take out interest-bearing bank loans. As recently as 1960 prominent elders in his own clan had condemned such an act as violating the religious law against usury. Abu Kamil told me that he preferred his former job as clerk-usher in the religious court but that his present job as contractor of machinery was more remunerative and had a future, whereas his previous job had none. He said he worked harder now, but his mind was not always as occupied. It seems ironical, but is also significant, for those who claim that tradition weighs too heavily on the minds of peasants that Shaykh Basim, the village magician, bought the "saint's tree" in the village, chopped it up for firewood, and sold it in his shop and that Abu Kamil, the son of the preacher, pious man and former clerk of the religious court, is repairing tractors and paying out usury (interest) to the bank.

Abu Fayid

Abu Fayid, age forty-two in 1960, is the civil court clerk referred to several times in the last chapter. In some respects he adheres to a traditional style of life: when in the village he wears the shawl and headband, he prepares sugarless coffee on a nightly basis in his guest house; he curtains the village by affording hospitality to its guests; he is recognized as a mediator; he gives advice to villagers about a wide variety of matters, and he responds to appeals based on patrilineal and matrilateral ties, though sometimes reluctantly and unenthusiastically.[21] It was Abu Fayid's extension of hospitality in his guest house in 1965 and the years following that allowed the Yasin mayor to maintain the full-blown mayorship, just as it was Abu Kamil's extension of hospitality that allowed it to operate before that time. Abu Fayid also practiced musayara—more so than the Yasin mukhtar, whom he chided on a number of occasions for berating members of the village publicly; it was also Abu Fayid who cautioned the mayor against going to the district officer in protest against the subdistrict officer's voiding of the school land sales contract. Thus Abu Fayid received a high rating in terms of old-style model behavior; he did not receive a top rating (see table 7), however, for his long residence outside the village had led to certain views that did not accord with traditional village views. Since the age of nineteen Abu Fayid had lived mainly outside the village. He had worked as a laborer, shopkeeper, and watchman in Palestine. With the Yasin mayor he had enlisted as a revolutionary in the Arab rebellion against the British in 1937, and he and the mayor were imprisoned for eight months by Jordanian authorities for continued support of the rebellion. He enlisted with the Arab Legion at the beginning of World War Two and served three years, during which time he was sent to Syria, Iraq, and Egypt. He was employed in the Jordanian customs in 1945 and lived in the border town of Ramtha; he was accused of taking bribes in this post and removed; subsequently, he was cleared by the courts and became a clerk of civil court, serving in various Jordanian towns for fifteen years. During this long period of employment outside the village he developed many "political" opinions which he was not reluctant to voice (this may have been the reason he was charged with bribery). These opinions are recorded in table 8 and will be discussed later. The significant fact here is that most villagers are either apolitical or antipolitical; they frown upon political party activity and political views attributed to it in all its forms. On the other hand, Abu Fayid possessed the key attributes of new-style model behavior: he was literate, had a government position, and many government contacts. He was giving his son a university education and was the leading entrepreneur in the village. He owned shares in a bus company, an electricity company, a gasoline station, a flour mill, and an oil press. He had over a hundred acres of land both in the village and the Jordan valley, all bought—he had inherited nothing from his father, who had died in prison after shooting a member of the local gendarmerie. His life history is that of a bucolic Horatio Alger for he started as a shepherd, became a sharecropper, then an urban laborer, then a soldier, then a government clerk, and finally, in village terms, a large landowner and investor; his income was almost double that of the next wealthiest man, Yusuf al-Tuluq. Although he had many attributes of a village way of life, he had many others that were distinctively a townsman's: he bought the daily newspaper, he took frequently unpopular political stands,[22] he discussed international affairs (e.g., the pros and cons of the Vietnam war), at work he always dressed in the garb of the bureaucrat—conservative European-style business suit, white shirt, necktie and shiny black shoes; and he firmly believed in status gained through achievement rather than ascription (as did most villagers).[23] Because of Abu Fayid's considerable external resources—his salary and his influence in government offices—and because he used them against the opposing village coalition (see his prominent role in the school lands and village council sequences), he was envied and disliked by many villagers in the other coalition. Because his resources were not only internal (the demographic and social organizational resources that came with land ownership and membership in a prominent and cohesive village lineage) but also external, he could not be got at through the tactics usually applied in village politics; only the destruction of his external resources would nullify his effectiveness. This is why the slanderous letter was sent to the authorities—if its charges had been accepted, his government position, his influence in government offices, and his salary would have been destroyed at one and the same time.

Sulayman Hasan

Sulayman Hasan, age forty-five in 1960, had twice served as mayor of the village. Since he was a member of Beni 'Amr and the mayorship had passed to Dumi and Yasin, he was not a substitute leader for either coalition, but he continued to be a man of influence. After Yusuf al-Tuluq, he was the largest landowner in the village. Like Yusuf his relative wealth had freed him from the necessity to travel or gain wide occupational experience outside the village. However he did have five years of primary school education in addition to three years of traditional Islamic instruction, and he maintained a guest house, where he prepared coffee on a regular basis. For the last fifteen years he had maintained a village grocery shop, while his sons tilled his land. Sulayman's social organizational resources were rated very low (see table 7), for his clan was plagued with grudges which prevented much cooperation for local political purposes. Sulayman had contributed to this internal dissension by refusing to certify a fellow clansman as an eligible marriage partner for a nubile girl of the clan—he had wished the girl to marry his own son. As a result of the furor his refusal aroused, he had to resign the mayorship and, rather embittered because of the incident, had refused to have anything more to do with the political activity of his own clan. Sulayman had a good knowledge of local history, tribal custom, and agricultural lore, and he rated high in terms of old-style model attributes of behavior: he was hospitable, a recognized mediator, and a giver of advice. However, he did not receive a top rating (see table 7), since as the marriage incident indicated, he did not practice musayara: he displeased his clansmen, indeed, told them off, resigned from his position, and withdrew from clan affairs rather than make the necessary accommodation. He also wrote the telegram accusing the village schoolmaster of unethical dealings—hardly an act of musayara. Although he was extremely intelligent, knowledgeable, effective in debate, and personally attractive, he did not rate high in terms of new-style model behavior (see table 7): although he was literate, his youngest son had failed his high school examinations and it was clear that he would not be able to receive the university education that his father could well afford. This was an especially bitter blow for Sulayman, for he had been in the same primary school class as Abu Fayid and had received the same amount of education, yet Abu Fayid had achieved local prominence, while he had remained in the village, and Abu Fayid's son was in medical school, while his own had not been able to finish high school. Moreover Sulayman was no entrepreneur; he had not invested his money in any enterprise outside of dry cereal farming. The idiosyncratic aspects of Sulayman's personality that made him fall short of the old-style model were also those that made him personally attractive: he was honest, straightforward, and independent-minded. These qualities extended to his dealings with government officials and others in authority. He told me that he once took a letter to the governor's office in the market town. In the waiting room a bureaucrat tried to take the letter from him, but Sulayman insisted on waiting and delivering it personally. It was a cold and rainy winter day and Sulayman went over to the stove and huddled next to it. A policeman came over and told him to get away from the stove. Sulayman replied, "Don't I have the right to this stove? I am cold and want to warm myself. Isn't this the property of the governate? Isn't it partly mine by right? Where am I to warm myself? My mother's brother does not live here.. My father's brother does not live here." The policeman acquiesced and pulled up a chair for him to sit on. The same atypical qualities of temperament that made Sulayman's relations with his own clansmen abrasive also made him specially appealing and effective when he dealt with those in authority.

Muhammad al-Yusuf

Muhammad al-Yusuf, age forty in 1960, was a shopkeeper and a prominent member of Beni 'Amr who aspired to take Sulayman Hasan's place as mayor of the village and representative of his clan. When I arrived in the village, he was in the process of collecting signatures on a nominations petition suggesting himself as a mayoral candidate. Muhammad did not succeed; indeed, he had never been a man of influence and he has been included here to dramatize the attributes he lacked, which the others possessed. Like Sulayman he was hampered by the demographic and social organizational weakness of his own clan; unlike Sulayman, however, he did not make up this deficiency by an abundance of economic resources—though he had much more land than most villagers—he had much less than Sulayman Hasan (one quarter as much) and his grocery shop had very little capital. He had a lackluster personality and he knew much less of custom than most of the influentials. In terms of old-style model behavior he was not a recognized mediator, was not pious, did not practice musayara, did not maintain a guest house, although he occasionally prepared coffee in his shop, and he was miserly. In terms of new-style behavior, although he was literate, he had not educated his sons beyond primary school, had no government position or government contacts, had not engaged in material modernization, and was not engaged in any kind of entrepreneurial activity outside dry cereal farming. Although he came from an important and fairly cohesive lineage within the clan, neither his own marriage nor that of his father, siblings, or children afforded significant sociopolitical ties outside it to make him a social structurally appropriate leader in the old style; and since he was neither young nor the possessor of important social links outside the village, he rated low in terms of new-style structural appropriateness (see table 7). This brief review of his resources illustrates that even a man of ambition, some land, and strong lineage ties cannot become a man of influence unless he possesses other attributes of influence and power.

Ikhleyf al-Muflih

Ikhleyf al-Muflih is another man who aspired to become a man of influence—he had run for mayor in 1956 and lost. Ikhleyf, age forty, was a shopkeeper from the same lineage of Yasin as Yusuf al-Tuluq. Like Muhammad al-Yusuf, he had only a mediocre knowledge of custom, did not practice musayara, and had a lackluster and slightly abrasive personality. Like Muhammad, although he was literate, he had no government position or government contacts, was not an entrepreneur, and had not engaged in material modernization. But he did have certain advantages over Muhammad al-Yusuf: he had more than twice as much land as Muhammad and a much smaller family to support, he came from one of the more important and cohesive lineages of Yasin, and he came from the largest and most cohesive clan in the village. Moreover, in terms of old-style structural appropriateness he had important affinal and matrilateral ties into other lineages inside and outside his clan. Most important, while Muhammad al-Yusuf enjoyed the reputation of a miser, Ikhleyf maintained a guest house and was active in curtaining the village by slaughtering livestock and entertaining such men as the Pasha and various government officials when they passed through the village. So active was he in this endeavor that Yusuf al-Tuluq, his lineage-mate, sneered at his efforts, implying that the scale of his hospitality would soon exhaust his resource base. But Ikhleyf lacked all the other attributes of old-style model behavior: he was not a recognized mediator—his abrasive personality and failure to practice musayara ruled him out—he was not pious, he was not a recognized giver of advice, and he had not cultivated the ties of kinship and clanship through personal diplomacy in the same way as the Yasin mayor. Since he lacked the attributes of new-style leadership, he could not compete effectively either for the mayorship or a position of influence in the village. Ikhleyf's case demonstrates that it is not sufficient to possess all the sources of power and even some of the leading attributes of influence if other conspicuous sources of influence are lacking. It also demonstrates that power is not automatically translated into influence, and the politically ambitious—those who actively seek to occupy formal positions—are by that very fact handicapped in the quest for influence.

The Mayors

Although a number of these influentials played an important role in local-level politics, the pivots for such politics were the mayors. Not only did their office necessarily involve the mayors in all important local political matters, but also the occupations of many of the other influentials restricted their opportunity to exert influence. Some, like Abu Kamil, owned most of their land in the Jordan valley and engaged in entrepreneurial activities that took them out of the village for much of the year. Others who had government positions, like Abu Fayid and Mahmoud Abd al-Qadir, exercised influence regularly, but their presence in the village was in part a matter of happenstance; there was no assurance—indeed, there was a probability—that they would be shifted to another locale in the future.

The life histories of the two mayors provide interesting points of similarity and contrast. Abu Tahir was the youngest of four brothers. After studying the Quran for one year in the village with the preacher and after completing six years of primary school education in Deir Abu Said, he looked after his father's land; since most of it was in the Jordan valley and he had three elder brothers, it is questionable whether he ever ploughed himself. At the age of fourteen he began smuggling Players cigarettes from Jordan into Palestine with the terminal point at Haifa. This was a profitable enterprise, for Jordanian tobacco was of high quality and smuggling avoided the payment of taxes. He claims to have made 150 pounds a month as a smuggler, an enormous sum at that time (1947); he quickly added that his father spent the entire income on the extension of hospitality in his guest house. When his father died in 1950, Abu Tahir finished out his term as mayor—he was only seventeen at the time. One of his brothers had served as a medic in the Arab Legion and had taught Abu Tahir how to administer various antibiotics by needle. Abu Tahir soon became a self-appointed medic in the area, traveling on his pure-bred horse to all the surrounding villages. Since he charged half what a doctor would have charged and since in any case there was no resident doctor in the area, peasants were eager to utilize his services. His practice as a medic remained his most stable source of income and his permanent occupation. His annual income from his land and his practice (250 pounds sterling), was above average for the village, but far from making him well-off. Abu Tahir's father had been a recognized leader or shaykh in the village during the period of single mukhtars (see chapter four) and had continued his own father's reputation as a generous man; Abu Tahir's grandfather had possessed 200 head of sheep. His father dissipated this capital, as well as the income Abu Tahir provided, in the extension of hospitality. The mayor said that the bread oven in their house was never closed, and in explaining his father's behavior, he said, "All their lives the Arabs have been known for their *karam*"—this term means at one and the same time generosity and nobility of character. When his father died, the family was left deeply indebted. Abu

Tahir closed his father's guest house—it remains barred to this day—and eventually paid off his father's debts. However much he might praise his father's behavior, it was quite clear that he rejected his father as a role-model. Abu Tahir is today as well known for his miserliness as his father was for his generosity. Abu Tahir's comment about the household's current state of affairs was as definite as it was satisfied: "We are somewhat at rest now."

Abu Yasin has a much more extensive and diverse occupational history. He was the eldest of three sons.[24] At the age of ten he became a shepherd for his father for two years and subsequently attended primary school for three years, following one year of Quranic instruction in the village. At the age of eighteen he became a plowman on his father's land, which he continued to do for the next seven years. While he was a shepherd, a catastrophe struck his lineage. One of its members claimed to be a prophet, had instituted changes in the form of prayer, and had won the allegiance of a number of peasants inside and outside the village. The head of the police post had ordered the man's beard shaved off after he refused to admit that he was an imposter. When in retaliation the police chief and three other policemen were killed, Abu Yasin's uncle and three other lineage members, including the uncle of Abu Fayid, were implicated. Government troops moved into Kufr al-Ma and occupied the village for fifteen days; they confiscated more than 300 head of livestock and most of the lineage's stored grain pending the arrest of the culprits, who had fled. Although the culprits were apprehended and either killed or jailed, most of the lineage's wealth was never returned and the poverty of Abu Yasin's family began at that time.

When Abu Yasin was a plowman on his father's land, he went frequently to Palestine in the off season or during the growing season in years of drought. There he took work as a builder, a watchman, a fisherman, a plasterer, a blacksmith, and finally he got a full-time job in Tel Aviv as the foreman of a building crew. During this period, 1931–36, he worked for Jews as well as Arabs; indeed he became infatuated with a Jewish girl whom he intended to marry until his father threatened to disown him. To facilitate his communication with Jews in Palestine he had gone for a short period to the Berlitz school to learn Hebrew. In the early part of World War Two he worked for the British army on the construction of the Eden line and later unloading ammunition from British ships in Haifa.

In 1935 he became involved in the growing Arab resistance to British mandatory rule in Palestine. Through much of 1936 and 1937 he was a guerrilla fighter and a gunrunner for the resistance, picking up guns in Aleppo and Damascus and smuggling them into Palestine. He was interned for seven months on one occasion and jailed for five months on another for participation in these activities. In 1942 he married and in 1943 he returned to Kufr al-Ma, where he worked as a plowman until 1948, when he reenlisted in the resistance. He was posted as head of the guard of the Arab Higher Committee, and when the Arab Legion entered Jerusalem in 1948, he was attached to it with the rank of sergeant-major. In the Legion he served in ordinance and demolition units. He returned to the village in 1951 and lived on his saved army earnings and by tilling his land until 1956, when the exhaustion of his savings and his meager landholdings forced him to supplement his income by sharecropping. He was selected as mayor in 1957 and continued as mayor through the 1960s, although his household continued in an impoverished condition (his annual income in 1960 was a hundred pounds sterling) until the middle sixties. At that time his two eldest sons enlisted in the Arab Legion and began receiving regular stipends. Most of these army earnings were saved for his sons' marriage payments, but some was used to buy land in the Jordan valley.

In some respects the economic history of these two families is remarkably similar. In the parental generation the families were relatively affluent, with sufficient land and much livestock (over 200 head of sheep in both cases). The fathers of both mayors followed the model of old-style leadership and expended their wealth in their guest houses on their relatives, covillagers, and honored guests. Although Abu Yasin's father never became a mayor, he was a shaykh renowned for his skill in mediation, his wise counsel, and his generosity; when he died, the usual three-day mourning period was extended by a week in order to accommodate all the men from surrounding villages who came to pay their respects. When the fathers died, the sons (in the one instance partly due to the catastrophe) were left impoverished. At the present time both mayors have improved their economic status, the one by pursuing his occupational specialty and the other by the contributions of his sons who are in the army. But the reaction of the two mayors to the family's impoverishment was startling different. While Abu Tahir boarded up his father's guest house, Abu Yasin continued to maintain the full-blown mayorship, sinking further into debt to do so, for his income was meager even by village standards. I sometimes witnessed him coming to the village shop to buy meat on credit to prepare a meal for an honored guest; shopkeepers always extended the credit, but with the individualization of household incomes and village customs they increasingly resented having to do so and gossiped about Abu Yasin's irresponsibility behind his back. Abu Yasin, then, followed in his father's footsteps by operating according to the governing attributes of old-style leadership—providing skilled mediation and profuse hospitality—while Abu Tahir rejected his father's style of leadership and offered neither.

The occupational histories of the two mayors are also quite different. Although Abu Tahir had gone to Palestine in his early days, he seldom went thereafter, and more important his visits were short—he never worked in Palestine. Abu Yasin worked there in diverse occupations over long periods; he came into contact not only with urban Arabs but also with Jews and Englishmen. This experience widened his social and political horizon and in Lerner's terms created a far greater empathy for and knowledge of other ways of life and other blueprints for living.[25] Evidence for this is found in table 8. Although Abu Tahir was able to give somewhat expanded answers to such specific questions as, "What is the most important problem facing the country?," "What is the most important foreign threat?," and "What is the reason for the loss of Palestine?," he answered questions relating to ideology (such as, "What is your definition of capitalism?," "What is your definition of communism?," and "What is your definition of Islam?") either by saying he didn't know or hadn't studied it or by giving a terse one phrase answer,—e.g., "Russia, we don't like it" or "Just Islam." Abu Yasin, on the other hand, answered every question regarding political ideology and in the case of communism and democracy elaborated his answer. Abu Yasin's life history also demonstrates his much greater involvement in and commitment to nationalism: several times he volunteered for service in the struggle for national independence. Among all the influentials described, no one approached his record of service as a soldier-patriot except Abu Fayid and even he did not equal it. As if to affirm his preeminence in this respect, Abu Yasin named five sons after Arab military heroes martyred in Jordan during the early Islamic conquests.

It is interesting to note in this regard that although only Abu Yasin, Abu Fayid, and Fayid al-Hamad had undergone military training and service, all the influentials interviewed in table 8 except one, Yusuf al-Tuluq, stipulated military force as the most important factor in history. Yusuf's selection of political leadership probably reflected his view that British political chicanery lost Palestine; but even he, after suggesting a possible political accommodation with Israel, stated that force was the only solution. Although Abu Fayid was not formally interviewed as were the influentials on table 8, it is apparent from other discussions that he far exceeded Abu Yasin and any other influential in the sophistication of his views regarding political ideologies; in this he was quite atypical. As I have already mentioned, his political views probably occasioned the bribery charges made against him during his service in the customs. These views were clearly republican: he said that in Italy the prime minister had only one car; he said that Omar Ibn al-Khattab (the second Muslim caliph) slept unguarded under a tree and that when others remarked on his lack of precaution, Omar replied, "I've ruled, done justice, felt secure, slept." Abu Fayid said that two days after Anthony Eden, the British prime minister, quit his position, the authorities refused to repair his car at government expense; he said that England would soon be a republic. Therefore although Abu Fayid excelled even Abu Yasin in some of the key attributes of old-style model leadership—maintaining a guest house, curtaining the village, and practicing musayara (see the discussion of Abu Yasin's deficiency in this respect), he was clearly not in accord with villagers' views regarding social (see the discussion of achieved status) and political ideology. As noted in table 8, not a single villager interviewed[26] answered in the affirmative the question, "If you were at a general meeting and a citizen rose to defend a point of view that you and the majority of those assembled considered to be against the best interests of the country and the people, would you allow him to speak?"

Abu Tahir, on the other hand, had no record of military service and more clearly reflected the traditional village view (a view that was losing currency in 1960) that soldiering was to be avoided and was suitable only for sons of poor peasants who lacked a steady income.

In terms of sources of power Abu Tahir's income exceeded that of Abu Yasin in 1960, but that position was reversed by 1967 (see table 7); however neither mayor was ever counted among the well-to-do. In fact during the first six years of Abu Yasin's mayorship his clansmen studiously avoided going to his guest house at mealtimes and in the evening, unless there was a special occasion, going rather to Abu Kamil's, Abu Fayid's, Yusuf al-Tuluq's, or some other clan elder's in order not to deplete Abu Yasin's resources further. Abu Yasin's lineage was three times the size of Abu Tahir's and it was far more cohesive.

In terms of idiosyncratic personality traits, Abu Yasin was as attractive as Abu Tahir was unattractive. The former was personally

Table 8
Ideological Views of Selected Leaders in Kufr al-Ma

ABU KAMIL

Definition of Democracy:	It proceeds according to the path of right and equality.
Most Important Factor in History: [1]	Military force
The Model Person: [2]	The pious, God-fearing man.
Definition of Socialism:	He (the socialist) is accursed; a communist.
Definition of Communism:	It contradicts religious and Islamic principles, a destroyer.
Definition of Capitalism:	That's what you have in America, we don't have any capitalists in Jordan.
Definition of Islam:	The pillars of faith: belief in God, the messenger, the angels, the revealed books, resurrection, the power of his good and evil.
Most Important Problem Facing the Country:	The Palestine problem; secondly the Algerian problem.
Most Important Foreign Threat:	Communism for the Arab countries; Israel for Jordan.
Reason for Loss of Palestine and Solution to Palestine problem:	The English sold out Palestine.
Freedom of Speech: [3]	No.

YUSUF AL-TULUQ

Definition of Democracy:	In the time of the Turks the British state; America, a country that is always neutral —it likes peace more than war because it is a mercantile state.
Most Important Factor in History:	Political leadership; politics attracts (in its wake) everything.

The Model Person:	The man working quietly for his people and the pious, God-fearing man, with the former slightly preferred.
Definition of Socialism:	Doesn't know.
Definition of Communism:	A destroyer: it rends honor; it opposes religion, honor and country. He (the communist) doesn't know his children, he doesn't know he has a sister, everything belongs to the government. You don't have land.
Definition of Capitalism:	America; they work, they have capital and commerce; it doesn't like war and it doesn't oppress the people.
Definition of Islam:	God is one; he has no partner. Muhammad is his messenger, and Jesus and Moses and every person follows his own path.
Most Important Problem Facing the Country:	The problem of Israel.
Most Important Foreign Threat:	Israel only.
Reason for Loss of Palestine and Solution to Palestine problem:	Politics lost Palestine—the politics of Britain. Solution: that refugees be safeguarded in their homes by America and Britain, that refugees take part of land back and Israel keep the rest. Solution: there is no solution—except occupying it by force.
Freedom of Speech:	No, we follow the majority.

ABU YASIN

Definition of Democracy:	Just rule; there is no compulsion, it is not like dictatorship; Jordan today is a democracy; Jamal (Nasser) has a dictatorship; he dominates the people; I have the right to complain to the public defender.

Most Important Factor in History:	Military force; when military force is sufficient, it organizes the country.
The Model Person:	The patriotic revolutionary.
Definition of Socialism:	It is close to communism but different; the Shadiriya may be socialist; they are a sect in norther Syria who share their wives with one another.
Definition of Communism:	There is no religion in the state; the people are prohibited from worship except in special circumstances; people are prohibited from seeing their sons; there is no individual private property; it is all to the state; it gives women freedom; neither her husband, nor her brother, nor her father can control her.
Definition of Capitalism:	The owners of companies in America; they are the capitalists.
Definition of Islam:	The profession of faith; the giving of alms; the pilgrimage; the distinctive sign of Islam in its true meaning is the reading of the Quran.
Most Important Problem Facing the Country:	The United Arab Republic.
Most Important Foreign Threat:	Communism; Israel.
Reason for Loss of Palestine and Solution to Palestine problem:	The Balfour Declaration and imperialism. Solution: the return of Palestine to its people.
Freedom of Speech:	No.

ABU TAHIR

Definition of Democracy:	I haven't studied it; I don't understand anything about it.
Most Important Factor in History:	Military force: because we are on a war border and need military strength.

The Model Person:	The patriotic revolutionary; we need a trustworthy person guarding his own land because we have many enemies—not just Nasser and Syria.
Definition of Socialism:	
Definition of Communism:	Russia; we don't like it.
Definition of Capitalism:	
Definition of Islam:	Just Islam.
Most Important Problem Facing the Country:	The problem of the liberation army because they enter Jordan as thieves and enter Israel and destroy; we can't allow that; we catch them and put them in jail; we are able to defend our own boundaries; we will settle with them one day; thievery doesn't harm Israel, only the Jordanian farmer who suffers retaliation.
Most Important Foreign Threat:	America when it aids Israel with arms and the atomic bomb; lack of agreement among Arab leaders.
Reason for Loss of Palestine and Solution to Palestine problem:	The English and the Balfour Declaration lost Palestine—no other reason. Solution: forceable return; what matters to us is that not a Jew remains in Palestine and that it be returned to its rightful owners who were dispersed.
Freedom of Speech:	No, not at all.

SAEED AL-SALIM
(a poor, marginally literate peasant)

Definition of Democracy:	
Most Imporant Factor in History:	Military force.

The Model Person:	The man working quietly for his people.
Definition of Socialism:	
Definition of Communism:	
Definition of Capitalism:	
Definition of Islam:	
Most Important Problem Facing the Country:	War from the outside; against Syria, Egypt, Ibn Saud.
Most Important Foreign Threat:	The attempted coup against Husayn; their cause—politics, the leadership of Faiq al Melki. Solution: purifying the people.
Reason for Loss of Palestine and Solution to Palestine problem:	The English. Solution: only by war.
Freedom of Speech:	No.

---

1. The specific question put to informants was as follows: "The factor which has had the largest effect in history is: military strength; thought; economic factors and classes; or political leadership? (Choose one)"

2. The specific question put to informants was as follows: "Of the following persons, which is closest to being the exemplar: the able successful merchant; the God-fearing and pious Muslim; the devoted revolutionary who struggles in his country's interests; the obedient contented citizen; the military hero; or the man working quietly and deliberately for his people? (Choose one)"

3. The specific question put to informants was as follows: "If you were in a public meeting and a citizen arose to defend a point of view that you and the majority of the assembled considered contrary to the interest of the country and the people, do you believe that he has the right to be heard?" I wish to thank Hanna Battatu for allowing me to use the above questions. They were part of a questionnaire which he developed and applied among high school students in Iraq. In every case I read the question to the informant without further comment and recorded his answer.

charming, gregarious, a good host, and an entertaining raconteur; of medium height, and powerfully built, he had a thick white mustache, a raucous voice and manner, a good sense of humor, and an infectious laugh; when angered, he would respond frankly and directly to the challenge. Abu Tahir, though handsome, was tight-lipped, and when he spoke, he was often sharp-tongued—he was able to put men, even government officials, on the defensive with his sarcastic remarks. In the guest house he seldom contributed to the conversation unless called upon; though he often smiled in a wry manner, he seldom laughed, and when provoked, he responded by silence or circumlocution. He openly envied the material goods that others possessed and he was not above borrowing items that he never returned. When he discovered that a person outside the circle of his relatives could not be of much use to him or refused to do him a favor, he tended to have little more to do with him. None of these qualities endeared him to others, and there was a substantial truth to a remark Abu Yasin made in a moment of anger, "Even his own relatives can't stand him."

Abu Tahir had a good knowledge of tribal law and mediation procedures and some knowledge of local history, not because he was particularly interested in them, but because he was necessarily exposed to such matters in the course of his father's service as shaykh. Abu Yasin, on the other hand, had an excellent knowledge of local history, tribal law, mediation procedures, nationalist struggles, and agricultural custom. His knowledge went beyond the merely theoretical, for he was an active mediator and had participated in the resistance. He was, moreover, a man of the world and a jack-of-all-trades on whom people called for practical advice and assistance: he was a carpenter (he specialized in making plough handles), a tinker, a tree surgeon (he also advised on various plant diseases), a gun expert, a charcoal-maker, an amateur veterinarian, a stonecutter, and a former smuggler.

With regard to social structural appropriateness for old-style leadership, Abu Tahir did not rate very high because of his age, parental status (he had no grown sons), and lack of critical matrilateral ties; however his own marriage gave him one critical affinal link with the largest independent family in the village, the Shuqayrat. Abu Yasin could not have rated higher on this attribute, since he was an elder and the father of two grown sons and a number of others who would soon reach maturity; he came from the most cohesive lineage of the largest clan in the village; and he had matrilateral and affinal ties with one Dumi lineage, one 'Amr lineage, and three independent families. With regard to new-style social structural appropriateness, Abu Tahir rated higher than Abu Yasin, for he was young and had effective links in the local-level bureaucracy in the subdistrict center; Abu Yasin had many links outside the village, but most were not within the bureaucracy and those that were seemed to be less effective.

With one outstanding exception, Abu Yasin followed the norm of old-style model behavior much more closely than Abu Tahir. He was a pious man who consciously attempted to adhere to the injunctions of Islamic ethics with regard to the undesirability of factionalism (construed in the local context as political party activity) and the desirability of the modesty of women and the honesty of men: after he had publicly denounced one villager to his face, he explained, "He gave false witness; he has no religion; I hate lying." Abu Tahir was not so concerned about religious ethics and his attendance at religious rituals was perfunctory; I sometimes saw him going over his accounts during the Friday congregational prayer, and on one occasion when I accompanied him on a Friday morning to the market town, he was more interested in buying clothes for his children than attending the Friday prayer, which he almost missed.

Abu Yasin expressed typical views about the value of large families, particularly the value of having male progeny. I once hazarded the opinion that his having seven boys and one girl was an unfortunate economic circumstance, since the marriage payment given to sisters was often used to provide the marriage payment for their brothers and that the sexual imbalance in his family would make it difficult to marry off his sons. He replied:

> I prefer boys. The girl requires more exertion—I must protect her more; she is naked, I must clothe her. I can't let her go to school without proper dress or let her go to work. The boy—it doesn't matter; he'll go to work with laborers and sleep on the ground and he can work. God sends the poor man boys. They will get married—brother will help brother—don't worry about the marriage payment. The girl can't walk to school; the boy—it doesn't matter. We have a saying here, "A house of men and not a house of riches. [*bayt rijāl wa la bayt māl*]."

In former times a man was judged according to the hospitality he offered to the world, that is, to those outside his nuclear family—storing one's provisions in the loft and depriving one's own family was a commendable act. Today, however, in part because the prayer leader preaches that true generosity necessarily includes one's own family and in part because of occupational mobility and registration of land in individual ownership, model behavior requires generosity to one's own family, one's relatives, and the honored guest. Abu Yasin was a generous man, both to the world and to his family; he went deeply into debt for the sake of both. By way of criticism it was said of Sulayman Hasan that he was good to the world but not to his relatives or his family. Although he often extended hospitality in his guest house, and in so doing curtained the village, and had good friends outside his clan, he did not get along with his relatives and refused a request to sign a statement of good character required for a marriage contract. Sulayman's son ran off to Beirut because his father refused to bribe officials in order to get him a position after his son failed the high school examinations. Rather than commending Sulayman for his honesty, village opinion construed this act as miserliness toward his own family. Abu Tahir was miserly both towards the world and towards his patrilineal kinsmen; they once tried to eject him from his domicile; he was simply not interested in establishing long-time reciprocal debt relationships by offering hospitality and doing favors with some undetermined payoff in the distant future. He was, however, generous to his nuclear family and solicitous of their welfare.

Abu Tahir recognized the price of kinship; he knew that continual hospitality to relatives and clansmen deprived one's own family and eventually brought impoverishment. Rather than pay this price, he sacrificed the prestige derived from such behavior, sloughed off such traditional obligations to his kinsmen, and became a practitioner of inward-looking individualism. This fact brings us to a consideration of some of the more strictly social psychological aspects of the two mayors' behavior. Abu Yasin valued his kinsmen and was conscientious about living up to traditional kinship obligations: he was proud of having provided his younger brother's marriage payment and his sister's sizeable trousseau, although her marriage was of the exchange type and did not require it.[27] He was meticulous about visiting his relatives, particularly all his kinswomen, on appropriate festival days; and he rendered innumerable services to his kinsmen *gratis*, including exemption from paying clan dues for those who were unable. He viewed clan-mate relationships as continuing debt relationships: one performed services for kinsmen—helped build their houses, plough, prune their trees, act as marriage go-between, mediate their disputes—without expecting immediate repayment in coin. Exploiting kinship ties to the hilt was part of Abu Yasin's political strategy. But to state it thus is to miss part of the truth. Abu

Yasin depended on the village's and especially his kinsmen's compassion.[28] The village was in a very real sense a security blanket for him as it was not for Abu Fayid, who had lived outside it most of his life, or for Sulayman Hasan, who had defied his closest kinsmen and gotten along quite well. Abu Yasin both wanted and sought the village's compassion; Sulayman Hasan would have dispensed with it, if he had been given the opportunity. Abu Yasin had been given the opportunity—he had many friends and contacts in the outside world, those provided by his variegated occupational history. He could have gotten permanent employment outside the village at a number of points in his career—for instance, he could have continued as a career soldier in the Arab Legion. But he chose to return to the village. Even though he had coped quite well in the outside world and had absented himself from it for long periods, the village afforded the comfort and security that no other milieu, however sumptuous, could provide. This need was expressed in an acute fashion by the poor illiterate peasant Saeed al-Salim (see table 8), who had gone to work in Lebanon where he did quite well economically, first in a cement factory in Beirut and then as a gardener in a village outside Tripoli. I asked him why he had returned. First he recounted the story of his inadvertent drunkenness in the vineyard (mentioned in chapter five); then he told me there was no mosque in close proximity, that they spoke a strange dialect, and that the food was not pleasing to him. He capped his explanation by saying, *tawaHHasht*, literally, "I became like an animal" and more generally, "I became desolate or lonely or unsociable." When a village man came to Abu Yasin to ask for his advice and aid, saying, "We are a minority; no one listens to us; we go to you because you will listen to us, because you and Abu Fayid must help us," or when a man like the nephew of Khalil Marwan (referred to in the last chapter) came to Abu Yasin and told him, "I cannot be disloyal to you; you have treated me like a son," he was receiving not only the village's compassion but also the accolades that only its sons can offer. Abu Yasin's dependence was also reflected in his not resigning from the mayorship despite the long-standing failure of certain clansmen to support the mayorship financially. It was reflected even more critically in his inability to ask his clansmen for money after signing official documents for them—a right given to him by the establishment of the contractual mayorship. The close psychological interdependence of Abu Yasin and his clansmen and its detrimental effects on his well-being and state of mind was epitomized in a statement he made about himself, "I am like a candle: I burn myself up to light the way for others."

Abu Tahir was not completely independent of the village's compassion. I once asked him why he never considered changing jobs and going to Beirut, which he had seen and which had attracted him. He replied, "How can I? I've been giving shots for twenty-two years. My homeland (*watan*) is dear to me." But Abu Tahir had reduced both his substantive and psychological dependence on his clansmen by cutting off hospitality (as villagers said, "He eats; he does not feed"), developing an independent source of income, operating a limited mayorship, and specializing in short-term payoffs for clansmen based on his ties with the local bureaucracy. Both his substantive and his psychological independence was reflected in his oft-repeated remark to villagers who mentioned that some elder or other was criticizing their behavior: "Who is so-and-so (referring to the elder)? Don't pay any attention to that kind of talk."

There is one respect in which Abu Yasin departed substantially from the old-style model of leadership—the practice of musayara. Although he was well aware of the necessity of establishing good will, receiving approval (*radā'*), and reconciling villagers, and though in fact he worked tirelessly for those ends, (he was a master of dyadic diplomacy in mediation sessions), he often violated a primary mode of village behavior—circumspection—and one of its primary goals—the preservation of social harmony. Instances of such behavior have been cited in previous chapters: he told off one of his supporters who failed to provide a promised payment; he beat up the bogus magician and the Rifa'i shopkeeper who was sponsoring him; he swore at Mustafa Gawayder and Mustafa Yusuf of Shujur; he summarily forbade villagers to sell water to the Bedouin; he brought government officials into the public roads and sheep incursion cases, which resulted in substantial fines against many of his own clansmen. Those who signed the petition against him in 1960 had been alienated by him in one direct confrontation or another over the years. He sometimes let his temper get the best of him; he lacked the patience that was regarded as an essential attribute of manliness (*murūwwa*). Abu Yasin's decidedly noncircumspect behavior arose from the fact that he was a man of principle and a trouble-shooter: he felt responsible for his community and was on the alert for violations of its best interest or the country's laws. The price he had to pay for such good "citizenship" was that his covillagers, including his clansmen (see Abu Fayid's comments), often condemned him for behavior they regarded as foolish, improper, headstrong, against the best interests of the village, and destructive of the harmony that prevailed within it.

Within the village Abu Tahir practiced circumspection to a fine point. In the very instances in which Abu Yasin had acted as a good citizen and a trouble-shooter, Abu Tahir had acted with what most villagers regarded as good sense—and Abu Yasin considered cowardice: he seldom, if ever, called in government officials to act against villagers; he had ridden out of town early on the morning the tax collector came to the village; he refused to accompany Abu Yasin to the house of the Rifa'i family that was selling water to the Bedouin; and he ducked down a side alley after Abu Yasin had rooted him out of bed in order that they both confront the bogus magician and his sponsor; he was not present when the altercation occurred and, therefore, did not become the object of criticism and abuse when the affair became public knowledge. Barnard's dictum that "men seek to avoid authority and responsibility" certainly applied to him.

With respect to new-style model behavior there is a curious turnabout. Although both were literate, neither Abu Yasin nor Abu Tahir had government positions or prominent contacts with bureaucrats in the market town or the capital. But both had attempted to form links with local-level bureaucrats in the subdistrict center. In dealing with them, Abu Yasin used traditional terms of respect and politeness formulas in the obsequious manner characteristic of most peasants who deal with government officials. In doing so he was clearly operating in terms of musayara. But Abu Tahir, who was so circumspect within the village, dispensed with many politeness formulas and dealt much more directly with government officials. While Abu Yasin was making one request of the subdistrict officer in an overly polite way, Abu Tahir was making three. This direct and almost impudent manner was an essential element in Abu Tahir's successful dealings with government officials, for it threw them off balance and put them on the defensive, as the incident regarding the school lands case dramatically illustrated. Abu Yasin's and Abu Tahir's rather low rating regarding new-style model behavior reflected not only their lack of government positions but also their lack of entrepreneurship and material modernization, although both had begun to do a bit of the latter. Abu Yasin bought chairs for his guest house in 1967 and Abu Tahir said that in the next year he was going to remodel and refurnish his own guest house. Nor had the two men educated their sons beyond the primary school level—Abu Yasin because he could not afford to and Abu Tahir because his children were still infants. However the successful enlistment of Abu Yasin's two sons in the army enhanced his standing from the new-style point of view.

There is no doubt that both mayors espoused and supported the aims of the central government regarding the material modernization of villages and in that respect were operating according to the new style. Abu Yasin believed that this was progress and he propagandized for it. "It is in the nature of things," he said, "that Kufr al-Ma should have a new school and electricity; the world was marching ahead and Kufr al-Ma would not be permitted to stay behind—progress would occur regardless of any group's opposition or nonopposition." The act of the subdistrict officer that gave him singular pleasure was his contacting the district officer by phone, thereby paving the way for Kufr al-Ma's hiring an additional teacher for the primary school. When the tax collector came to Kufr al-Ma to collect the annual village improvement tax (which was later spent on village projects), Abu Yasin practically dragged some of his clansmen, including his closest relatives, to the tax collector and made them pay. Although he did not propagandize for it with equal fervor, Abu Tahir was equally committed to material modernization. He held that any group of responsible townsmen—and not just landowners—could sign a petition obligating the village to support the building of a new school and he favored bringing in the police to exact payment from villagers who were recalcitrant about paying the village improvement tax. When the government brought piped water to the village entrance and said it would extend the pipes up into the village *gratis* if twenty-five villagers bought water meters, various grumblings arose. Some said that any water loss from the pipes was going to be charged to villagers; others said the water company was making money on the villagers, charging more than was appropriate for pipes and meters. Abu Tahir scoffed at these ideas and told the villagers that the water company was not a profit-making enterprise, that they weren't merchants, and that it wasn't even their money—it was the International Bank's; Abu Tahir clearly did not accept the traditional view that the government was out to milk the peasant.

On the other hand, in certain critical respects both Abu Tahir and Abu Yasin—literate, town-wise, and forward-looking men—departed from the model of new-style behavior. Abu Tahir once told me that livestock was the best capital investment; on another occasion he told me that the best investment was land. He had in fact bought both land and livestock with his savings, his only other large investment being his pure-bred horse. These investments represented traditional village values, par excellence. There was no indication that Abu Tahir entertained the notion of new-style investments, such as those of Abu Fayid, or of entrepreneurship of the kind in which Abu Kamil was engaged.

An aspect of Abu Yasin's traditional world-view came out in a discussion he had one evening with Abu Fayid, Yusuf al-Tuluq, and other elders regarding the relative merits of achieved and ascribed status. I recorded the discussion as follows:

> Abu Fayid began the conversation by quoting Al-Hajjaj, a famous governor of Iraq in the early Islamic period, on the importance of character and piety—not origin (*aSl*). When I asked him the meaning of asl, he replied that a man of good character was better than Abu Qasim (one of the poor relatives of the Wazir family living in the village—the Wazirs being the notables of the subdistrict and having been so for many generations). Yusuf al-Tuluq said he wouldn't give his children in marriage to the children of Salih Wazir because they were of bad character. He said that it was pedigree (*nasb*) and origin (asl) that he searched for. I asked him how many ancestors he could trace. He laughed and Abu Yasin interjected, "What we mean is that we observe their habits." An elder chimed in, "We don't marry gypsies; we don't marry blacks—they have no nasb." On another occasion Yusuf al-Tuluq said of the Wazirs, "We must remember their origin; yes, feudalism is gone, but their origin is known." Abu Fayid retorted, "That kind of talk is for bygone days; if you plant on the dung heap you get a good plant." Yusuf al-Tuluq replied, "Not like the plant on good soil." Abu Fayid continued, "Learning (*ʿilm*) builds everything." Yusuf al-Tuluq replied "[In the old days] there was no learning." Then he quoted the Quran, "We have raised you with respect to degree over one another in rank and means of living (*rafaʿnakum darajātan fil jāh wal rizq*)."[29] Abu Fayid replied, "No, only in means of living (*rizq*). Yusuf said, "The leader (*zaʿīm*), the leader. He has his worth and there cannot but emanate from him understanding (*fahm*).[30] I asked Abu Fayid, "Then you don't respect all those descended from the family of the Prophet (*bayt al-Hashimi*)?" He replied, "The Zubiyya and the Rifaʿiyya (lineages in Kufr al-Ma and a neighboring village) are descendants of the Prophet's family and we don't respect them more than others." An elder interjected, "Strangers who took women of the Rifaʿiyya in marriage had to pay 2,000 Turkish piastres extra in recognition of their honorable origin. The payment was called, 'the fall of honor' (*saqt sharf*)." Abu Fayid began talking

about a famous black Bedouin warrior who made the shaykhs of the Jordan valley take flight. Yusuf interjected. "But could he take one of their daughters in marriage? Not for a thousand pounds!" "He did take them in marriage," replied Abu Fayid, but he added, "Of course he was the son of Imhaydi," "Ah," said Yusuf "you have fetched the origin." (The implication of this remark was that the black warrior had a noble pedigree, since his father was a noble white warrior and that was what counted in a society that reckoned according to patrilineal descent). Yusuf continued, "Horses are of different kinds: pure-bred (*aSīl*), ploughhorse (*kaddīsh*), and mule (*baghl*) and the proof is on the race track." Then Abu Fayid talked about a ploughhorse that had defeated pure-bred horses. I asked, "How is it that the genius occurs? Was his father or grandfather a genius?" Abu Yasin said, "If a ploughhorse can run he must have been crossed with a pure-bred horse." He continued to explain how the pure-bred horse had become pure-bred and the ploughhorse a ploughhorse: there was a fig tree and Satan circled around it and spit on it; the Lord removed the spit; there were four horses. Satan went to them and told them that the tree would become man and oppress them and ride them. One horse charged and tried to get the tree—the spit turned into a dog, the horse into a ploughhorse, and the remaining horses stayed pure-bred. Abu Yasin concluded, "God created the freeman and the slave and God created the pure-bred—that is, the freeman of horses and the ploughhorse is the slave of horses—we plough with it and ride it." Abu Fayid said that some horses were ploughhorses because men used them for ploughing but that others were used for raids. An elder interjected, "Horses are pedigrees, pedigrees!" Abu Yasin said that they take pure-breds and plough with them and the people call them, kaddish, but if they turn them loose on the racing ground, they would run true. Yusuf said, "Take the Shiites (*Mitewli*) of Deir Abu Said, who will give them women in marriage [the inhabitants of the area were almost all Sunni Muslims and looked down on the Shiites]? No one. The people of Deir Abu Said take from among their own women but don't give to them (the Shiites). Abu Yasin said that the Shiites gave women to the inhabitants of Deir Abu Said because they had an excess of women. An elder interjected, "They [the Shiites of Deir Abu Said] used to pray [when they made their prostrations] on a ball of earth, but now they have taken up Sunni Islam [and do not do so]." An instance was brought up of an exchange marriage between a Shiite and Sunni family in Deir Abu Said (which if confirmed would have weakened the case for the importance of origins). Abu Yasin denied that the girl had been given to a Shiite family, insisting it was a Sunni family. "They (the Shiites) say (in the profession of faith), 'And I bear witness that Ali is the friend of God (*wa ashhad an ʿali wali allah*),'" said Abu Yasin. He continued that one of the local Shiites had been a butcher at first, but then a member of the Wazir family had told everyone that meat slaughtered by them could not be eaten and that this verdict had been affirmed by the local preacher. But then the member of the Wazir family had been bribed to say that he was a Sunni and the people ate his meat. Yusuf said that the Pasha had been invited to a meal by a Shiite and he had cautioned against eating meat slaughtered by them. Abu Fayid interjected, "Who would you give your daughter to in marriage, to the son of the Pasha or to Dr. Salim?" An elder chimed in, "Would we give her to a gypsy? No." Yusuf said that the Pasha once pulled a revolver on a Christian member of Parliament, telling him to shut up, though that Christian was more learned than all of them. He said the Pasha said to him, "Who are you, telling us we don't understand— your father is a furrier." Abu Fayid retorted, "It was the Turks who set up the *zaʿims*; they selected one man from each area and left a few mounted troops with him, and they asked each zaʿim to send his son to Istanbul [for training]. The zaʿims did not owe their position to their origin." On another occasion an elder told me that once a boy wanted to kill his father and he waited in the doorway until the father returned from the mosque. The father returned and on passing the window of the house was addressed by his wife, "Your son is waiting for you, gun in hand, aiming to kill you." The father asked, "Is he really our son [i.e., not a bastard]?" She replied, "Yes." The father continued on his way and entered the house. On seeing his son, he said, "Throw down your gun," and the son threw down his revolver and started crying. On another occasion Abu Fayid began reciting poetry attributed to the same Al Hajjaj mentioned above. The final verse was as follows: "The courageous man is he who says, 'I am so and so and not he who says my father was . . . .'"

I have no substantial evidence that Abu Tahir would have disagreed with the traditional position taken by Abu Yasin, Yusuf al-

Tuluq, and the elders in this account. However one aspect of Abu Tahir's personal and political style does place him much closer to the new-style model of leadership and accounts for his higher rating on table 7—his orientation toward machine politics. Inside the village he supported the village council not only because he thought it would insure dominance of his coalition, but also because it would afford rewards in money and contracts. Outside the village he acted as a successful fixer and pork-barreler in terms of short-term payoffs: he was able to get local sinecures for members of his coalition and to avoid the consequences of some government policies. His adroitness in playing machine or contractual politics led both his opponents and his followers to exaggerate his effectiveness. Yusuf al-Tuluq attributed the proportions given to the clans in the 1960 fodder distribution to Abu Tahir's chicanery when it simply reflected administrative policy. When in 1966 there seemed to be some possibility that Kufr al-Ma would join the municipality of Deir Abu Said, it was widely rumored that after the adhesion Abu Tahir would get hold of 2,000 needles and give free shots, thus winning all the votes in the next election. If Abu Yasin was a master go-between within the village, Abu Tahir was a master manipulator in government offices where new-style behavior counted for more.

Abu Tahir was abetted in his practice of machine politics by his practical frame of mind and Abu Yasin was prevented from practicing it by his commitment to principles and ideal norms. In 1960, after the most serious case of honor to shake the village and the subdistrict in the past thirty years—a case involving the murder of a young woman, the imprisonment of three men, and the reputation of a leading family in the subdistrict—Abu Yasin told me that there was no solution to the case short of a revenge murder by the victimized group; he said that the victimized group would absolutely refuse to accept money compensation and reconciliation. I asked Abu Tahir about the same case, and he said that under government prodding the victimized party would finally yield to pressure and agree to a reconciliation with a payment of a very large sum by the offender's group as compensation. When I returned to the village in 1965 the disposition of the case had been as Abu Tahir had predicted, not as Abu Yasin had insisted.

An important conclusion of this analysis is, then, that there is a close fit between the personality of each mayor, and the political strategy each has chosen. Abu Tahir's sharp tongue, directness, quickness and sarcasm in dealing with government officials, his miserliness, circumspection, and use of circumlocution in dealing with villagers suits his strategy: machine politics (in the subdistrict center, village council, and new contractual mayorship), the watered-down mayorship, increasing confrontation and encounter, utilization of the power of numbers, a practical evaluation of the gentleman's agreement, and the individualization of all claims based on the moral authority of the elders. Abu Yasin's generosity, his skill in mediation, his mastery of custom, his jack-of-all-tradesmanship, his personal charm, his gregariousness, his piety, and his seeking the village's compassion suits his own strategy: clan paternalism, the full-blown mayorship, the rejection of subversion or even muted renegadism, the exploitation of clanship, kinship, and quasi-kinship ties for all they are worth, and the ethical evaluation of the gentleman's agreement, the politics of hospitality, and the idiom of discrepancy. As was the case with their strategies, the personality of each mayor bore a serious flaw: Abu Tahir's notoriously self-seeking life style alienated his own clansmen and relatives; he had few friends; villagers did not trust him and many quite openly said that he was "no good" and of "no benefit" to the village—in spite of the substantive payoffs he had won for it. On the other hand, even the members of the opposing coalition agreed that Abu Yasin was a good man, but they sometimes doubted whether he was a wise man—his penchant for pursuing justice rather than harmony tarnished his reputation for leadership. But, more important, his dependence on the village's compassion made it impossible for him to make the most of the new contractual basis of politics that had already been established for the mayorship and in an incipient fashion for the village council: it was too painful for him to ask his kinsmen and affines for money for services rendered.

The Dilemma of a Transitional Society?

Having analyzed the strategy of the Yasin coalition and the influence of its leaders, particularly its mayor, we can now ask to what degree the difficulties and problems of that coalition are a consequence of the incongruous juxtaposition of the logistical, economic, social structural, cultural, and social psychological elements of a transitional society? Otherwise stated, was the seeming failure in the Yasin mayor's strategy as evidenced by the incipient shift in power in the village council, the difficulties in maintaining the full-blown mayorship, and the comparative success of Abu Tahir in winning payoffs for the village a result of his falling between two worlds, from neither of which he could benefit fully? Recent law had made payment of annual mayorship dues, makhtara, voluntary and many had ceased to give; on the other hand, village custom still held that the mayor ought to prepare and sign documents *gratis*. Abu Yasin was unable to make up by contracts (individual payments for documents drawn up, mathbata) what he lost in regular annual contributions. This inability was related in part to his following the old-style personality model—he was still expected to be (and he expected it of himself) a good man—generous to his relatives. He would not solicit pecuniary contributions from them if they did not give voluntarily. The contractual mayorship, then, weakened him as the head of a clan movement and sharpened intraclan and intravillage antagonism without adding substantially to his economic or political base. Moreover the gentlemen's agreement had not been scrapped so as to furnish the basis of a voluntaristic political system based on mutual advantage, personal contracts, and free choice. The logistics of the mayorship was modern (Amman and Irbid were the important centers of power, not Der'a in Syria), as was its economics and legal base (the contractual mayorship), but its social structural (clan paternalism), cultural (ethic of generosity), and social psychological (seeking the village's compassion) underpinnings were not.

Of course there were some indications that the integration of initially noncongruent elements was coming about: the watered-down gentleman's agreement which permitted muted renegadism but not subversion, the mixed complexion of financial support for both mayors (both had mathbata as well as mukhtara payments—see table 5); and the occasional oscillation from one tactic to another (with the reduction of financial contributions for the mayorship, Abu Yasin occasionally pressed some of his supporters outside the clan for contributions). But for the Yasin mayorship such adjustments were piecemeal and not fundamental. If what is meant by a "transitional society" is some state of affairs that stands at a half-way point between two ends of a continuum and the two ends of the continuum are defined as movement politics and machine politics, then the Yasin mayorship was not at that half-way point. If, on the other hand, transitional society means a state of affairs in which the noncongruency of elements is the defining characteristic, then the Yasin mayorship was transitional, as indicated by the idiom of discrepancy which its leaders espoused not only as a component of strategy but also as an article of belief: "We curtain the village, but you wish to rule us."

With respect to the attributes of power and influence listed on table 7, can it be said that either of the mayors or any influentials are transitional in either of these senses? In a study of local-level leadership by mayors (*muhtars*) in Turkey, Scott has presented some data that aid in answering this question.[31] He contrasted the attributes of old-style village mayors with a new-style mayor in a village close to a city.[32] The former was usually a native villager, a cultivator, and the beneficiary of religious training and a primary education only. The mayor served as muhtar on a part-time basis only. The post involved a great deal of paperwork and was not sought after; there was a high rate of turnover for those who accepted the position. The traditional occupant of the post tended to be either an elder from a large kin group who was a successful mediator, and hence basically a social equal, or an agha (titled landlord) and thereby of higher status than the peasantry. The new-style village mayor was comparatively wealthy and comparatively young (age forty). He came from a smaller kin group, but one that had diversified assets, traditional and modern. He himself made most of his income from a brick factory. The new-style mayor was not mainly engaged in "fixing" but rather in winning a larger share of the pie for the group he represented essentially as an equal.[33] He had served in the army, was a cardplayer, and attended the village coffeehouse for that purpose. He had held office for fourteen years. In all these respects this mayor differed from the old-style mayor. However Scott also pointed out a number of traditional attributes that he possessed: he had a large family (seven children); he respected the honor code; he was both serious and gregarious; his father had been muhtar before him; he had a traditional religious education—though far longer than usual; and he was a successful mediator. Thus the new-style village mayor in Turkey represented a combination of attributes, some traditional and some modern.

In Kufr al-Ma the old-style mayor, Abu Yasin, also presented a combination of attributes: he was hospitable, generous, pious, an excellent mediator, an elder, the father of a large family with many sons, a member of a large and cohesive patrilineage, a good advisor, and a master of custom; on the other hand, he was a literate, man-of-the-world, jack-of-all-trades, resistance fighter, patriot, and propagandist for material modernization. In what sense can either Abu Yasin or the Green Village mayor be considered "transitional" in their sources of power and influence? The balance of attributes for Abu Yasin was clearly on the traditional side, while the balance of attributes for the Green Village mayor was clearly on the new-style side. But the significant fact in both cases is that new attributes and sources of power and influence were added to the old without the replacement of the latter. For instance, the Green Village mayor's army service, his cardplaying in the coffeehouse, his role as innovator, and his new source of income did not diminish his respect for the honor code, the strength of his religious beliefs, or his skill as an arbitrator; and Abu Yasin's diverse occupational history, his involvement in the nationalist movement, and his dedication to material progress in no way weakened his skill as a mediator, his base of support in his clan and lineage, his reputation for generosity, his adherence to Islamic ritual, or his belief in Islamic ethics. These two men are "transitional leaders," then, in different degrees, if what is meant by that phrase is the combination of new and old sources of power and influence. They are not transitional leaders if what is meant by that phrase is the replacement of some old sources by some new. Change of leadership patterns is cumulative with respect to sources of power and influence but the resulting combination of sources is not necessarily integrated either functionally or cognitively.

Conclusion

This study has focused on the local-level political process or, somewhat invidiously put, "practical politics," that is, on the choice situation itself, the strategies available for use and those selected, the maneuvering of politicians (here mayors), and the implications of such choices for winning or losing the competition. But in carrying out this study it has been necessary to deal at length with the "environment of politics," with those factors considered critical in either establishing constraints or providing opportunities for leaders or men of influence. Part of that environment is largely outside the village and includes demographic and geographical constraints, the ideology of national-level bureaucrats, the structure of local-level administration, and particular roles (subdistrict officer, policeman). Part exists within the village itself and includes the immediate numerical (personnel), economic, social organizational, and ideological resources available to the competitors, idiosyncratic differences of personality, and certain aspects of social relations, such as multiplexity and cross-cutting ties. Part spans several arenas and includes occupational differentiation, rural-urban migration, Islamic law and ethics (interpreted at the local level by the preacher and outside the village by the religious judge), and the role of the Pasha (who operates simultaneously as an outsider, due to his inherited charisma and official position, and as an insider, due to his personal history of residence and leadership within the village and his affinal ties with its members). It is only by considering such factors in the environment of politics that I have been able to investigate such problems and processes as the in-built limits to the development of factionalism, the costs of utilizing the external arena, the articulation of arenas with respect to personnel, tactics, and prizes, and the simultaneous and opposing tendencies toward cyclical change on the one hand and cumulative change on the other.

The analysis has recorded a number of indices in the environment of politics as well as the actual process of competition—indices of the change from movement to machine politics: the growing individualization of the village as attested to by the decline of hospitality at all levels of the social structure, the increasing tendency to spend savings on items of conspicuous display, and the increasing importance of the subdistrict arena for social control. In a more strictly political context there is the increasing tendency to confrontation and encounter as evidenced by the 1960 petition against the mayor and the 1965 breaking of the gentleman's agreement, as well as the 1964 change in the official basis of the mayorship (from status to contract). The analysis has also recorded a number of indices of cyclical change: the feedback process by which political confrontations and encounters are usually resolved within the framework of social control, the return of Shujur to their own coalition, the accommodation of the mayors with one another, and the return to the observance of the gentlemen's agreement by all parties to the competition. The analysis has concluded that the crisis over the establishment of the village council is fundamentally a result of the coincidence of these two simultaneous and opposite processes and trends: the trend of ideological neutrals to be incorporated into movements (the clans and their component lineages) and the trend for all followers of movements (clan members) to be incorporated as "supporters" in machines. Viewed in terms of the competing coalitions, the resulting incongruity was revealed in the idiom of discrepancy: "We curtain the village and you wish to rule us." Viewed in terms of the two mayors' life styles and their contrasting modes of political competition, the incongruity was reflected in the Yasin mayor's inability to make movement politics work (as evidenced by the continuous decline of mukhtara payments) and his equal inability to break loose from it (because he sought the village's compassion) and capitalize on the opportunities the contractual mayorship created.

There are three important methodological conclusions of this book. An incisive study of the political process depends on paying much more attention to the structure, composition, and, most important, operation of the fundamental competing units, whether these units be corporate groups, corporate-like groups, or factions. A related conclusion is that whatever the formal structure or the ideology may be, these units seldom act in a unified fashion in the process of competition. Indeed where partible allegiance is an accepted principle of politics, it could not be otherwise. Therefore to view the competition in terms of core and support elements or in terms of refinements of these concepts (primary and secondary core/support, etc.) is not intellectual hairsplitting but rather an attempt to develop concepts that are not only more appropriate to the empirical facts of political competition but also more amenable to its analysis.

The second methodological conclusion is that the study of politics in small communities, even when that study explicitly focuses on competition for public prizes (control over mayorship, village council, temple, school committee), necessarily involves an investigation of private institutions (the family, household, or social network). As was demonstrated in chapter six, the history of interpersonal relationships and the particular decisions of individuals with respect to such matters as marriage, divorce, inheritance, magic, robbery, and land are directly pertinent to the outcome of political competition over public institutions and prizes.

Third, this study has substantiated the methodological importance of studying situations, communities, or societies that on the face of it—both in terms of the investigator's observations and the evaluations of the people themselves—are not wholly appropriate for the investigation of a particular problem or the application of a particular conceptual framework. Kufr al-Ma was neither an obvious nor easy locale for the study of local-level politics, but for that very reason perhaps the study is more valuable.

The most important substantive contribution of this book to the study of politics is the detailed description of one of its neglected subtypes—low-key politics. In low-key politics: followers are free to resort to the external arena but not leaders; followers are freer to switch than leaders are to recruit; confrontations tend to be generalized and passive rather than specific and active; signal confrontations rather than challenge confrontations preponderate; acts that are construed as innocent in many communities are construed as signal confrontations in communities with low-key politics; most significant encounters are *in absentia*. Low-key politics utilizes mechanisms for institutionalized deconfrontation—in Kufr al-Ma the gentleman's agreement, encounters-by-mediation (which render ambiguous who won and who lost), and the tip-off ploy (telling your opponent what you are about to do in the hopes that he will agree with you or, at least, not object). Low-key politics is characterized by muted subversion, muted renegadism, muted encounter (since it is often *in absentia*), and avoidance. In low-key politics the competitors often deny the reality of the competition either before, during, or after the fact, or deny an emotional investment in its out-come. Low-key politics usually involves prizes of lesser importance and therefore smaller investments of resources.

Precisely which factors in the political environment or in the competitive situation itself lead some communities, such as Kufr al-Ma, to develop low-key politics and others, such as those among the Central African Ndembu or Swat Pathans, to develop intense and abrasive political competition has yet to be determined. It is a problem that no serious student of politics can afford to ignore in the future.

Notes

Preface

1. National-level elections were held in 1967, though not during the period of my residence in the community. My observation was that the permanent residents of the community were generally uninterested in the outcomes of such elections and certainly spent little or no time engaged in political activity.
2. See Bruce Borthwick, "The Islamic Sermon as a Channel of Political Communication in Syria, Jordan and Egypt" (Ph.D. thesis, University of Michigan, 1965).
3. Robert Levine in Raoul Naroll and Ronald Cohen, *A Handbook of Method in Cultural Anthropology* (New York: Natural History Press, 1970), p. 185.

Chapter One

1. The recent literature of social anthropology has proliferated studies of the opposite type—studies of abrasive politics—in which violence is often featured and/or in which confrontations are frequent and open. Examples include Victor Turner's *Schism and Continuity in an African Society* (Manchester: Manchester University Press, 1957), Fredrik Barth's *Political Leadership among Swat Pathans* (London: Athlone Press, 1959), Napoleon Chagnon's *Yanomamo: The Fierce People* (New York: Holt, Rinehart and Winston, 1968), Thomas Kiefer's *The Tausug: Violence and Law in a Philippine Moslem Society* (New York: Holt, 1972), Anton Blok's, *The Mafia of a Sicilian Village 1860–1960 A Study of Violent Peasant Entrepreneurs* (New York: Harper and Row, 1974), and Mervyn Meggitt's *Blood Is Their Argument Warfare Among the Mae Enga Tribesmen of the New Guinea Highlands* (Palo Alto: Mayfield, 1977).
2. Antoun, Richard T., "Pertinent Variables in the Environment of Middle Eastern Village Politics," in Richard T. Antoun and Iliya Harik, *Rural Politics and Social Change in the Middle East* (Bloomington: University of Indiana Press, 1972).

3. Antoun, Richard T., *Arab Village: A Social Structural Study of a Trans-jordanian Peasant Community* (Bloomington: University of Indiana Press, 1972).

4. The use of the term "scarce" ends and resources does not signify acceptance of the marginalist economic view of scarcity. The ends themselves are scarce only in relation to the unique distribution of values in each society.

5. Robert Dahl, as quoted in William A. Gamson, *Power and Discontent*, (Homewood, Illinois: Dorsey Press, 1968), p. 96.

6. See Harold Laswell, *Politics: Who Gets What, When, How* (New York: Meridian Press, 1958).

7. William Gamson, *Power and Discontent*.

8. David Easton, *A Framework of Political Analysis* (Englewood, New Jersey: Prentice Hall, 1965).

9. M. G. Smith, "A Structural Approach to Comparative Politics," in Easton, David, Editor, *Varieties of Political Theory* (Englewood, New Jersey: Prentice Hall, 1966).

10. Jeremy Boissevain, "The Place of the Non-Group in the Social Sciences," *Man* 3, 4 (December 1968).

11. The concept of "corporation" and its applicability to the local-level social structures anthropologists generally describe has been the subject of recent debate. Cochrane has argued for a restricted usage of the term based on its historical meaning in English law. Goodenough has argued for a wider usage referring to groups that are unitary parties to jural relationships. The usage of the term in this book is closer to Goodenough's. However today the clans of Kufr al-Ma, even in Goodenough's terms, are not corporate groups, although they may have been in the past. For a discussion of the former corporate functions exercised by the clans and the village with respect to land, see Antoun, *Arab Village*, Chapter One. For the debate between Cochrane and Goodenough, see the *American Anthropologist* 7, 5 (October 1971): 1114–1155.

12. Fredrick Barth, "Models of Social Organization," Royal Anthropological Institute Occasional Paper No. 23, (London: Royal Anthropological Institute, 1966).

13. See Talal Asad, "Market Model, Class Structure and Consent: A Reconsideration of Swat Political Organization," *Man* 7, 1 (March 1972).

14. Anton Blok, *The Mafia of a Sicilian Village*.

15. Anatol Rapoport, "The Use and Misuse of Game Theory," *Scientific American* 207, 6 (December 1962).

16. Frederick G. Bailey, "The Study of Politics in Village India," unpublished mimeograph, n.d.

17. As I have pointed out in "Pertinent Variables," like any analyst seeking to work out the conceptual framework in its early stages, Bailey has used the same terms with somewhat different meanings in various published and unpublished works.

18. Frederick G. Bailey, *Politics and Social Change Orissa in 1959* (Berkeley: University of California Press, 1963), p. 138.

19. Gamson, *Power and Discontent*.

20. Sydel Silverman, "Bailey's Politics," *Journal of Peasant Studies* 2 (1974).

21. Frederick G. Bailey, *Strategems and Spoils* (New York: Schocken, 1969), pp. 121–32.
22. James Reston, *New York Times*, 5 October 1967.
23. A game format is not to be confused with "game theory" and all of its mathematical implications.
24. Silverman, "Bailey's Politics."
25. Bailey's *Caste and the Economic Frontier* (Manchester: University of Manchester Press, 1957); *Tribe, Caste and Nation* (Manchester: University of Manchester Press, 1960); and *Politics and Social Change.*
26. Alfred Kroeber, *The Nature of Culture* (Chicago: University of Chicago Press, 1952).
27. I am in general agreement with Elliot Liebow's view of the significance of *ex post facto* analysis: "It could be argued, I believe, that the timing of hypothesis formulation is irrelevant; that regardless of whether hypotheses are generated *pre* or *post factum*, the test of their validity always rests on future replication; and that the only proper restriction of the generation of hypotheses or explanations is that they fit the data." See Liebow, *Tally's Corner* (Boston: Little, Brown Co., 1967).

Chapter Two

1. This estimate is quoted in Raphael Patai, ed., *Jordan* (New Haven: Human Relations Area Files, 1956), pp. 21–27.
2. See the *Proceedings of the Conference on Middle East Agricultural Development*, Report No. 6, p. 23.
3. A *shaykh*, strictly speaking, is any elderly man. The term shaykh is also applied to any man of religious learning regardless of age. Shaykh Luqman, the imam of Kufr al-Ma (who led the prayers in the mosque), for instance, was only thirty years old and received this appellation. In this monograph, however, unless otherwise indicated, the term will be used to designate the political leader of a descent group or village or combination of descent groups or villages in a certain area. This man usually based his authority on his military prowess, his competence in settling disputes, and the size and distinction of his lineage. In Weber's terms, he was both a "traditional" and a "charismatic" leader (see Max Weber, *The Theory of Social and Economic Organization* (Glencoe: The Free Press, 1968), pp. 341–86). The shaykh supported his authority with the loyalty of his armed kinsmen, with exactions in kind from peasants, and with the munificence of his hospitality to his followers (see below and chapter four). After 1922, with the establishment of the central government, the authority and the stature of the shaykh were reduced, while the importance of another political leader, the *mukhtar*, grew. By comparison the mukhtar was a dwarfish figure. Although he represented his own clan and his own village, he was tied to the central government as its functionary. He was selected by his clan and village, not for the number of guns his kinsmen could command or the nobility of his pedigree, but for his knowledge of town ways and his ability to

manipulate government officials. When referring to the dominant shaykh of the "peoples of Tibne" the word "shaykh" is capitalized.

4. Key Arabic words frequently repeated in the course of the text will not be italicized and their long vowel marks will not be transliterated after first mention. Proper place names will be spelled according to their common usage.

5. A. Grannot, *The Land System in Palestine: History and Structure* (London: Eyre and Spottiswoode, 1952), p. 213.

6. The reconstruction of the musha' system presented here is based on written accounts such as Grannot and Weulersse as well as information collected from village informants who participated in this land tenure system before its abolition in 1939. Neither the authors who have written about the system nor the present writer have observed it in operation. Therefore all statements regarding the system must be regarded as tentative.

7. Grannot, *The Land System in Palestine*, p. 228. Of course such a statement is conjectural and assumes a minimum of buying or selling of shares since their original assignment at the time of the founding of the village.

8. Ibid., p. 246.

9. See Antoun, "Conservatism and Change in the Village Community: A Jordanian Case Study," *Human Organization* 24 (Spring 1965).

10. The percentage engaged in subsistence agriculture is probably smaller and the percentage engaged in nonagricultural occupations outside of the village is probably higher, for many falling in the latter category were not present in the village during my stay and therefore were not recorded in the occupational census.

11. For a fuller description of the social structure of Kufr al-Ma, including a discussion of the household, marriage, and social control, see Antoun, *Arab Village*.

12. For the precise spatial relations of the lineages of the village including the few exceptions to the pattern stipulated, see the map facing p. 90 in Antoun, *Arab Village*.

13. For the precise spatial relations of the clans of the village, including the few exceptions to the pattern stipulated, see Antoun, *Arab Village*, map facing p. 74.

14. For the distribution of land according to descent groups in 1960, together with land sales since 1939, see Antoun, *Arab Village*, map facing p. 24.

15. The translation "mayor" for mukhtar is not entirely appropriate, since, unlike his American counterpart, he does not represent a legal corporation (municipality), rather an administrative unit; moreover he is not this unit's sole representative—in Kufr al-Ma there is a second mayor. Furthermore he is not elected, nor is he subject to renomination and reelection in order to continue his tenure; he is chosen by a consensus of clansmen and confirmed by the central government. His tenure ends only when that consensus changes or when the district officer declares him no longer able or willing to discharge his duties fairly. Despite these differences it would even be more misleading to

translate mukhtar as "headman," since he performs few of the tasks performed by a headman in the literature of sub-Saharan African ethnography (whether ritual, economic, or social). Moreover he is not necessarily or even usually a first among equals in terms of power of influence; other clan elders often exert more influence in clan and village-wide policy-making.

16. A multiplex relationship is one that serves many interests, e.g., economic, political, religious, recreational. See Max Gluckman, *The Judicial Process Among the Barotse of Northern Rhodesia* (Manchester: University of Manchester Press, 1955), p. 18 for a discussion of the concept.

17. The external resources are discussed in chapter four and again at length in chapter five.

18. One acre equals approximately four dunums.

19. See chapter one for a definition of confrontation and chapter six for further illustrations and analysis of the concept.

20. An analysis of the clerk's role appears in chapters six and seven.

21. *Politics and Social Change*, p. 138.

22. Ibid., pp. 140–141.

23. Ibid., pp. 141–142 and pp. 152–154.

24. Actually the tribesmen did not commit apostasy; they simply refused to pay the traditional *zakat* or Islamic tax. However since the payment was a pillar of the faith, the act was regarded as tantamount to apostasy, hence the phrase.

25. See chapters one and three for a definition of these concepts.

26. The single known instance of outright renegadism is discussed in chapter six.

27. Bailey alludes to the concept in his 1965 paper delivered to the Working Conference on Indian Politics at Sussex University, but he does not devote much space to its elucidation. The concept of collusion developed in *Strategems and Spoils*, pp. 121–32, has implications for partible allegiance without being in any way synonymous with it.

28. Since chapter five is devoted to the subject of external resources, including the effect of national-level policy-making on the village, no discussion of the subject occurs here.

29. The confrontations involving the establishment of the village council are discussed in chapter six.

30. Kufr al-Ma is not the only recorded case of such a shift in the political process among Middle Eastern peasants. Emrys L. Peters's reports on the village of Juba᾿ in Lebanon ("Aspects of Rank and Status among Muslims in a Lebanese Village," in J. Pitt-Rivers, ed., *Mediterranean Countrymen* (Paris: Mouton, 1963); and "Shifts in Power in a Lebanese Village," in Antoun and Harik, eds., *Rural Politics and Social Change*), imply such a shift. I have analysed Peters's data in my essay "Pertinent Variables."

31. For a full analysis of these events, see chapter six.

32. A number of anthropologists have analyzed local-level factional politics including Alan R. Beals and Bernard J. Siegel, "Pervasive Factionalism," *American Anthropologist* 62 (June 1960); Janet Bujra,

"The Dynamics of Political Action," *American Anthropologist* 75 (February 1973); Raymond Firth, "Factions in Indian and Overseas Indian Societies," *British Journal of Sociology* 8 (December 1957); Paul Friedrich, "The Legitimacy of a Cacique," in Marc J. Swartz, ed., *Local-Level Politics* (Chicago: Aldine Press, 1968); Adrian C. Mayer, "Factions in Fiji Indian Rural Settlements," *British Journal of Sociology* 8 (December 1957); Ralph Nicholas, "Factions," in Eggan and Gluckman, *Political Systems and the Distribution of Power* (New York: Praeger, 1965); Moshe Shokeid, "Immigration and Factionalism," British Journal of Sociology 19 (1968); and Melford Spiro, "Factionalism and Politics in Village Burma," in Marc J. Swartz, ed., *Local-Level Politics*. The concepts of "machine" and "faction," while not synonymous, have certain important implications for one another. These implications will be discussed in chapter six.

Chapter Three

1. "Political Activity in Village India," pp. 2–3.
2. "Para-political Systems" in Marc Swartz, ed., *Local-Level Politics*.
3. See Bailey, *Strategems and Spoils*, p. 28 and pp. 38–48.
4. Ibid., p. 46.
5. Bailey, "The Study of Politics in Village India," mimeographed, n.d.
6. Bailey, *Strategems . . .* , p. 45.
7. "Political Activity in Village India," p. 25.
8. There are certainly other points of view. For instance, I have completely neglected a social psychological point of view which would focus on the emotional disposition of individuals toward leaders irregardless of overt postures of support.
9. See Horton, "A Syrian Village in its Changing Environment," (Ph.D. dissertation, Harvard University, 1960). For an analysis of some of Horton's data from the point of view of local-level politics, see Antoun, "Pertinent Variables." Actually Horton uses the term "sib" rather than clan to describe the above-mentioned groups. In order to be consistent with the usage generally adopted in this monograph for like groups, I have used the term "clan." As mentioned in the previous chapter, the term "sib" has been given another meaning.
10. In Atareb a lineage can trace its descent to a common ancestor, two or three generations removed from the oldest living generation, i.e., it is usually a five-generation group figured from the present set of fifteen-year-olds. Each lineage is known by the name of a lineage ancestor. In Atareb a clan is a patrilineal descent group that lives in a certain area of the village (unlike the lineages which are scattered within the clan area), cannot trace ties to a common ancestor but claims such an ancestor, whose name designates the clan. The clan is characterized by social integration and common group sentiment. Wives who have married into the clan from other clans are not considered clan members, but wives taken from within the clan are members. According to Horton, lineages of clan status trace common patrilineal ancestry but have no collateral branches. They live in

their own residence area and have their own part of the threshing floor. In certain respects they are treated as clans by others as well as themselves, and frequently they push for clan status and thus become the object of political jockeying by both alliances. Unattached families, either nuclear or extended, reside in the area of other descent groups and are usually considered to be in sympathy with those among whom they live. But Horton notes that such families are normally considered to be outside the framework of political struggle and are involved, unwillingly, only in times of crisis.

11. This summary and interpretation of Horton's data necessarily omits a great deal of relevant ethnographic data. Interested readers should consult the original dissertation.

12. In this book ideology does not refer to some ideal and hence unrealizable set of beliefs, nor does it suggest a polarity between some real set of factors and some other presumptively false set of beliefs about them. Rather ideology refers to beliefs men have about what their individual, social, or metaphysical circumstances are. These beliefs may or may not be true. In the present context, the point of view for distinguishing core and support is ideological because all members of the clan define themselves as members of the clan by fact of ascription. Statements such as "I am of Beni Yasin" and/or "We are brothers and sons of brothers" are simply definitive of social membership and are not normative statements on the one hand or necessarily historical (true) statements on the other.

13. Bailey, *Politics and Social Change*, p. 141.

14. *Politics and Social Change*, Chapter 6.

15. See Antoun, "On the Significance of Names in an Arab Village," *Ethnology* 7 (1968) for the importance of nicknaming in social control.

16. Henry Maine, *Ancient Law* (New York: Henry Holt Co., 1878), pp. 164–65.

17. In describing this type of nonpaying support, the mukhtars used the following phrases: "All his work is with me" (*kul shughlū maʿī*); "They stamped with me" (*khattamū ʿendi*); "All of his transactions are with me" (*muʿāmālātu kullu maʿī*). I solicited the information recorded on this table from the two mukhtars. Although it is possible that my informants misled me as to the degree of economic support from the village households, and indeed some underrating of certain support categories occurred (see chapter six), the degree of inaccuracy was minimized by the fact that I solicited this information after fifteen months of field work in the village, when I had the good will of my informants. I was, moreover, in a position to cross-check the accuracy of the statements. However there is no question that the responses of the Yasin mukhtar were more detailed and qualified than those of the Dumi mukhtar and in that sense more accurate. While the Yasin mukhtar often told me, "He pays me two measures of wheat and two measures of barley every year" or "He doesn't pay me on the threshing ground, but for each document I draw up for him he pays me ten piastres" or "He stopped paying me two years ago," the Dumi mukhtar simply said, "He comes to me for documents" or "He comes to me for documents and pays" or simply "He is for me."

18. These fourteen categories are my own rather than those of informants. Table 5 much more closely reflects the statements of informants, although not entirely so.

Chapter Four

1. I am basing my account of the shaykhdom mainly on Munib Madi and Sulayman Musa's, *The History of Jordan in the Twentieth Century* (*tārīkh al-irdun fi al-qarn al 'ashrīn*) (Amman, 1959), Frederick G. Peake's *The History of East Jordan* (Jerusalem, 1935), and the accounts of village informants. Most men above the age of fifty were familiar with the district political structure before it collapsed in 1922. But the details of its operation are not clear. The account of this political structure is frankly conjectural at a number of points, but I have attempted to make sense out of the facts available.
2. Of course the Arab Legion demonstrated that with proper incentives, training, and understanding leadership, Bedouins make good soldiers.
3. It should be noted that in Kufr al-Ma the government did not give the mukhtar an official stamp as the mark of his authority until 1959.
4. This revenue total is all the more interesting considering that 1959–60 was a drought year while 1964–65 was not.
5. The pertinent laws are as follows: "Law for the Administration of Villages (No. 5) for the Year 1954"; "Law for Mayors within Regions, Municipalities and Local Districts (No. 52) for the Year 1958"; "Regulation for the Acceptance of Payments and Fees by Mayors in Towns and Villages (No. 62) for the Year 1964"; and "Directives for the Selection of Mayors" issued in 1959. Each of these laws was published in the Official Gazette of the Hashemite Kingdom of Jordan in the year of promulgation.
6. See Max Gluckman, John Barnes, and J. Mitchell, "The Village Headman in Central Africa" *Africa* 19 (1949); also Gluckman, *Custom and Conflict in Africa* (Oxford: Oxford University Press, 1956); and "Inter-Hierarchical Roles: Professional and Party Ethics in Tribal Areas in South and Central Africa," in Swartz, *Local-Level Politics*.
7. See "Law for the Administration of Villages (No. 5) for the Year 1954," Article 5, Paragraph One.
8. Here I wish to record my debt to the writings of Raymond Firth on "social organization," the writings of Max Gluckman on intercalary leaders, and conversations with Emrys Peters for clarifying my own views on local-level leadership.
9. Bailey, "The Study of Politics in Village India," p. 4. See chapter one for a definition of these and the following terms.
10. The term arena is not found with the present meaning in Bailey's first two books, *Caste and the Economic Frontier* and *Tribe, Caste and Nation*. However the analyses of the position of the Boad Outcastes in the first book and the concept of "bridge actions" in the second are closely related to the development of the concept in the third book. The concept of arena receives very little attention in Bailey's latest book, *Stratagems and Spoils*, where it is only mentioned briefly in

relation to "umpires" and to the transformation of "teams" into "arenas."

11. See Victor Turner, *Schism and Continuity in an African Society* (Manchester: University of Manchester Press, 1957).

12. Other such societies include those of the Swat Pathans studied by Fredrik Barth in his monograph, *Political Leadership among Swat Pathans* (London: Athlone Press, 1959), the Sicilian Mafia studied by Anton Blok in his work, *The Mafia of a Sicilian Village 1860–1960* (New York: Harper and Row, 1974) and the Filipino Muslims studied by Thomas Kiefer in his book, *The Tausug: Violence and Law in a Philippine Moslem Society* (New York: Holt, 1972).

13. Turner, *Schism and Continuity*, p. 94.

14. It could be argued that the lesser multiplexity of Dumi, its lesser social organizational unity, and its weaker sense of ideological unity had always made movement politics less effective than for Yasin, and that the switch to the contractual mayorship only accentuated the drift.

15. In reality, two independent lineages and part of a third supported the coalition, while one ʿAmr lineage and one independent lineage supported Yasin.

16. I wish to thank my colleague Fuad Khuri of the American University of Beirut for bringing this folk saying to my attention. Although I never heard villagers state it in this manner, they would have understood it, agreed with it, and, based many of their actions upon it.

Chapter Five

1. In a previous publication (Antoun "Conservation and Change in the Village Community," *Human Organization* 24, 1 (1965) I discussed the problem of stability and change in the village community without tracing out specific implications for local-level politics.

2. I have recorded in detail a number of the problems caused by occupational mobility and economic differentiation particularly among siblings and close cousins in *Arab Village*. See in particular, cases 3, 4, 6, and 7.

3. I am drawing heavily here on an incisive conference paper given by George Grassmuck to the Conference on Local Government in Mediterranean Countries in Beirut, Lebanon in September 1966. Its title is "Regional and Local Government in the Hashemite Kingdom of Jordan" (mimeographed).

4. In 1965 an administrative reorganization of the kingdom (Law No. 125 for 1965) established four tiers of administration for some areas—the muhafatha, the liwa, the qadaʿ, and the nahiyah. But in many areas the second and fourth tiers were lacking. In the part of the district (Ajlun) where Kufr al-Ma was located (Al-Kura) no intermediate second tier existed. That is, the subdistrict officer (qaimaqam) dealt directly with the muhafith in the district capital (Irbid). According to the *Statistical Yearbook 1964*, the total population of the Ajlun district in 1961 was 273,976; its area covered 3,885 square kilometers

with about 66 persons per square mile; it numbered 64,975 urban inhabitants, 190,838 rural inhabitants and 18,163 scattered tent dwellers.

5. This description and Chart 3 were adopted from "An Administrative Review of The Ministry of Interior. The Ministry of Municipal and Rural Affairs" by Griffenhagen Kroeger, Inc., Consultants in Public Administration to the Hashemite Kingdom of Jordan, (Amman, January 1966), p. 5.

6. Grassmuck, "Regional and Local Government," p. 31.

7. Speech of the Minister of Interior for Municipal and Rural Affairs, 2 March 1966 (mimeographed, in Arabic).

8. Grassmuck, "Regional and Local Government."

9. Rimawi, 2 March 1966, p. 32.

10. Griffenhagen and Kroeger, as quoted in Grassmuck, "Regional and Local Government," p. 35.

11. In April 1966 Dr. Rimawi addressed a letter to the governor of the Ajlun district requesting an explanation for the fact that only 7 of 61 villages with a population of 800 or more had councils. In a speech earlier in the year (2 March 1966) Rimawi called attention to the fact that although 70 village councils had been formed throughout the kingdom during the year, there were 204 villages (over 800 in population) to which the law applied. The Griffenhagen-Kroeger Report published earlier (January 1966) and reporting for all villages (and not just those over 800 in population) cited 121 villages with councils and 751 with mukhtars (i.e., without councils). Reporting in a conference on "Local Government and Cooperative Development" later in the year (September 1966), Qutub reported that 135 village councils had been formed throughout the kingdom out of a total of 966 villages or about 15 percent of all village settlements (see Qutub, "Local Government and Cooperative Development," pp. 7–8 and Griffenhagen-Kroeger, "An Administrative Review," p. 17).

12. Gubser cites a number of instances of this kind in his study of the Jordanian town of Al-Kerak, *Politics and Change in Al-Kerak, Jordan* (London: Oxford University Press, 1973).

13. I am indebted for much of the information on the office of the muhafith and for the following table on the Griffenhagen and Kroeger review referred to above.

14. In the following paragraphs I have drawn upon Grassmuck's characterization of the decentralization policy in Jordan in the middle sixties.

15. This was a conclusion of the Griffenhagen-Kroeger review, p. 17.

16. Grassmuck noted that in the office of one muhafith, of the six telephone lines four were to appointed officers of the central government in the region or the capital; only two were local lines. (Grassmuck, "Regional and Local Government," p. 25)

17. See Grassmuck's comments on this point. The rise of the Palestinian movement in Jordan has made Grassmuck's comments of ten years ago even more apropos.

18. See Antoun, "Conservatism and Change" for an elaboration of this point.

19. See pp. 70–73 of the "Village Projects and Services Law, Law No. 27,

1957" in *The Collection of Laws and Regulations for Jordan Until 1960*, part 3, Amman, 1962.

20. Other factors mentioned in the next chapter also dissuaded villagers in Kufr al-Ma from participation in the Committee for Village Improvement.

21. I am using the term "roles" here and in what follows to mean "social identities" in Goodenough's sense; see Ward Goodenough, "Rethinking 'Status' and 'Role,'" in M. Banton, ed., *The Relevance of Models for Social Anthropology* (London: Tavistock, 1965).

22. In 1935 several villagers killed a number of policemen at the local police post after the police had taken a respected villager who claimed to have special religious charisma and shaved off his beard.

23. These items are considered delicacies. I do not mean to suggest that all or even most policemen act in such a manner. Indeed no policeman recruited from a rural area and understanding the norms of hospitality and reciprocity could have acted so. Furthermore I have witnessed many high-echelon bureaucrats refuse lavish offers of hospitality, either because such offers do not accord with their own "modernized" value systems or because they realize the implications of the politics of hospitality for their own actions or because of both considerations.

24. Peter Gubser, *Politics and Change in Al-Karak, Jordan, 1973*. See particularly pp. 139–145.

25. I do not wish to indicate that the Pasha was universally respected and acclaimed; a few government employees were hostile to him and others ambivalent; although he was respected and acclaimed by the vast majority of peasants, a few claimed to have been victimized by him.

26. Pp. 118–121.

27. Lloyd Fallers, "The Predicament of the Modern African Chief: An Instance From Uganda," *American Anthropologist* 57 (April 1955).

28. This fact distinguishes the situation in Al-Kura from that described by Gubser for Kerak, where, he states, the Majali family act as a unified body in political contexts; see Gubser, *Politics and Change in Al-Karak, Jordan*, p. 85.

29. For an elaboration of the implications of rural-urban migration, see Antoun, "Conservatism and Change."

30. Gubser indicates that in some of the rural areas of Al-Karak district, this tendency to resort to supplication and passivity in the face of men of higher status and power remains; see Gubser, *Politics and Change in Al-Karak, Jordan*, pp. 141–42.

31. A more detailed discussion of the implications of this incident for both village politics and the personal styles of village politicking follows in the next two chapters.

32. The estimate of 150 days appears in a UNESCO report on the Wadi Zglab watershed, in which Kufr al-Ma falls.

33. See Ishaq Y. Qutub, "Impact of Rural Credit and Thrift Cooperative Societies on the Traditional Social and Economic Structure of Rural Jordan—A Study of Three Villages," paper presented at the University of Malta under the auspices of the Mediterranean Social Science

Research Council, December 1965 (mimeograph), pp. 6–7 and pp. 23–24.

34. See Qutub, p. 23. In spite of these factors Qutub points out that once cooperatives were set up and cultivators were persuaded to join them, a large majority of peasants regarded them as superior to traditional sources of credit (Qutub, "Impact of Rural Credit," p. 24).

35. Gubser, *Politics and Change in Al-Karak, Jordan,* p. 141.

36. One such handicap is minority ethnic status. Abner Cohen, for instance, describes the situation of the Hausa migrants in Yoruba towns in southern Nigeria. For a time the Hausa of the Sabo quarter in Ibadan supported a political party purportedly representing their ethnic interests. However they quickly found that such a party could not be effective because of the overwhelming Yoruba majority in the area. They reverted to the strategy of intensifying their economic and social relations within their Sabo quarter—a quarter which had already been recognized as a partially autonomous under the British policy of indirect rule. Quarter endogamy was intensified, pressure was increased to attend the quarter mosque (rather than the congregational mosque in the city center), and the Sabo Hausas adopted a special brand of Islamic mysticism, that of the Tijaniyya order. The elaborate rituals enjoined by the order led to increased social as well as ritual contact; they also led to a more cohesive social organization, since activities relating to mediation, the signing of contracts, and the offering of advice on ethics and Islamic law were directed by 119 full-time religious specialists (malams) within the quarter. The intensification of ritual and social activity encouraged economic activity not only by proliferating and intensifying contacts within the community and by establishing a firm basis of trust for transactions that were usually carried out orally but also by making the ethnic boundary between Sabo Hausa and other Muslims more significant and precise, thereby reinforcing the monopoly the Hausa already had in the cattle trade and were attempting to establish in the kola nut trade. See Cohen's study of politics and ethnicity, *Custom and Politics in Urban Africa* (Berkeley: University of California Press, 1969).

37. See Gubser's comments on political parties in Al-Karak and Ann Dearden, *Jordan* (London: Robert Hale, 1958) for a general description of the political parties in Jordan during this period.

38. See Pickthall's translation of the Quran, 5:59, 11:17, 13:38, 18:12, 19:37, 23:54, 35:6, 40:5, 40:30, 58:19, and 58:22.

39. As mentioned before, however, the collection of taxes was not on a strictly universalistic basis: certain villagers were excepted from payment for what was regarded as just cause. Thus the traditional village value of "just priority," literally, "I am 'closer' or 'more deserving' (*ana awla*) usually invoked on the basis of kinship, descent, friendship, propinquity, or, in this instance, economic status, almost inevitably creeps into relationships governed by universalistic criteria.

40. The terms "orthogenetic" and "heterogenetic" are used by Redfield and Singer to distinguish different kinds of ideological change, particu-

larly with respect to the development of cities in India; see Robert
Redfield and Milton Singer "The Cultural Role of Cities," *Economic
Development of Cultural Change* 3 (October 1954).

41. An even more pronounced instance of orthogenetic change with respect
to a case of honor occurred in 1925. After three policemen had been
killed by villagers at the police post, the army descended on the village, confiscated all the animals, seeds, and furnishings of the culprit's close patrilineal kinsmen, camped in the village for fifteen days,
engaged in some willful damage of property, and finally, after the culprits were caught, kept one-half of the confiscated property as
blood-money (*diya*). The soldiers' behavior in the village was in general accord with the expected behavior of a victimized tribal group
during the traditional "boiling of the blood" (*fawrat al-damm*) period, although in this instance the period extended beyond the traditionally accepted three-day period.

42. See the section on "the arena" in chapter four for a further discussion of
prizes.

43. Bailey, "Political Activity in Village India," p. 23. See also Bailey,
Strategems and Spoils, p. 179.

44. See Bailey, "Political Activity in Village India," pp. 159–60.

45. Actually the personnel allowed to compete are drawn from all the peoples of Tibne, for in a historical sense they are all "sons of the village"; this fact helps to explain why villagers are willing to embrace
the Pasha as an ally but not other agents in the external arena.

46. Pp. 271–75.

47. In *Strategems and Spoils* (1969), Bailey gives some evidence that this did
happen. He refers to one Pan who was organizing children's sports in
the village "hoping to gather a few votes by demonstrating his
selflessness and public spirit."

48. It is a fight because the Pans violated both the rules governing personnel
eligible to compete and the rules governing tactics. It is a competition
because many Pans still value the prize available in the internal arena
and because by the "collusion" of both sides certain critical economic relations between them have not been endangered.

49. Bailey, *Strategems and Spoils*, p. 151.

50. Ibid.

51. See Iliya Harik, *The Political Mobilization of Peasants* (Bloomington:
Indiana University Press, 1974).

52. See Abner Cohen, *Arab Border-Villages in Israel* (Manchester: Manchester University Press, 1965).

53. This is not strictly true, since the Jordanian rules establish a minor
property qualification for some offices and individuals with records of
criminal or blatant political party activity are excluded.

54. It is questionable, however, that the members of Beni Dumi and Beni
'Amr affirm across the board structure B's views regarding the eligi-
bility of personnel. I can imagine many situations, apart from the
village council, in which they would insist equally with Yasin that
such and such a matter was the concern of the village's notables and
not others.

Chapter Six

1. See M. G. Smith, "Segmentary Lineage Systems," *JRAI* 86 (1956); Fredrick Barth, "Segmentary Opposition and the Theory of Games: A Study of Pathan Organization," *JRAI* 89 (1959); and Janet Bujra, "The Dynamics of Political Action: A New Look at Factionalism," *American Anthropologist* 75 (1973).
2. See Bailey, *Strategems and Spoils*, p. 94.
3. Ibid., pp. 29–30.
4. See Bailey, "Political Activity in Village India," pp. 4–5.
5. In his "Political Activity in Village India," "Parapolitical Systems," and *Strategems and Spoils*.
6. See Bailey, *Strategems and Spoils*, p. 98.
7. Ibid., p. 123.
8. See Anatol Rapoport, "The Use and Misuse of Game Theory," *Scientific American* 207, 6 (December 1962): 2 and chapter one for a discussion of the difference between fights and games.
9. See Antoun, *Arab Village*, map facing 74.
10. The sequences of competition can also be marked off in a way entirely unrelated to external authorities. In the Atareb case, analyzed in chapter three, the phases of competition were determined by the cultural framework of the village arena, which identified certain periods as "times of peace," others as "times of dispute," and still others as "times of corruption." More specifically, in Atareb the type of political competition was related to the phase of conflict development. Thus during Horton's time of peace and his time of corruption it was inappropriate and perhaps impossible to fish in troubled waters, i.e., to subvert clans and lineages from the opposite alliance. However during the intermediate time of dispute pragmatic rules allowed such subversion, although normative rules (the gentlemen's agreement to refrain from interfering in the opposite alliance's affairs) forbade it.
11. The term "cases" is used here in a very general sense to refer to separable clusters of incidents. There is no intention of analyzing these incidents within the framework of social control or the sociology of dispute.
12. For an indication of Shujur's numerical strength, see table 3; for further information about this lineage and its role in village affairs, see Antoun, *Arab Village*.
13. If a charge of contention and dispute is upheld, the judge can declare a judicial separation which terminates the marriage. If the charge of wifely obedience is upheld, the wife must return to her husband.
14. The consent of the woman is required by Islamic law for a valid marriage contract.
15. Etymologically the term *hajjāb* means "maker of amulets," but since the individual described here does far more than that and claims to possess power over supernatural beings and forces, the term magician has been used to describe his occupational specialty.
16. Although a funeral was not mentioned in any of the five cases, the first petition presented by Yasin to attach the village to the municipality

of Deir Abu Said took place on the occasion of one member's funeral. One of the most significant acts that led to the termination of Shujur's secession occurred during the religious festival celebrating the end of Ramadan (see chart 16).

17. *American Anthropologist* 62 (June 1960).
18. Ibid., p. 397.
19. Nicholas, "Factions: a Comparative Analysis," in F. Eggan and M. Gluckman eds., *Political Systems and the Distribution of Power* (New York: Praeger, 1965), pp. 44–46.
20. Graham, "The Succession of Factional Systems in the Uttar Pradesh Congress Party, 1937–66" in M. Swartz, *Local-Level Politics*, p. 323.
21. In M. Swartz, ed., *Local-Level Politics*, pp. 409–20.
22. *American Anthropologist* 75 (February 1973).
23. Following Mayer's 1966 usage, quasi-groups are ego-centered sets of people who interact in successive contexts of activity.
24. Unfortunately Bujra's essay deals mainly with the oppositional context and the local socioeconomic context but very little with the external political context.
25. Bujra, "The Dynamics of Political Action," pp. 146–47.
26. Ibid., p. 150.
27. Boissevain, "Of Marbles and Men: Factionalism Reconsidered," 1975.
28. See chapter four and Turner, *Schism and Continuity in an African Society*.
29. Ernestine Friedl, "Lagging Emulation in Post-Peasant Societies," *American Anthropologist* 66 (June 1964).

Chapter Seven

1. For an analysis of the significance of names for individual differences as well as for social control, see Antoun, "On the Significance of Names in an Arab Village," *Ethnology* 6, 3 (April 1968).
2. For an example of such an interpretation, see Antoun, *Arab Village* 1972, case 7.
3. See Friedrich's introduction to Part III of Swartz's *Local-Level Politics*, p. 204.
4. Ibid.
5. The present chapter does not attempt to examine personality by a configurational, basic, or modal approach; in short, it is not a personality study.
6. Many definitions of influence have been ignored in the following brief discussion in favor of those definitions which illuminate my data. Also ignored are attempts to operationalize the concept. See, for example, William A. Gamson, *Power and Discontent* (Homewood, Ill.: Dorsey, 1968).
7. Chester I. Barnard, "The Acceptance of Authority," in L. A. Coser and B. Rosenberg, eds., *Sociological Theory: A Book of Readings* (New York: Macmillan Co., 1957), p. 144.
8. Ibid., p. 148.

9. Ibid., p. 151.

10. Robert Bierstadt, "The Analysis of Social Power" in Coser and Rosenberg, *Sociological Theory*, p. 159.

11. Ibid., p. 161.

12. William Lloyd Warner and Paul S. Lunt, *The Social Life of a Modern Community* (New Haven: Yale University Press, 1941); William Lloyd Warner, M. Meeker, and K. Eels, *Social Class in America* (Chicago: Science Research, 1949); William Lloyd Warner and Associates, *Democracy in Jonesville* (New York: Harper, 1949).

13. Social structural appropriateness can also be construed as an element of power in its social organizational aspect. Since the main thrust of the analysis deals with influence rather than power, this aspect will be neglected.

14. Linda Zecher, "The Men of Influence and The Exercise of Influence in Nabatieh Lebanon" (M.A. dissertation, American University of Beirut, 1967).

15. Ibid.

16. Ibid.

17. See Antoun, "The Social Significance of Ramadan in an Arab Village," *The Muslim World* (January and April 1968) for a detailed account of the offering of hospitality and charity during Ramadan.

18. According to Islamic and folk beliefs, jinn are noncorporeal humanlike beings.

19. As an example of his untraditional way of looking at things, Mahmoud criticized a young villager just returned from a work journey to Kuwait for squandering his earnings on a high marriage payment (£50 more than usual); he said he would have done better investing it in a grocery shop or in education.

20. His life history is given in greater detail in Antoun, "Social Organization and the Life Cycle in an Arab Village," *Ethnology* 6, 3 (July 1967).

21. For more information on Abu Fayid, see Antoun, "The Social Significance of Ramadan in an Arab Village." He is the villager who finally lived up to the Ramadan obligations concerning visiting among kinsmen.

22. For instance, he backed the Palestine Liberation Organization when almost all other villagers were against it under the leadership of Shukairi.

23. See the later discussion among the Yasin mayor, Yusuf al-Tuluq and Abu Fayid on the subject of marriage, the breeding of horses, and achieved and ascribed status.

24. It is interesting to note that one son in each family is a black sheep. Abu Yasin's middle brother is a baker living in Amman with his mistress. One of Abu Tahir's middle brothers was jailed twice for political activities and was released on condition that he return to his home village and stay there. Neither Abu Yasin nor Abu Tahir visit these brothers, nor do the brothers visit them.

25. See Daniel Lerner, *The Passing of a Traditional Society* (Glencoe, Ill.: The Free Press, 1958) for a discussion of empathy and its application to the modernization of individuals in a Middle Eastern setting. For Lerner the four phases of modernization are urbanization, literacy,

mass media participation, and political participation (*The Passing of a Traditional Society*, chapter 2). Although Abu Yasin had a much wider social and political horizon than Abu Tahir and a greater degree of empathy, he was not able to operate as effectively as the latter in dealing with town bureaucrats in gaining benefits for the village. This fact suggests that the emergence of particular individuals as "new peasants"—able to demand from bureaucrats what is theirs as a matter of right rather than favor—may be related to personality differences as much or more than geographical or social mobility. For a stimulating discussion of the emergence of the new peasant in the Middle East, see Reinhold Loeffler, "The Representative Mediator and the New Peasant," *American Anthropologist* 73, 5 (October 1971).

26. With the exception of Shaykh Luqman, whose responses are not recorded on table 8.

27. See Antoun, *Arab Village*, chapter 3 for further details on sister-exchange marriages.

28. Beqiraj has argued that one social psychological attribute of peasantry is their social psychological dependence on their covillagers. Although I believe this was the case for Abu Yasin, it was not the case for other villagers, as is pointed out later; therefore Beqiraj's generalization, while having an element of truth, is false, even for the universe constituted by a single village. For further details, see Mehmet Beqiraj, *Peasantry in Revolution* (Ithaca: Center for International Studies, 1966).

29. In fact, no such verse is to be found in the Quran. Several verses refer to God's elevating some men over others, but the nature of that elevation is left unspecified (e.g., Quran, 2:253, 6:165, 32:43). One verse specifies preference with respect to means of living (16:71). I have found no Quranic reference whatsoever to the concept of rank (*jāh*) in any of the above contexts. The quotation, then, is a garbled mingling of the parts of one Quranic verse with another concept (*jāh*) which is alien to the Quran, though it may appear in Commentaries of the Quran, Traditions of the Prophet, or sermons of the village preacher.

30. The use of the term *za'īm* suggests that the leader Yusuf has in mind is the traditional political leader with a local power base, e.g., the Pasha.

31. See Richard B. Scott, *The Village Headman in Turkey* (Ankara: Institute of Public Administration, 1968).

32. Scott gave the village a pseudonym, Green Village.

33. He once had an interview with the premier of the republic for this purpose.

Bibliography

Antoun, Richard T. "Conservatism and Change in the Village Community: a Jordanian Case Study." *Human Organization* 24 (Spring 1965): 4–10.
————. "The Social Significance of Ramadan in an Arab Village." *The Muslim World* 58 (January 1968): 36–42; (April 1968): 95–104.
————. "Social Organization and the Life Cycle in an Arab Village." *Ethnology* 6, (July 1967): 294–308.
————. "On the Significance of Names in an Arab Village." *Ethnology* 7 (April 1968): 158–170.
————. *Arab Village A Social Structural Study of a Transjordanian Peasant Community*. Bloomington: Indiana University Press, 1972.
————, and Harik, Iliya F. *Rural Politics and Social Change in the Middle East*. Bloomington: Indiana University Press, 1972.
————. "Pertinent Variables in the Environment of Middle Eastern Village Politics," in Antoun, R. and Harik, I., *Rural Politics and Social Change in the Middle East*, Bloomington: Indiana University Press, 1972.
Asad, Talal. "Market Model, Class Structure and Consent: A Reconsideration of Swat Political Organization." *Man* 7, 1 (March 1972): 74–94.
Bailey, Frederick G. *Caste and the Economic Frontier*. Manchester: Manchester University Press, 1957.
————. *Tribe, Caste and Nation*. Manchester: Manchester University Press, 1960.
————. *Politics and Social Change Orissa in 1959*. Berkeley: University of California Press, 1963.
————. "The Study of Politics in Village India." Unpublished mimeograph, n.d.
————. "Political Activity in Village India." Paper delivered at the Working Conference on Indian Politics and Political History, University of Sussex, August, 1965.
————. "Parapolitical Systems." In Marc Swartz, editor, *Local-Level Politics*. Chicago: Aldine, 1968.
————. *Strategems and Spoils A Social Anthropology of Politics*. New York: Schocken, 1969.
Barnard, Chester I. "The Acceptance of Authority." In L. A. Coser and B.

Rosenberg, editors, *Sociological Theory: A Book of Readings*. New York: Macmillan, 1957.

Barth, Fredrick. *Political Leadership Among Swat Pathans*. London: Athlone Press, 1959.

———. "Segmentary Opposition and the Theory of Games: A Study of Pathan Organization." *Journal of the Royal Anthropological Institute of Great Britain and Ireland* 89 (1959): 5–21.

———. *Models of Social Organization*. Royal Anthropological Institute Occasional Paper No. 23. London: Royal Anthropological Institute, 1966.

Beals, Alan R. and Siegel, Bernard J. "Pervasive Factionalism." *American Anthropologist* 62 (June 1960): 394–417.

Beqiraj, Mehmet. *Peasantry in Revolution*. Ithaca: Center for International Studies, Cornell University, 1966.

Bierstedt, Robert. "An Analysis of Social Power." In L. A. Coser and B. Rosenberg, editors, *Sociological Theory: A Book of Readings*. New York: Macmillan, 1957.

Blok, Anton. *The Mafia of a Sicilian Village 1860–1960   A Study of Violent Peasant Entrepreneurs*. New York: Harper and Row, 1974.

Boissevain, Jeremy. "The Place of the Non-Group in the Social Sciences." *Man* 3, 4 (December 1968): 542–556.

———. "Of Marbles and Men: Factionalism Reconsidered." Paper delivered for the symposium on The Anthropological Study of Factional Politics, York University, Canada, April 1975.

Borthwick, Bruce. *The Islamic Sermon as a Channel of Political Communication in Syria, Jordan and Egypt*, Ph.D. Thesis, University of Michigan, 1965.

Bujra, Janet. "The Dynamics of Political Action: A New Look at Factionalism." *American Anthropologist* 75 (February 1973): 132–152.

Cochrane, Glynn. "The use of the Concept of the "Corporation": A Choice Between Colloquialism or Distortion." *American Anthropologist* 73 (October 1971): 1114–1149.

———. "Juristic Persons, Group and Individual Tenure: A Rejoinder to Goodenough." *American Anthropologist* 73, 5 (October 1971).

Cohen, Abner. *Arab Border-Villages in Israel*. Manchester: Manchester University Press, 1965.

———. *Custom and Politics in Urban Africa*. Berkeley: University of California Press, 1969.

Dalil al-muwātin qawānin wa al-anthima al muta' alaqa bi al-hukm al-maḥali wal intikhābat al-niyābiya (Citizen's Guide A Collection of Laws and Regulations Relating to Local Government and Parliamentary Elections in the Hashemite Kingdom of Jordan). Amman: The Cooperative Society Worker's Press, 1963.

Dearden, Ann. *Jordan*. London, Robert Hale, 1958.

Easton, David. *A Framework of Political Analysis*. Englewood, New Jersey: Prentice Hall, 1965.

Fallers, Lloyd. "The Predicament of the Modern African Chief: An Instance from Uganda." *American Anthropologist* 57 (April 1955): 290–305.

Firth, Raymond. "Factions in Indian and Overseas Indian Communities." *British Journal of Sociology* 8 (December 1957): 291–295.

Friedl, Ernestine. "Lagging Emulation in Post Peasant Societies." *American Anthropologist* 66 (June 1964): 569–586.

Friedrich, Paul. "The Legitimacy of a Cacique." In Marc J. Swartz, editor, *Local-Level Politics*. Chicago: Aldine, 1968.

———. Introduction to Part III of Marc J. Swartz, editor, *Local-Level Politics*. Chicago: Aldine, 1968.

Gamson, William, A. *Power and Discontent*. Homewood, Illinois: Dorsey, 1968.

Gluckman, Max, Barnes, John, and Mitchell, J. "The Village Headman in British Central Africa." *Africa* 19 (1949).

Gluckman, Max. *The Judicial Process Among the Barotse of Northern Rhodesia*. Manchester: Manchester University Press, 1955.

———. *Custom and Conflict in Africa*. Oxford: Oxford University Press, 1960.

———. "Inter-Hierarchical Roles: Professional Party Ethics in Tribal Areas in South and Central Africa." In Marc Swartz, editor, *Local-Level Politics*. Chicago: Aldine, 1968.

Goodenough, Ward. "Rethinking 'Status' and 'Role': Toward a General Model of the Cultural Organization of Social Relationships." In M. Banton, editor, *The Relevance of Models for Social Anthropology*. London: Tavistock, 1965.

———. "Corporations: Reply to Cochrane." *American Anthropologist* 73, 5 (October 1971).

Graham, B. D. "The Succession of Factional Systems in the Uttar Pradesh Congress Party, 1937–66." In Marc Swartz, editor, *Local-Level Politics*. Chicago: Aldine, 1968.

Grannot, A. *The Land System in Palestine: History and Structure*. London: Eyre and Spottiswoode, 1952.

Grassmuck, George. "Regional and Local Government in the Hashemite Kingdom of Jordan." Paper delivered at the Conference on Local Government in Mediterranean Countries, The American University of Beirut, September 1966.

Griffenhagen-Kroeger, Inc. "An Administrative Review of the Ministry of Interior, The Ministry of Municipal and Rural Affairs." Mimeographed, Report No. G-K/Jordan 66-1.1, Amman, 1966.

Gubser, Peter. *Politics and Change in Al-Karak, Jordan*. London: Oxford, 1973.

Harik, Iliya F. *The Political Mobilization of Peasants*. Bloomington: Indiana University Press, 1974.

Horton, Alan. "A Syrian Village in its Changing Environment." Ph.D. Thesis, Department of Anthropology, Harvard University, 1960.

Kiefer, Thomas. *The Tausug: Violence and Law in a Philippine Moslem Society*. New York: Holt, Rinehart and Winston, 1972.

Kroeber, Alfred. *The Nature of Culture*. Chicago: University of Chicago Press, 1952.

Laswell, Harold. *Politics: Who gets What, When, How*. New York: Meridian, 1958.

Lerner, Daniel. *The Passing of a Traditional Society*. Glencoe, Illinois: The Free Press, 1958.

Levine, Robert A. "Research Design in Anthropological Field Work." In

Naroll, R. and Cohen, R., *A Handbook of Method in Cultural Anthropology*. Garden City, New York: Natural History Press, 1970.

Liebow, Elliot. *Tally's Corner*. Boston: Little Brown, 1967.

Loeffler, Reinhold. "The Representative Mediator and the New Peasant." *American Anthropologist* 73 (October 1971): 1077–1091.

Machiavelli, Nicolo. *The Prince*. Middlesex, England: Penguin, 1964.

Madi, Munib and Musa, Sulayman. *Tārīkh al-irdun fi al-qarn al- ashrīn* (The History of Jordan in the Twentieth Century). Amman: 1959.

Maine, Henry. *Ancient Law Its Connection With The Early History of Society, and its Relation to Modern Ideas*. New York: Henry Holt, 1878.

Mayer, Adrian C. "Factions in Fiji Indian Rural Settlements." *British Journal of Sociology* 8 (December 1957): 317–328.

———. "The Significance of Quasi-Groups in the Study of Complex Societies." In M. Banton, editor, *The Social Anthropology of Complex Societies*. London: Tavistock, 1966.

Meggit, Mervyn. *Blood Is Their Argument   Warfare Among the Mae Enga Tribesmen of the New Guinea Highlands*. Palo Alto: Mayfield, 1977.

Naroll, Raoul and Cohen, Ronald. *A Handbook of Method in Cultural Anthropology*. Garden City, New York: Natural History Press, 1970.

Nicholas, Ralph. "Factions: a Comparative Analysis." In F. Eggan and M. Gluckman, editors, *Political System and the Distribution of Power*. New York: Praeger, 1965.

Northrup, F. S. C. "The Nature of Concepts, Their Interrelation and Role in Social Structure." Stillwater: Stillwater Conference, 1958.

Patai, Raphael, editor. *Jordan*. New Haven: Human Relations Area Files, 1956.

Peake, Frederick G. *The History of East Jordan*. Jerusalem: 1935.

Peters, Emrys L. "Aspects of Rank and Status among Muslims in a Lebanese Village." In J. Pitt-Rivers, editor, *Mediterranean Countrymen*. Paris: Mouton, 1963.

———. "Some Structural Aspects of the Feud Among the Camel Herding Bedouin of Cyrenaica." *Africa* 37 (July 1967): 261–282.

———. "Shifts in Power in a Lebanese Village." In R. Antoun and I. Harik, editors, *Rural Politics and Social Change in the Middle East*. Bloomington: Indiana, 1972.

Pickthall, Mohammed M. *The Meaning of the Glorious Koran*. New York: Mentor, 1959.

Qutub, Ishaq Y. "Impact of Rural Credit and Thrift Cooperative Societies on the Traditional Social and Economic Structure of Rural Jordan—A Study of Three Villages." Paper delivered at the Mediterranean Social Science Research Council Conference, The Royal University of Malta, December 1965.

———. "Local Government and Cooperative Development in Jordan." Paper submitted to the General Assembly organized by the Mediterranean Social Science Research Council, held at the American University of Beirut, Beirut, Lebanon, September 1966.

Rappaport, Anatol. "The Use and Misuse of Game Theory." *Scientific American* 207, 6 (December 1962): 108–118.

Redfield, Robert and Singer, Milton. "The Cultural Role of Cities." *Economic Development and Cultural Change* 3 (October 1954): 53–73.

Reston, James. *New York Times.* 5 October 1967.

Rimawi, Qasim al-. Speech delivered by the Minister of Interior for Municipal and Rural Affairs. Amman, 2 March 1966 (mimeographed in
Arabic).

Scott, Richard B. *The Village Headman in Turkey.* Ankara: Institute of Public Administration, 1968.

Silverman, Sydel. "Bailey's Politics." *Journal of Peasant Studies* 2 (1974):
111–120.

Shokeid, Moshe, "Immigration and Factionalism: An Analysis of Factions
in Rural Israeli Communities of Immigrants. *British Journal of
Sociology* 19 (1968): 385–406.

Smith, M. G. "Segmentary Lineage Systems." *Journal of the Royal Anthropological Institute of Great Britain and Ireland* 86 (1956):

————. "A Structural Approach to Comparative Politics." In D. Easton,
editor, *Varieties of Political Theory.* Englewood Cliffs, New Jersey:
Prentice Hall, 1966.

Spiro, Melford. "Factionalism and Politics in Village Burma." In Marc
Swartz, editor, *Local-Level Politics.* Chicago: Aldine, 1968.

Statistical Yearbook 1964. No. 15. Amman: Department of Statistics Press,
n.d.

The Collection of Laws and Regulations for Jordan Until 1960. Part 3.
Amman: n.d.

*The Proceedings of the Conference on Middle East Agricultural Develop-
ment.* Agricultural Report No. 6. Cairo: Middle East Supply Center,
1944.

Turner, Victor. *Schism and Continuity in an African Society.* Manchester:
Manchester University Press, 1957.

Warner, William Lloyd and Lunt, Paul S. *The Social Life of a Modern Community.* New Haven: Yale University Press, 1941.

————, Meeker, M., and Eels, K., *Social Class in America: A Manual for
Procedure for the Measurement of Social Status.* Chicago: Science
Research, 1949.

————, and Associates. *Democracy in Jonesville.* New York: Harper, 1949.

Weber, Max. *The Theory of Social and Economic Organization.* Glencoe,
Illinois: The Free Press, 1968.

Weulersse, Jacque. *Paysans de Syrie et du Proche-Orient.* Paris: Gallimard,
1946.

Zecher, Linda. "The Men of Influence and the Exercise of Influence in
Nabatieh, Lebanon." M.A. thesis, Department of Sociology and Anthropology, American University of Beirut, Beirut, 1967.

Index